Technology, Com|
Radical Polic,
The Case of Brazil

QUEEN ELIZABETH HOUSE
INTERNATIONAL DEVELOPMENT

TECHNOLOGY, COMPETITIVENESS AND RADICAL POLICY CHANGE

The Case of Brazil

JÖRG MEYER-STAMER

FRANK CASS
LONDON • PORTLAND, OR
Published in association with the
German Development Institute, Berlin

First published in 1997 in Great Britain by
FRANK CASS & CO. LTD.
Newbury House, 900 Eastern Avenue,
London IG2 7HH

and in the United States of America by
FRANK CASS
c/o ISBS
5804 N.E. Hassalo Street
Portland, Oregon 97213-3644

British Library Cataloguing in Publication Data
A catalogue record for this book is available from the British Library

Library of Congress Cataloging-in-Publication Data
Meyer-Stamer, Jörg, 1958–
    Technology, competitiveness and radical policy change : the case
of Brazil / Jörg Meyer-Stamer.
        p.   cm. — (GDI book series : no. 9)
    "Published in association with the German Development Institute,
Berlin."
    Includes bibliographical references.
    ISBN 0-7146-4379-3
    1. Technological innovations—Brazil. 2. Technology and state—
Brazil. 3. Competition—Brazil. 4. Import substitution—Brazil.
I. Deutsches Institut für Entwicklungspolitik. II. Title.
III. Series.
HC190.T4M49   1997
338'.064'0981—dc21   97-8178
                                                               CIP

Printed and bound in Great Britain by
Creative Print and Design (Wales), Ebbw Vale

Contents

Part II Technology, Innovation and Industrial Competitiveness: The Discussion in the OECD-Countries – Prospects for Brazil

Figures in the Text

Abbreviations

ABICOMP	Associação Brasileira da Indústria de Computadores e Periféricos (Brazilian Federation of Computer and Peripherals Industry)
ANPEI	Associação Nacional de Pesquisa e Desenvolvimento das Empresas Industriais (National R&D Federation of Industries)
BEFIEX	Comissão para Concessão de Benefícios Fiscais a Programas Especiais de Exportação (Tax Incentive Program to Promote Exports)
BNDES	Banco Nacional de Desenvolvimento Econômico e Social (National Bank for Economic and Social Development; until 1982 BNDE)
CAD	Computer-aided design
CAM	Computer-aided manufacturing
CAP	Computer-aided planning
CDI	Conselho de Desenvolvimento Industrial (Council for Industrial Development)
CIM	Computer-integrated manufacturing
CNC	Computerized numerical control
CNPq	Conselho Nacional de Desenvolvimento Científico e Tecnológico (National Council for Scientific and Technological Development)
CUT	Central Única dos Trabalhadores (biggest umbrella trade union)
DC	Developing country
FINAME	Agencía Especial de Financiamento Industrial (BNDES agency to finance investments in capital goods)
FIPE	Fundação Instituto de Pesquisa Econômica (economic research institute)
FUNCEX	Fundação Centro de Estudos do Comércio Exterior (economic research institute)

IBGE	Instituto Brasileiro de Geografia e Estatística (Office of Statistics)
ICMS	Imposto sobre Circulação de Mercadorias e Serviços (VAT in federal states)
IEDI	Institute Econômico de Desenvolvimento Industrial (Industrial economic research institute)
IC	Industrialized country
INPI	Instituto Nacional de Propriedade Industrial (National Institute for Patent Law)
IPEA	Instituto de Pesquisas Econômicas Aplicadas (economic research institute)
IPI	Imposto sobre Produtos Industrializados (Federal VAT)
ISI	Import-substituting industrialization
MBI	Movimento Brasileiro para a Informática (Brazilian movement in the field of informatics)
MCT	Ministério para Ciencia e Tecnologia (Ministry of Science and Technology)
MINICOM	Ministério de Comunicações (Ministry of Communication)
MSTQ	Measurement, standards, testing, quality assurance
NC	Numerical control
PBQP	Programa Brasileiro da Qualidade e Produtividade (Brazilian Program for Quality and Productivity)
PC	Personal computer
PCI	Programa de Competitividade Industrial (Program for Industrial Competitiveness)
PCT	Programa da Capacitação Tecnológica (Programm to Strengthen Technological Capability)
PFL	Partido do Frente Liberal
PMDB	Partido do Movimento Democrático Brasileiro

PNBE	Pensamento Nacional de Bases Empresariais (Association of Modern Small and Medium-Sized Enterprises)
PPS	production planning systems
PT	Partido dos Trabalhadores
R&D	Research and Development
SBPC	Sociedade Brasileira para o Progresso na Sciência (Brazilian Society for Progress in Science)
SEBRAE	Serviço Brasileiro de Apoio à Pequena e Média Empresa (Brazilian Promotion Service for Small and Medium-sized Enterprises)
SEI	Secretaria Especial de Informática (Special secretariat for Informatics)
SENAC	Serviço Nacional de Aprendizagem Comercial (national vocational training organization in the service sector)
SENAI	Serviço Nacional de Aprendizagem Industrial (national vocational training organization in the industrial sector)
SNDCT	Sistema nacional de desenvolvimento científico e tecnológico (national system for scientific and technological development)
SUDAM	Superintendência do Desenvolvimento da Amazônia (Development Agency for the Amazonas region)
SUDENE	Superintendência do Desenvolvimento do Nordeste (Development Agency for the Northeast)
SUFRAMA	Superintendência para a Zona Franca de Manaus (Development Agency for the Free Production Zone of Manaus)

Introduction

Technology, industrial competitiveness, and radical policy change are the key issues of the present study.

Radical policy change. In the past developing countries undertook efforts to diminish their dependence on imponderables of the world market by building up a more or less complete national industrial base and protecting it with a variety of tariff and nontariff import barriers. The theoretical foundation and justification of these attempts was the concept of import-substituting industrialization (ISI) developed at the beginning of the 1950s. In many countries ISI policies gave rise for a protracted period to high rates of economic growth and the development of a large-scale industrial base. But they also led to distortions and immanent problems, and these, based as they were on one-sidedly inward-looking policies, ultimately proved ISI to be a dead-end street. Following attempts in the 1960s (which for the most part failed) to achieve a more pronounced outward orientation, and some isolated radical reorientations in the 1970s, most inward-looking countries, at the latest since the eruption of the debt crisis, came under strong pressure to alter their policies radically. Core elements of structural adjustment programs imposed on these countries from outside, or developed by them on their own initiative, included reduction of the level of state intervention, strengthening of market forces, and a radical shift in foreign trade policy.

Industrial competitiveness. Various semi-industrialized countries found that the efficiency levels of their firms and their ability to adjust rapidly to altered framework conditions and heightened competition were low (Esser 1992, 11f.). Business collapses, sometimes even culminating in the demise of entire industries, were not rare. Competitiveness is thus a difficult challenge even for industrially advanced developing countries – the existence of an industry offering random-quality products at high prices in a sheltered domestic market is one thing, the existence of an efficient and competitive industry up to the levels of efficiency and quality customary in the world market is quite a different matter.

At the company level, competitiveness is measured in terms of the ability to satisfy simultaneously four criteria. The firm must supply products of adequate quality, and at competitive prices; it must be in a position to provide sufficiently differentiated products to meet a differentiated demand situation; and it must be able to respond quickly to changes in demand behavior. Beyond this, market success is contingent on a firm's ability to build up an effective marketing system, to establish a brand name, and so on. At the level of the economy as a whole, the OECD defines competitiveness as follows: *"... the degree to which a nation can, under free and fair market conditions, produce goods and services which meet the test of international markets, while simultaneously maintaining and expanding the real incomes of its people over the long term."*[1]

But how is it that firms become competitive? The orthodoxy of structural adjustment postulates that the main concern is the right macroeconomic framework: if the economic-policy framework is designed in such a way as to generate competitive pressure, firms have no choice but to become competitive (Thomas 1991). This view is the reverse conclusion drawn from experience made in the phase of import substitution, when it became evident that, despite any and all state intervention (e.g. in technology policy), very little competitiveness is able to emerge in the face of low levels of competitive pressure. A macroeconomic framework that generates competitive pressure would therefore seem to be the necessary condition for the emergence of industrial competitiveness.

Yet, for two reasons, this condition is not a sufficient one. First, frameworks that generate competitive pressure do not necessarily produce incentives toward the development of entrepreneurship.A soberly calculating entrepreneur may come to the conclusion that under the prevailing conditions, i.e. in spite of stable macroeconomic conditions, it is not worthwhile to build up an industrial firm. This would particularly be the case when there are no specific locational advantages (e.g. especially cheap inputs) that afford a firm, in its learning phase, an edge over outside competition. In a constellation of this sort, which, for instance, seems to prevail in Bolivia (Messner 1993b), no industrialization process will get underway without an active industrial policy that includes protection for infant industries (Hillebrand 1991).

Second, even when the initial conditions are less unfavorable for dynamic entrepreneurs, they continue to be faced with the problem that in the absence of any active support they are forced to compete, in the domestic and the world market, with firms that, at home, enjoy ample state support of various kinds. A firm left to its own resources in important areas – e.g. vocational training, technological support, foreign trade information – will find itself in competition with a firm that is tied into a dense network of support firms, technology institutions, training facilities, export-promotion agencies, and so on, and can thus capitalize on various positive externalities. The former firm will have a chance of survival in this competition only when it enjoys advantages denied to the latter one, e.g. the already mentioned specific locational advantages; the Chilean furniture industry, for example, with its weak network structures, profits from favorable production conditions for its main intermediate product, wood (Messner et al. 1991). Yet this restricts it in its development potentials, for the more strongly factors other than low prices – e.g. technological competence and innovativeness in developing new products, design competence or promptness in responding to market changes – determine the pattern of competition, the greater will be the problems confronting the first firm.

Technology policy. An industrialization process going beyond any simple cashing in on given comparative advantages will overburden firms acting in isolation. Aside from elements such as the ability to establish a brand-name image, it is above all technological factors that decide on a firm's success, since the price and quality of a product are contingent on the organization of the development and production processes, i.e. depend on a firm's technological competence. The latter in turn is to a large degree affected by external effects (exchange of personnel and information among firms, R&D cooperation among firms and research institutions, and so on). Positive external effects, in particular technological externalities, can either emerge on their own owing to chance historical factors, or be created on an interfirm level without any intervention on the part of the state; the experiences made in industrial districts point in part in this direction (Schmitz and Navdi 1994). But it is more often the state that plays an important part – not least to the extent that many external effects emerge from activities typically assigned to the state, e.g. training or scientific research. Technology policy in this way takes on the role of a key factor for the emergence of industrial competitiveness.

This study's core thesis is: lack of success in capacity-building or strengthening of technological competence is linked causally with the one-sidedly inward-looking development model that has been pursued in the majority of developing countries (DCs). This model led to incentive structures that induced the great majority of industrial firms to undertake efforts in the direction of technological development which proved both inadequate and distorted. Low levels of innovation efforts furthermore imply that there was no need to develop any networking between basic research and applied research and development in universities, research institutes, and firms, which has meant a lack of development of innovation systems of the kind familiar in the industrialized countries. The question that ensues is, then: What potentials for and approaches to the development or strengthening of technological competence exist in DCs after the end of inward-looking development models, i.e. in a situation in which the firms are exposed to pressure to lose no time in boosting their competitiveness?

Part I of the study advances the arguments for this thesis. The section begins by pointing out that technology transfer from the industrialized countries (ICs) is no substitute for technological efforts undertaken by DCs themselves. The section discusses – with special reference to Latin America – the failure of the model of import-substituting industrialization (ISI) and the connection between ISI and, first, technological development and, second, governance patterns as a means of explaining the limited successes met with by technological efforts in DCs. The thesis is then illustrated with the case of Brazil. This country is, for various reasons, well suited as a case study. Among the DCs Brazil is the country with the largest industrial base;[2] it has pursued an explicit technology policy in different industrial sectors; it exhibits a number of the defects typical of ISI; and it has undertaken efforts since

1990 to realign its industrial development. The guiding question in investigating Brazil is: What was the nature of the link between industrialization and technological development in the variant of ISI specific to Brazil? This question is addressed with an eye to Brazil's history of industrialization as a whole. The section furthermore looks into the connection between the crisis of ISI and the crisis of the Brazilian political system; this is the precondition for being able to asses the governing capacity of the Brazilian state.

Part II examines approaches available to DCs following the end of ISI to strengthen technological competence, in particular in industry. The section starts out by summarizing the present state of the technology-oriented debate. The central questions here include: What rules does the process of technological change follow? What are the current patterns of technical change? What is the institutional environment that shapes the process of technological change? What possibilities of political governance exist? And, finally, the question most germane to the present study: What implications does this have for the development or the strengthening of the competitiveness of industries in advanced developing countries? In answering these questions, the section refers not only to the discussion current in the field of political science but also to various strands of the current economic and sociological discussion. Taken on its own, none of these strands is able to explain exhaustively the process of technological change and provide guidelines on technology policy. But taken as a whole they do complement one another, making possible a number of propositions on more and less promising policy interventions and the underlying institutional arrangements involved. The discussion on theoretical-conceptual models is followed – again with an eye to Brazil – by an examination of the question involving the strengthening of technological capability and enhancement of industrial competitiveness following the end of import substitution. This entails looking into both adjustment processes at the company level and new technology-policy initiatives. Aside from an evaluation of the relevant literature, the Brazil sections are based on interviews of political-administrative decision-makers at the federal and state level, decision-makers in firms, and academic experts. The interviews were conducted in the course of five sojourns in the field (August 1989, June 1990, February–April 1991, April–May 1993, and June 1994).

What is Technology?

Any discussion of the experiences made with and approaches to technology policy must be preceded by a conceptual definition of the actual subject – technology – particularly in view of the fact that there is no universally accepted definition of the term that might serve as a natural point of departure. Definition is not made any easier by the fact that the semantics of the term technology differs in German and English – the former emphasizing the science of technology, the other the application of technical knowledge.[3] Summing up the widely accepted definition, it is possible to delimit two variants – a narrow definition and a broad one.

In the more narrow sense technology is the know-how required to develop and apply technical methods. It appears in a bound form in machines and plants, in an unbound form in blueprints, and manuals (Helmschrott 1986, 3). Technology transfer is the transmission of this know-how. The term technology transfer is frequently used as a synonym for the *international* transfer between industrialized countries or from industrialized countries to developing nations; yet it is not seldom that a transfer of know-how within the boundaries of one country is referred to as technology transfer.

The narrow definition refers to technical artifacts. At first glance it has the advantage of being handy. But its drawback is that its use entails the risk of loosing sight of the complementary factors. Complementary factors, without which the employment of technical artifacts makes no sense, are above all *qualification* (of the people who work with artifacts) and *organization* (i.e. the process of tying artifacts into social contexts and operational sequences).

This leads to three conclusions:

(1) Technology should not be seen in isolation from the environment in which it emerges, or from the organizational structures in which it is used. Technology does not come about in a vacuum, it always develops in concrete social contexts. It is therefore never neutral, and is always developed on the basis of given (economic, social, political) interests. The utilization of technology is contextual: in a crime-related context technology will tend chiefly to be used for criminal ends; in a society blessed with ample resources technology can be used to feign modernity; in a competition-oriented society technology will be used to heighten efficiency and thus to increase welfare.

(2) Technology often embodies organizational factors. A closed process in the chemical industry or a production line in the metal-processing industry, for instance, consists not only of technical knowledge of individual processing sequences, it also implies organizational knowledge about possible transitions between these sequences. This is even more clear-cut in information technology: In computers, sequences that previously were performed by people on the basis of accumulated organizational knowledge have been translated into programs to control machines.

(3) Any narrow definition, accompanied by the view and approach that go along with it, can thus be tantamount to a guaranty that projects will fail – in development cooperation no less than in many international high-tech corporations, many of which have gone down in recent years flying the colors of one-sidedly technology-minded rationalization projects.

The discussion on development policy and the field of development cooperation has in recent years experienced a general acceptance of the broad definition of technology, one that does justice to the problems outlined here. This definition includes four components:[4]

(1) technical hardware, i.e. a specific configuration of machines and equipment used to produce a good or to provide a service;

(2) know-how, i.e. scientific and technical knowledge, formal qualifications and tacit knowledge;

(3) organization, i.e. managerial methods used to link hardware and know-how;

(4) the product, i.e. the good or service as an outcome of the production process.

The advantage of the broad definition is that it can help to avoid barren discussions in that it prevents, for instance, any equating of technical artifacts and technology. It to this extent mirrors experience gathered, for example, in development cooperation – in view of this definition it is obvious that technology can not be transferred in package form. At the same time it is, against this background, easier to comprehend that technology is involved whenever production goes on – even when seemingly primitive technical artifacts are utilized in the process,[5] for "no country is without technology, not even the most primitive." (Enos 1991, 169)

Still, this definition is not entirely satisfactory in that it is not inclusive enough. True, it is plausible to break down the definition into the elements technical hardware, know-how, and organization; yet the fourth element, the product, resists this schema. It would thus appear that the schema is in need of modification; a useful definition should distinguish between the elements and the objects of technology (Figure 1). The elements that remain are technical hardware, know-how, and organization. The object is on the one hand the production process, on the other the product itself. This breakdown mirrors the experience that in the production process very different goods can be manufactured with similar combinations of elements, i.e. process technology, organization, and know-how are, within a given framework, independent of the good produced; an example would be the production of furniture and automotive parts which can be manufactured in factories with machines and organizational patterns that are on first, and possibly even at second, glance very similar. On the other hand, the same product can be manufactured with very different combinations of the three elements; to go on with the example cited above: a furniture component of identical quality can be produced both by a qualified joiner using traditional tools and by a qualified machine operator making use of a computer-controlled manufacturing center.

Figure 1:

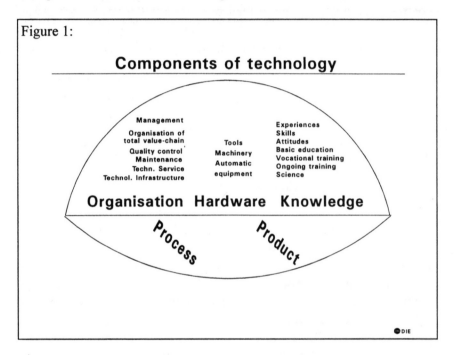

Components of technology

Management		Experiences
Organisation of total value-chain	Tools	Skills Attitudes
Quality control Maintenance Techn. Service Technol. Infrastructure	Machinery Automatic equipment	Basic education Vocational training Ongoing training Science

Organisation Hardware Knowledge

Process *Product*

Ⓓ DIE

Technological and economic development are linked inseparably – sustained economic growth results in particular from increasing the efficiency of inputs, i.e. from the introduction of new, better machines, through organization improvements, successful learning processes, and enhanced qualifications – in short: through technological progress. This insight has all along left its mark on the discussion and the practice of development policy; the latter has regarded technology transfer, beside the transfer of capital, as an approach crucial to overcoming underdevelopment. This goal has been achieved in very few countries; all in all, the welfare gap between industrialized and developing countries has widened. There is no doubt today that more than technology and capital are required for dynamic development. Political and economic framework conditions, sociocultural factors, and an eye for specific ecological conditions are what decide on the success or failure of development strategies.

That is not to say that technology is a secondary element. Quite on the contrary, technology is more than ever a central factor of economic development. Technology is the link between the *inputs* capital and labor and the *output*, the product. Technology can be the lubricant that makes for efficient production; but it can also be the sand that clogs up the process, causing that, in the end, what comes out will be less than what went in.

What is Technology Policy?

The subject of this study is technology policy. This is of course a somewhat fuzzy concept. True, anyone can conjure up an association of what technology policy might be; yet the likelihood that two persons will come up with the same association is slight. Differences in the understanding of technology policy result from that fact that technology policy can refer both to "generic" technologies, i.e. universally applicable methods and know-how, and sector-specific technologies (in agriculture, industry, certain areas of the service sector). It can furthermore refer to different phases of the process of research and development. And technology policy can also attempt to steer the emergence and application of technologies, though it can at the same time restrict itself to the mere creation of favorable framework conditions.

There is one more complicating factor: technology is an inclusive category, and for that reason technology policy is an inclusive policy that resists any cut-and-dried delimitation from other policy fields. Technology policy overlaps with numerous other policies:

- industrial policy, which is commonly taken to mean all those political interventions that are used to modify market events and shape industrial structures;

- research and/or science policy, i.e. the shaping of the areas of an innovation system more remote from practical application;

- educational policy, which is used to mold person-related technical and organizational qualifications;

- agricultural policy, where certain instruments of technology policy – e.g. extension services – have for the first time been used successfully;

- competition policy, although the relationship meant here is more conflictual than complementary, since its aim, with an eye to technology-policy objectives, is to promote larger-scale business units and foster close cooperation between competitors;

- trade policy, which is significant in determining what incentive structure, and thus what innovation pressure, firms are exposed to;

- structural or regional policy, in which technological components play a major part in improving the business environment;

- infrastructure policy, to the extent that the procurement policy of the (for the most part governmental) agencies in charge of infrastructure has at all times been a central instrument of technology policy – used both to strengthen local firms and to control the direction taken by the process of technological change.

The present study is concerned with the areas of technology policy geared to improving industrial competitiveness. This throws up new definitional problems, for this sphere of technology policy overlaps with industrial policy. And the latter in turn is a concept that is not exactly marked by lucidity. For some it is identical with deep-reaching state intervention, not unlike investment guidance; for others it is a collection of incentives and instruments used to improve microeconomic competitiveness. It in any case includes more than merely technology-related instruments, viz. also financial instruments, competition policy, infrastructure policy, and the like. When the present study refers to industrial policy, this category is meant – in particular in the empirical section – to be understood in analogy with the way (which is somewhat fuzzy in analytical terms) in which it is used in the Brazilian discussion; industrial policy is here not understood as synonymous with technology policy.

The concern here is to arrive at a working definition of the term technology policy, not some hyperexact delineation of the concept. The term is used here as follows: technology policy is the totality of the measures designed to strengthen industry's technological competitiveness. Trade policy, regional policy, or competition policy not specifically used to support or discipline individual branches of industry are to be as strictly distinguished from it as programs designed to strengthen firms financially or to promote their exports.

Part I Technology and Industrial Competitiveness in the Context of Import Substitution - General Reflections and Experience from Brazil

1 Import Substitution, Technology Development, and Technology Policy in Developing Countries

Regardless of the definition used: technology is invariably a central issue in the discussion on development, for development is, among other things, a synonym for the transformation of modes of production, and this in turn implies change in the underlying technology (regardless of whether hardware or, as here, the totality of hardware, organization, and know-how are meant).

The discussion over technology and development has for the most part been confined to the field surrounding two elements: technology transfer, i.e. the transfer from industrialized countries of know-how and knowledge embodied in machinery to developing countries, and the strengthening of technological capability in developing countries (capacity building). The one aspect can look back on a long history, since even the introduction into Europe of gunpowder or porcelain constitutes cases of technology transfer; and all examples of late industrialization, beginning with France and Germany, have in large measure rested on the transfer of technology from more advanced countries. At the same time, however, it has always been clear that any successful transfer of machines, know-how, and organizational patterns presupposes a substantial measure of capability on the part of the recipient; that is to say, that technology transfer and the strengthening of technological capability are complementary processes. Nevertheless, one of the hallmarks of the initial decades of development was that more attention was paid to technology transfer than to capacity building. There were two reasons for this. First, most developing countries were marked by an extensive lack of modern technology, and thus technology transfer seemed to be the obvious solution to the problem presented by their productivity lag; and second, the dominant view was that many technologies could be regarded as "mature" technologies, i.e. that they, on principle, could be mastered with the aid of textbooks. Seen in this way, capacity building was synonymous with the preparation for an understanding of canonical knowledge.

1.1   Possibilities and Limitations of Technology Transfer

1.1.1   Altered Framework Conditions for the Transfer of Technology from Abroad

Because technology transfer (understood in what follows as border-crossing transfers) was viewed as a central instrument to be used in overcoming underdevelopment, it was entirely logical that developing countries, beginning at the end of the 1970s, called for a narrowing of the North-South technology gap via unhindered and prefreably cost-free transfer of technology from the North to the South. But this demand met with little willingness in the industrialized countries. Accords going in this direction (e.g. the Law of the Seas agreement of 1982, which was not ratified by the leading industrialized countries) (Wolf 1986). have remained the exception; a technology fund which was agreed in principle in 1979 at the Vienna Conference on Science and Technology for Development and was to be endowed with funds amounting to billions of dollars, never came to fruition (Standke 1987).

In dealing with this topic, international organizations have undergone a process of fundamental change. Until the mid-1980s the adoption of a code of conduct topped the agenda. It was intended to put an end to abusive practices associated with technology transfer, e.g. excessive license fees. Today, what is under discussion is no longer how to *control* technology transfer but how to *stimulate* it (UNCTAD 1990a).

This reflects changes in North-South technology relations, for in practice the access of developing countries to technology appeared to be growing more difficult in the 1980s (UNCTAD 1988a). The process of technological change accelerated, new technologies (microelectronics, biotechnology/genetic engineering, new materials) were developed and employed. The availability of technology and the ability to harness it for the rapid development of new processes and products became one of the central competitive factors both for individual firms and for entire economies. Technology also came more and more to be developed in the private sector; in many important industrialized countries the private share of overall R&D spending continued to grow (Germany 1985/89: 61.8/65.9 %; Japan 1984/88: 66.9/70.5 %) (OECD 1991). The transfer of and access to technology was controlled by private actors in accordance with their interests.

That is not to say that DC access to technology had become generally impossible; South Korean and Taiwanese firms, for example, had no trouble obtaining process and product know-how for microchips (Meyer-Stamer 1991). However, unstable economic and unpredictable legal framework conditions, signs of economic crisis, and weak recipient structures did diminish the attractiveness of the great majority of DCs as recipients of privately organized technology transfers. At the same time the debt crisis sapped the financial capacity of most developing countries to purchase technology (UNCTAD 1992) – a problem that has yet to be solved and is exacerbated by apparent rises in the quotients used to calculate license fees (UNCTAD 1991a, 10).

Technology transfer is effected in different manners (Table 1). The most important in quantitative terms are conventional mechanisms in which the technology donor may play either an active role (foreign direct investment and joint ventures, licensing agreements, engineering services, and the sale of turnkey plants) or a passive role (purchases of machinery). In addition, successful newly industrialized countries (NICs) have made particular use of specific nonconventional mechanisms; these may include imitation (reverse engineering) and noncontractual technology transfers between a firm and its customer (learning by exporting, e.g. in subcontracting). Some of these instruments are of course difficult to distinguish from criminal (brand-name piracy) or hazardous practices (e.g. low-quality copies of airplane or automotive parts). It is for this reason that the industrialized countries, both in bilateral relations and in international forums, exercise strong pressure on semi-industrialized countries, the intention being to induce the latter to implement a level of patent and copyright protection in accord with that in effect in the North (although it must be admitted that the industrialized countries have themselves, in the process of their development, engaged in the pirating of ideas on a grand scale, a practice which was sometimes even legally sanctioned) (UNCTAD 1988b).

Table 1: Types of Technology Transfers

	Active role of the technology donor	Passive role of the technology donor
Formal (market-mediated)	Foreign direct investment, joint ventures, turnkey plants, engineering agreements, licenses	Purchases of machinery
Informal (not market-mediated)	"Learning by exporting"	Imitation, evaluation of journals, scientific exchange
Source: Fransman (1984).		

This aspect, among others, was included in the just concluded GATT round in a negotiating group on so-called TRIPS (trade-related intellectual property rights) (Wiemann 1992). Further negotiations dealt with the limitation or prohibition of trade-related investment measures (TRIMS). The objective was to ban restrictive measures that have been used, among other things, to ensure a more effective transfer of technology by foreign direct investors. In both of these cases the impacts of the GATT agreements in the end proved less dramatic than originally feared (Anand 1992). TRIMS are in any case being rescinded in many countries in the wake of the general process of liberalization and with an eye to improving the conditions for foreign investors. The TRIPS regulations provide leeway for political intervention; "*the Agreement allows compulsory licences when the rights holders fail to license pat-*

ented technology 'on reasonable commercial terms'. "[1] Moreover, their purpose is to ensure what many semi-industrialized countries have already implemented – as a result of pressure from abroad, but also in their own well-understood interest, i.e. in order to protect their own innovation efforts (Sherwood 1990).

The discussion on environment and development has furthermore given rise to a countertrend against restrictive tendencies in the international setting (ECOSOC 1994). Politicians from the South were quick to grasp what chance this meant: no environmental protection without technology, no technology without technology transfer, no technology transfer without money.

The know-how for environmentally friendly technologies (end-of-pipe plants on the one hand, integrated environmentally sound production processes on the other) is chiefly the property of private firms. This is the point of departure of thoughts under consideration in developing countries: How is it possible to ensure that these firms will (1) transfer technology at all and (2) will transfer it at an acceptable price? Both of these considerations constitute a problem: a technology monopolist will as a rule have invested substantial sums in the development of the technology concerned and will therefore be interested in selling licenses at the highest possible price (price problem). Many firms, having earlier failed with projects, today have reservations about transferring technology to developing countries. This is one reason why the transfer of technology from the North to the South declined sharply in the 1980s; the firms prefer to transfer technology only to countries that provide a minimum of certainty that the technology will be used effectively (access problem).

The industrialized countries are thus faced with the challenge of providing financial support in particular for those developing countries whose technological competence is adequate to ensure an effective utilization of environmentally friendly technology. This is, seen on the global scale, an enterprise worthwhile in ecological terms: since the environmental standards in these countries have tended to be low, it is possible to achieve substantially higher reductions of emissions with a given volume of investment than would be possible in the industrialized North, given its high filter density. The Montreal Protocol (on the reduction of CFC production), signed in 1987, took a first significant step: it created a fund earmarked for the support of developing countries in their conversion efforts. The 1992 framework agreement on climate change (Climate Framework Convention, CFC) has proposed far-reaching, albeit not sufficiently precise, regulations on the obligation of the ICs to step up the transfer of environmentally friendly technologies to DCs.[2] Firms in the industrialized countries furthermore discovered that it can be wholly to their financial advantage to pay compensation for environmental-protection measures in developing countries instead of increasing the degree of pollution abatement in plants in their own countries, e.g. for waste gases from 95 % to 99 % (which is generally far more costly than an increase from, say, 35 % to 40 %); this approach is under discussion in the context of Climate Framework Convention under the heading of *joint implementation*.

1.1.2   Success Factors and Limitations of Technology Transfer

In the end it is not the altered international framework conditions that call forth skepticism when the potentials of technology transfer are viewed today. What is more significant are the inherent limitations of technology transfer.

The mechanism most significant in quantitative terms is the transfer of technology bound in the form of machinery and plants. The second most important area is the transfer of technology within the framework of foreign direct investment or joint ventures; it is estimated that payments for licenses constitute only 5–10 % of what, on the whole, is accounted for by internal firm-level transfers (Reddy and Zhao 1990, 297). Aside from technology, foreign direct investment also entails the transfer of organizational know-how, and foreign firms are undertaking substantial efforts to develop the qualifications required in the host country.

A number of studies (Reddy and Zhao 1990) have noted that foreign investors transfer production technologies and organizational patterns which they use at home without making much effort to adapt them to specific environmental conditions. They tend more – e.g. by building up supply networks – to attempt to adapt the environment to their own needs. This can represent an important contribution to development (for instance, transfer of modern production technologies required for local supplier companies); it is, however, not seldom that in the end this type of behavior proves detrimental to development (Tetzlaff 1986). Efforts geared to adaptation are for the most part restricted to reducing the scale of production. It is seldom that foreign firms set up R&D departments in their affiliates in developing countries (apart from small units designed to ensure that the transferred technology is utilized effectively).

The mode in which technology is transferred – this applies especially for technology for nonaffiliated firms – depends mainly on four factors:

- the technology donor's competitive position (technology available only to a limited number of firms is rarely transferred abroad);

- the importance the technology has for the technology donor (the less important the technology is for a given market position, the more likely it is that it will be transferred abroad);

- the age of the technology (the older the technology, the more likely it is that it will be transferred abroad);

- the character of the technology (transactions between affiliated firms involve especially high technology).

It must thus be assumed that nowhere near every technology that could be transferred will in fact be transferred – neither among industrialized countries nor between industrialized and developing countries.

Factors crucial to the success of technology transfer include:

- the durability of the relationship between the donor and the recipient of technology;

- the transfer of components above and beyond technical hardware;

- the recipient's training;

- the donor's experience with technology transfer and foreign operations;

- an adequate level of technological development on the part of the recipient.

Successful technology transfer thus presupposes a number of factors the presence of which cannot be assumed in all developing countries. The last-named factor is particularly important (Enos 1991). In solving the problem of the chicken and the egg, this experience stipulates that what technology transfer from abroad should represent is not the starting point in the development of technological competence but a complementary element of it.

The transfer of technology is furthermore associated with specific fundamental problems, for *"technology is never fully specified in blueprints or equipment; it is not easily imitable, and experimentation and uncertainties regarding modifications complicate all strategies."* (Rath 1990, 1435) Three principle problems can be identified here:

> *"First, technology is in large measure 'tacit' in that the operating characteristics of a given technology are not fully codified and hence cannot be perfectly known ex ante (...). Second, imitation of a given technology is not trivial, but in fact demands considerable effort on the part of the imitating firm. Finally, given technologies are not well understood, such that production experience is crucial to their efficient operation. These characteristics are present, to varying degrees, in all technologies."* (Herbert-Copley 1990, 1459)

In view of this problem the discussion has shifted in the course of time from the possibilities and problems of technology transfer to the investigation of the determinants of endogenous technological competence. Also, the insight gained in recent years that development cooperation displays a tendency to ignore technology available in DCs – e.g. local knowledge on ecosystems, endogenous technical change among small producers (Gamser et al. 1990; Maldonado and Sethuraman 1992; Islam 1992; and Stewart and Ranis 1990).

1.2   Technology Policy in the Face of Framework Conditions Inimical to Innovation

Since the 1970s at the latest, the development of technological capability (endogenous capacity building) has been a frequently postulated goal. Yet it is evident that this goal has, at least to any appreciable degree, been achieved only in a limited number of industrially advanced DCs. These are without exception countries whose industrialization strategy has been keyed to international competitiveness. On the other hand, countries that have pursued a one-sidedly inward-looking industrialization strategy have at best developed islands of technological capability. This, the following argument will postulate, is a direct consequence of the immanent logic of the model of import-substituting industrialization. This connection long received too little attention in the discussion on technology and industrialization in developing countries (Herbert-Copley 1990, 1461). The discussion proceeded from the infant-industry argument, i.e. the observation that protection against overly powerful foreign competition is an important precondition for late industrialization. One distinguishing feature of successful cases of late industrialization, in particular those in East Asia, is, to be sure, that new industries have at the same time been protected and exposed to pressure to perform; in Korea, for instance, firms were sheltered from foreign competition in the domestic market, while, at the same time, the state exercised great pressure to achieve international competitiveness within very brief periods of time (Hillebrand 1991, 116f.). This simultaneity of protection and pressure is a *sine qua non* of successful industrialization.

1.2.1   Import Substitution and Technological Development

In the case of import-substituting industrialization (ISI) of the type pursued in Latin America, on the other hand, protection far outweighed pressure. In Latin America ISI began during the World Economic Crisis, when Latin American exports collapsed, followed by the onset of a spontaneous process of industrialization geared to replacing the imports that failed to materialize. It was only after the Second World War that ISI was formulated as an explicit concept by the UN Economic Commission for Latin America (Kaufman 1990, 117). It at that time seemed unlikely that the developing countries could assert themselves "actively" by exporting to the world market, in this way achieving integration with it, since continuing deterioration of the terms of trade was expected for raw materials, and the industrial base that had been built up by then appeared inadequate to the task of competing seriously with the industrialized countries. It was only after a period of extensive import substitution, which also entailed a strengthening of technological capability, that appreciable exports of industrial goods could be expected (Thorp 1992, 188ff.).

But in practice this hardly ever happened – import substitution failed to create the groundwork for later exports of industrial goods. Instead, the immanent problems involved in this strategy undermined efforts to achieve industrial competitiveness (Cardoso and Fishlow 1992). These problems, which were responsible for the failure of the strategy of import substitution, can be summed up in five points (Messner and Meyer-Stamer 1992):

–   **Growth crisis**: Very high tariffs, a variety of nontariff barriers, and exaggerated exchange rates discouraged exports, since they raised the prices of exported goods either indirectly (import tariffs, lack of inexpensive imported inputs) or directly (overvaluation, export tariffs). Industry was restricted to the – for the most part too narrow – domestic markets, thus rendering it impossible to cash in on the benefits of mass production.

–   **Productivity crisis**: The insulated domestic economies lacked the internal and external competition that would have heightened efficiency and modernization . Consequently the gap between international and Latin American productivity levels continued to widen. The successive process of "growing into the world economy" that was envisioned in the theoretical concepts was for this reason all but unable to materialize.

– **Social crisis**: Low rates of productivity growth narrowed the scope for increases of real wages, further diminishing internal growth potentials. It proved impossible to alleviate the existing sharp social contrasts. Moreover, the surpluses available for investment were limited, which made these countries dependent on foreign savings.

– **Debt crisis**: The development strategy gave rise to structural balance-of-payments problems. The industrial sector itself hardly took in any foreign exchange, whereas its need for imports of primary products and capital goods was high. The faster the industrial sector grew, the more foreign exchange was therefore needed. The industrialization process was thus forced to rely on export revenues from the agricultural and raw-materials sectors plus external indebtedness. When, at the beginning of the 1980s, the debt crisis set in and raw-materials prices began to decline, this arrangement proved untenable.

– **Crisis of the state**: ISI overburdened the (often administratively weak) state with control tasks, created a subsidy mentality among firms, and led to corruption, clientelism, and permanent budget deficits that were often financed through galloping inflation.

The following section will look into two of these problems, namely those that are central to the context involved in analyzing technology policy: the productivity crisis and the crisis of the state.

1.2.2   Import Substitution and Productivity Crisis

The productivity crisis can be traced back to two factors: insufficient technological development owing to a lack of incentives and a "perverse adaptation" of technology to distorted framework conditions.

The industrialization concept pursued in the context of import substitution was in large measure based on technical considerations. The central objective was to develop a complete industrial base – the span extending from the processing of raw materials and manufacture of intermediate products to capital goods and consumer goods. In this context it seemed tantamount to wasting scarce resources when an identical product was manufactured by a number of firms. Competition among firms seemed a luxury beyond the reach of a poor country. And in certain branches of industry the goal of reaching the minimum-efficient plant size suggested a level of technical rationality before which thought of competition necessarily paled. Examples of this include the petrochemical industry with its low level of demand elasticity, and which is furthermore marked by technical rigidities to the extent that the decomposition of a unit of crude oil yields shares of products such as gasoline, heating oil, and naphtha that cannot be varied at will; or the fertilizer industry, where demand is determined by the agricultural technology in use and thus remains relatively stable. These are industries in which, first, the minimum efficient plant size is relatively large and, second, the fixed-cost share of overall costs (and thus the constraint to operate at consistently high rates of capacity utilization) is great.

There furthermore existed an economic logic that led to the formation of conglomerated groups of firms and heightened vertical integration, for this reduced transaction costs, which were high in view of the relatively weak development of national markets (Leff 1979, 52f.). This, it is true, grew more and more dysfunctional to the extent that

–   markets developed, i.e. the great measure of uncertainty and risk declined that is associated with weakly developed markets;

- specialized suppliers and service firms developed that are able to produce certain inputs or services much more efficiently than a firm integrated horizontally and vertically;

- interfirm networks emerged.

The benefits of business integration were more and more exceeded by the costs of integration , i.e. the internal transaction costs that arise due to high coordination costs, complicated decision-making processes, and bloated overhead, blocking flexibility and diminishing response times. This was exacerbated by the detrimental effects that business concentration exercises on competitiveness. But it is competition that constitutes the driving force of economic development: competitive pressure induces firms to improve processes and products on a continuous basis; and only in this way do the productivity increases materialize on which economic prosperity rests. The consequence of strategies à la *one firm/one product* was, on the other hand, defensive attitudes toward innovation that tended more in the direction of consolidation of a productivity level that had once been attained.

This is not to say that the countries which pursued ISI failed entirely to initiate technological learning processes. The problem is, rather, that the learning processes were systematically distorted. Their aim was not to improve economic efficiency but to adjust to specific framework conditions:

> *"Typical R&D efforts would be determined by the need to use different raw materials, scale-down (to smaller) plant size, diversify the product mix, change the product design, use simpler, more universal, less automated and lower capacity machinery, stretch out the capacity of existing equipment, etc."*
> (Teitel 1987, 109)

The outcome of import substitution was an attitude toward innovation that was, first, inadequate and, second, distorted; and this attitude was, in particular, not geared to achieving international competitiveness. Katz is thus mistaken when he notes:

"There is no immediate reason on account of which the rate of productivity growth deriving from such locally-undertaken technology-generating efforts should necessarily be greater or smaller than the one attained by comparable plants operating in relatively more advanced countries. In principle there is nothing to prevent a particular Brazilian, Mexican or Argentine firm from improving its relative position by means of intensive adaptive technological search efforts and gradually closing up the relative productivity gap which originally separated it from international standards, eventually reaching a position of potential competitiveness in foreign markets." (Katz 1987, 46)

In fact there are two reasons why this assessment is incorrect. First, it is not at all certain that optimization processes and incremental innovation come about at all under the conditions of import substitution; it is at least necessary to create artificially an incentive of the type otherwise introduced by the competition mechanism. Second, however, and in particular, the concern is not just any optimization process, it is an effort to come closer the international level of efficiency and not an "idiosyncratic" process of improvement and adjustment to a distorted environment. There is nothing to indicate that any optimization aimed at adjusting to distorted conditions represents an interim stage on the road to the international efficiency level. On the contrary, it must be assumed that this was an entirely different form of optimization, a form that went in a wholly different direction and often widened the gap separating such firms from the international level of efficiency.

The consequences stemming from lack of competition amounted not only to an inadequate level of production, they also entailed grave shortcomings in the quality of industrial products that consumers, for lack of alternatives, were forced to accept; Katz' formulation seems more a euphemism than an analytical insight:[3] *"Sheltered from external competition local firms feel somewhat less compelled to improve their product's quality."* In fact, a study on the adjustment pressure stemming from measures designed to open up markets in Latin America demonstrated that measures keyed to improvement of quality were given the highest priority; *"most managers admitted that product quality had not concerned them before the reforms."* (Corbo and Melo 1985, 14)

But in the past a clear view of the effects of ISI was hampered by the fact that there were firms which undertook innovation efforts despite low levels of competition in their national markets and low exports. Their behavior was incentive-incompatible; yet this behavior gave rise to doubts as to what, precisely, the incentive structure was. Their behavior often rested on the personal ambition and professional *ethos* of scientists, engineers, and technicians who were guided by a scientific-technical rationality rather than an economic rationale; or rested on entrepreneurial initiative in Schumpeter's sense of the term, in which innovation was, as it were, simply the seasoning required; or on a shared understanding of "national mission," which, in particular in state-owned monopoly enterprises, at times led to a well-developed innovation culture. The singular experiences made by such firms, often themselves the focal point of business journalism and scholarship, at times made it difficult to perceive the more average firms.

1.2.3   Reasons for the Failure of Traditional Technology Policy

Within the context of import substitution there were a variety of attempts to formulate technology policies aimed at building technological capacities in industry, though most of these met with little success. The reason was not solely neglect of the political-economic framework; in particular the lack of incentives owing to inward-looking attitudes and framework conditions inhospitable to innovation. A number of other factors are responsible for a situation in which efforts aimed at strengthening technological competence made little headway in most counties concerned, though not all of these factors are causally related to the problems of ISI. They instead generally occur under social conditions not characterized − as in the case of the East Asian NICs − by a primacy of economics, in particular the primacy of rapid industrialization with the aim of achieving international competitiveness:

- Other, reasonably grounded, priorities at the political level (e.g. debt management, structural adjustment, short-term crisis management) or stop-and-go economic policies (i.e. short-term measures geared to overcoming acute bottlenecks and problems, e.g. rapid rises in inflation or a balance-of-payments crisis) prevented the emergence of any long-term capacity-building in science and technology.

- The political elite's understanding of technological problems was often inadequate, and hence the resources actually made available were insufficient.

- In the face of generally scarce resources, efforts concentrated on fields of major military potential or great prestige (nuclear technology, aerospace technology), although these attempts generated few economically exploitable spinoffs.

- Scientific scholarship concentrated more on basic research than on applied research. This was in line with the prevailing incentive structures in that the prestige of the scientists concerned resulted from their presence in the international scientific community and research funds tended more to be made available by national and foreign foundations than by firms interested in applied research. This orientation was reinforced by the flawed assumption (not specific to Latin America) of a science push, i.e. the assumption that investments in basic research would sooner or later give rise to technological breakthroughs that could be harnessed for commercial ends (Vessuri 1990, 1544).

- There existed a sharp, in part culturally conditioned, partition between the research/technology community on the one hand and the state/economic planning and the economic community/firms on the other, and this disparity was often even deepened by political divergencies (in particular between the left-leaning faction among scientists and right-wing military dictators).

- Networking was inadequate not only between science and technology institutes and industry but also within the research system itself, because institutes were often compelled to compete for scarce resources, and this often meant that healthy rivalry was quick to degenerate into counterproductive animosity; and because scientists tended more to keep up their contacts with their alma mater in the First World (the incentives here being easier access to research funds in international cooperative ventures and the opportunity to travel abroad) than to cultivate contacts at home.

–   The problem of insufficient networking was exacerbated by problems inherent in the international system of development cooperation, which played an important part in developing universities and science and technology institutes. The significant aspects here included tied aid that led to the supply of incompatible equipment; the pressure to achieve short-term success with projects (which, instead of building up technological competence, led to substitution strategies since foreign experts were assigned line functions and were thus unable to act in a capacity of trainers and moderators) (Mytelka 1990); and inadequate networking among projects and lack of orientation in terms of the structure-shaping aspects of projects (Hillebrand, Messner, and Meyer-Stamer 1994).

The core of many of these problems is best sought in the specific political constellation that developed in the context of import substitution.

1.2.4   Import Substitution and the Crisis of State

ISI was a development model in which the state – especially following the exhaustion of the "simple" phase (Kaufman 1990, 116) – was assigned a central role as the stimulator, financier, and regulator of the industrialization process and as the instance responsible for providing compensation for the concomitant socioeconomic symptoms. In many Latin American countries a "state-centered matrix" emerged along the boundaries marking two conflicting fields (state and market, state and society) (Cavarozzi 1992, 671ff.).

The relations between state and market were characterized by two features: on the one hand, the state compensated for the absence of markets, e.g. a capital market, or the lack of functioning competition, especially in scale-intensive industries. On the other hand, the state intervened in existing markets that in part functioned, for instance the labor market. What emerged was a highly complex and inhomogeneous situation marked by marketlike and nonmarketlike transactions, although the market was never completely abolished. The state was confronted with more and more demands, for, in a growing number of transaction areas (growing on account of the "deepening" of import substitution, i.e. the development of new industries with increasing requirements vis-à-vis their institutional setting), its visible hand was forced to replace the invisible hand of the market. The state had, for instance, to seek to prevent administered prices from deviating too sharply from "realistic" levels; and it was forced to set up numerous instruments and supervisory institutions so as to be able not only to threaten price controls but to implement them as well.

The relationship between state and society, earlier marked primarily by clientelist relations, grew more and more differentiated as a result of the establishment of corporativist structures and the emergence of populist patterns of power. Corporativist structures at the same time cleared away the obstacles facing the state's claim to political legitimacy and the control exercised by important social groups, which often were forcibly incorporated into existing or newly created associations. Clientelist structures were not replaced by corporativism, they were supplemented by them. Populist patterns of power were often at odds with the established clientelist and corporatavist structures; politicians sought in this way to develop an electoral base so as to be able to outplay their competitors, who themselves sought to safeguard their own support via clientelist structures and corporativist associations.

The state-centered matrix unfolded along the lines of an additive logic; in cases of doubt conflicts were resolved through cooptation, i.e. by integrating new actors in the corporativist nexus. New political actors *"made increasing demands which were appended, in successive waves, to pre-existing ones. These sequential and often antagonistic demands, and the conflicts they generated, tended to be negotiated within isolated arenas; that is, each actor, or cluster of actors, was linked to the state through exclusive channels.*" (Cavarozzi 1992, 674) What in this way emerged was not a competitive system of represented interests with clearly perceptible mechanisms in the determination of winners and losers but "*a pattern of accumulation of multi-dimensional conflicts and oppositions that can be characterized as one of conflict sedimentation. Successive and multiple layers of conflicts were erected one on top of the other without developing mechanisms for settling disputes in a negotiated and orderly fashion. This is not to say that conflicts were never resolved; in fact, sometimes they were. The pattern of resolution, however, was overly dependent on arbitrary state decisions.*" (Cavarozzi 1992, 675) One consequence of conflict avoidance was high inflation, for in creating money to finance spending the state was able to avoid increasing taxes, thus avoiding to burden given social groups with the costs of the industrialization process.

This pattern had three immediate consequences. First, it preserved established social structures instead of overcoming them, i.e. the anticipated social "modernization process" took a distorted course. Traditional agrarian oligarchies were frequently able to assert their positions of political power even when they failed in the project of economic modernization. The industrial middle class that emerged in the wake of the industrialization process did, it is true, begin to articulate its political interests, but it was generally unable to achieve a hegemonic position. Second, the matrix implied a low degree of flexibility and responsiveness to new chances and challenges, for it was in any case difficult enough to cope with the accumulated conflicts; far-reaching changes of a development model of the type discussed in and partly practiced by Argentina and Brazil in the 1960s with an eye to a more pronounced external orientation proved unsustainable in this context. Third, and this is important with regard to scientific-technological development, the arbitrary character of decision-making generated an incentive system that encouraged individual short-term strategies of utility maximization instead of fostering long-term orientations.

This political structure had far-reaching implications as regards the concept of neostructuralism which was expected to overcome the limitations of import substitution; this concept was under discussion in particular in the second half of the 1980s (Eßer 1987a). It presupposed an actor both rational and able to act in accordance with long-term strategies, the, as it were, classical "development state." This actor, however, was nowhere to be found, for in the course of import substitution the state had long since become the captive of clientelist and corporativist interests. It was not possible simply to push through against the latter any orientation geared to international competitiveness, for one of the main interests of corporativist actors was precisely to seek shelter against competitive pressure in order to be able to pursue, over the long term, the soft option of easy profits in a protected environment.

This arrangement was not accessible to voluntarist attack. The only possibility of breaking it up was, it would seem (even though this interpretation may appear to smack of functionalism), a profound crisis that pulled the material and political rug from beneath the old model; in Chile, for example, a great number of firms went broke during the crisis of the 1970s (O'Donnell 1993, 1366). The Latin American crisis of the 1980s was not consciously induced by the proponents of competitive orientation, it emerged because the import-substitution model was exhausted, because the point of time had come when the "simple" solutions (inflation, foreign debt) no longer worked (hyperinflation, debt crisis), and the ability of the societies concerned to learn, adapt, and transform was low.

2   Import Substitution in Brazil: Industrialization and Technological Development in the Face of Weak Competitive Pressure

Brazil's industrialization long appeared to be a pronounced case of success. A country that at the beginning of the 1950s still had an agrarian character turned, in the course of 30 years, into one of the world's major industrial states.[1] At the end of the 1970s there was hardly any doubt that the country would close the gap separating it from the OECD countries, much in the same way that South Korea and Taiwan in fact did in the 1980s. Yet from 1979 on Brazil lapsed into a rapid succession of acute crises and brief periods of growth, and these can, on the whole, be interpreted as the structural crisis of the ISI model.

Brazil's history of industrialization can be broken down into three broad phases: a chiefly "spontaneous" industrialization process lasting until 1929, the phase of import-substituting industrialization from 1930 to 1990, and the transition to a world-market orientation beginning in 1990. Since in the phase of import substitution industrial, scientific-technological, and political constellations emerged which sharply curtailed the process of transition, this process is still going on.

2.1   Origins of Brazil's Industrialization

The origins of Brazil's industrialization extend back into the late 19th century. The coffee export boom stimulated the building (above all in the state of São Paulo) of factories for agricultural machinery, burlap sacks, and so on. The areas in which sugarcane is grown experienced the building of sugar refineries, and firms were established in the northeast to process locally produced cotton (Suzigan 1986, 70f.). The crucial factor, also as concerns the financing of imports, was coffee production; this holds without reservation for the years up to 1913, and the development continued, less pronounced, until 1929 (Suzigan 1986, 345). Although the state did provide support for the industrialization process (above all via high tariffs and the *similares* rule introduced in 1890, which banned the import of products that could be produced domestically), it neither initiated nor advanced the process – the tariffs were used above all to finance the state budget and were compensated for (as far as the development of import prices is concerned) through changes in the exchange rate; in addition, the *similares* rule was not applied consistently (Moreira 1993, 10, note 9). Furthermore, the state failed to stimulate the creation of the financial institutions required and an adequate educational system. Even infrastructure development was keyed primarily to the interests of the coffee sector and not to those of industry.

2.2   Import-Substituting Industrialization in Brazil

2.2.1   The First Phase of Import Substitution, 1929-54

The world economic crisis of 1929/32 marks the first turning-point in Brazil's history of industrialization – the transition to import-substituting industrialization. This was initially the pragmatic solution for the problems created by the collapse of the world market and the decline of export revenues resulting from it. The state started to play a more active role in industrialization policy, although, until after the Second World War, the view prevalent in government was that export of raw materials was Brazil's natural mission and that industrialization was not necessarily the right policy (Kaufman 1990, 119). The shape given to economic policy was crucial for the dynamism of the process of import substitution: Brazil struck out on the path of devaluation, but without much willingness to compete in the field of austerity. Current accounts were kept in balance with the aid of stringent foreign-exchange and import controls, and an expansive fiscal policy was used to stimulate domestic economic development.

> *"The success of this policy in sustaining income levels, adjusting the BP* (balance of payments, JMS) *and boosting manufacturing investment seems to have left a permanent mark on Brazilian policy makers. From then on, except for a few short*

periods, import and foreign exchange controls would be a key element of the government's policies whatever the ideological colours of the incumbents. " (Moreira 1993, 13)

This approach was used to stimulate the development of both the existing light industry (production of nondurable consumer goods) and a new heavy industry. The latter furthermore profited from the policy of overvaluation which was pursued after the Second World War and brought down the prices of imports of primary products and investment goods. An additional factor was selective state interventions during the Second World War, when the county's first steel mill was built. The share of industrial imports fell from some 45 % in the 1920s to roughly 25 % in the 1930s and to a figure below 20 % in the 1950s (Moreira 1993, 8, Figure 1). To be sure, this did not lead to the emergence of a competitive industry, for:

> *"In Brazil, during 1930-55, external competition was totally removed but nothing was put in place to push firms down the learning curve. Firms had, then, incentives to expand to fill the gaps left by imports, but little incentive to increase efficiency given the technologically poor domestic competition."* (Moreira 1993, 15)

The state's capacity to induce firms to step up their efficiency and engage in learning processes was limited. Because the state – thanks to the coup d'état of 1930, which was directed against the traditional, regionally anchored agrarian oligarchies – was without a reliable political base, the implementation of individual policies depended on its ability to forge ad hoc alliances; and Brazil's national industry, already in large measure beholden to trade capital and a segment of the coffee bourgeoisie (Mathieu 1991, 170), was an important ally. The payoff for industry was unimpeded access to the domestic market; performance criteria were perceived in this system as irrelevant. This pattern of a state buying political support by handing out economic sinecures is one of the red threads trailing through Brazil's history of industrialization.

The lack of competitiveness on the part of industry found expression in, among other things, the low level of exports of manufactured goods; industry's 1949 export share was no more than 2.3 % (Moreira 1993, Table A 7). The industrialization process thus remained dependent on exports of primary goods, above all coffee (1950: 63.9 % of overall exports) (Moreira 1993, Table A 6). The problems facing industry were further exacerbated by the fact that the state failed to implement flanking policies – development of financial institutions, infrastructure, formation of human capital.[2] To make things worse, certain legal framework conditions generated negative effects; a 1933 law, for instance, that limited the interest rate for credit to a maximum of 12 % frightened off potential lenders in view of an average inflation rate of 13 % (1940-55) (Moreira 1993, 17). The firms therefore had no other choice than to finance their investments through excessive prices – which were easy to push through in the absence of import competition (Baer 1965, 110ff.). Apart from a budget balanced by issuing new money, this was the second most important cause of the inflation that has accompanied Brazil's development process.

2.2.2   Active Industrial Policy and Crisis, 1955-64

The beginning of the 1950s marks a turning-point in the economic-policy discourse; the latter was dominated no longer by liberals but by structuralists under the influence of CEPAL (Bielschowsky 1991). One consequence was a stronger state role in the secondary sector and in the shaping of the institutional framework of industrial development – this phase saw the establishment of the first state-owned firms in the energy sector (Petrobrás in the oil industry and various electricity utilities) and the creation of the national development bank (BNDE). A second consequence – after the inauguration of President Kubitschek – consisted in the elaboration of a state-controlled industrialization project, the *plano de metas*. This plan defined quantitative targets in the sectors of infrastructure, heavy industry, food production, and training; the lion's share of investments, 43.4 %, went into the power-generation sector (Moreira 1993, 20f.).

There were few institutional innovations connected with the plan. A national development council was to operate as the central planning authority, but before long it had disintegrated into a number of sectoral agencies (*grupos executivos*) composed of public- and private-sector actors; the state's autonomy of action remained limited on account of the diffuse political base involved, and ad hoc coalitions continued to dominate the picture, thus preventing the state, in practice, from operating in the capacity of "overall capitalist." Coordination between sectoral activities was low. The state's weight within a number of sectors, in particular infrastructure and heavy industry, nevertheless grew, because, due to the insufficient supply of capital, private firms were hardly able to finance the investments required here. BNDE's activities were of little help, for it, for the most part, directed its credits to state projects; it was only since the middle of the 1960s that the credits made available to private firms took on a larger scope (Frischtak and Atiyas 1990, 64).

The implementation of the *plano de metas* was inhibited by overall economic development. While the plan implied growing imports of primary products and investment goods, increasing debt service and deteriorating terms of trade restricted the country's import capacity. The introduction of a graduated system of tariffs (ranging from 0 to 150 %) and the implementation of the *similares* rule brought little relief since the level of protection was already high. Various incentives aimed at attracting investments from foreign corporations were introduced; the latter became active in the production of durable consumer goods. The flow of capital not only helped to alleviate the current-accounts problems. Moreover, the development of these branches of industry also proved costly; any development by national firms would have proceeded at the expense of other sectors, thus colliding with the basic bargain of the industrialization model, namely not to disadvantage any sector in absolute economic terms (Mathieu 1991, 176). In fact, in no phase of the industrialization process after 1945 was the significance of foreign investment – measured in terms of overall investment in manufacturing industries – as great as it was in this phase (Table 2).

Table 2: Trends of Foreign Direct Investments, 1948-88 (1)			
	Million US-$ (2)	Percentage of investments in manufacturing industries (3)	Percentage of net capital inflow (4)
1948	16.5	no data	45.9
1952	8.6	no data	14.0
1956	84.4	29.6	30.9
1960	104.4	21.7	20.0
1964	47.4	5.9	12.7
1968	99.4	10.3	12.3
1972	486.5	14.5	10.9
1976	1,036.3	14.9	12.5
1980	1,461.0	22.6	11.3
1984	366.4	no data	4.1
1988	95.8	no data	5.9
(1) Three-year moving average. (2) Total FDI plus reinvestments minus withdrawals, debt-swaps and Brazilian investment. (3) 1970 prices. (4) Net FDI plus medium and long term loans. Source: Moreira (1993), p. 79, Tab. A.12.			

The rise in inflation had to be seen in the same context: rising govern-ment spending was financed not through tax increases but with the aid of credits provided by the Banco do Brasil, the country's largest state-owned bank; these credits were generally neither serviced nor repaid (Moreira 1993, 26). Attempts on the part of the state to limit rising inflation by means of a restrictive price policy of public-sector firms burdened the latter with losses, thus further increasing the budget deficit; also, this practice restricted the investment capacity of the state-owned firms. It likewise led to distortions in relative prices, which no longer provided information on relative costs and efficiency levels and therefore favored the misallocation of resources.

In quantitative terms, the targets of the *plano de metas* were for the most part met or even exceeded (Moreira 1993, 28), and economic development was, at an average GDP growth rate of 9.4 % (1955-61), dynamic. Various shortcomings, however, were not only not overcome, they were not even seriously tackled; this was true in particular of the nonexistent R&D infrastructure and the system of education and training. The costs of this – albeit partial – success were, to be sure, high: the state budget deficit grew, thus pushing up inflation, and price distortions increased in scope. The crisis of the early 1960s – galloping inflation, current-account crisis – was thus a direct outcome of the apparent success of the 1950s.

Moreover, an opportunity was missed – that is, to gear to exports the industries that had already been operating for a time and were thus no longer infants. In view of the pronounced scarcity of capital, and bottlenecks in human capital, the growth potential in these less capital-intensive industries was greater than in heavy industry and the production of durable consumer goods, where foreign firms (e.g. in the automobile industry) had begun producing; also, a more national entrepreneurship could have emerged here (Moreira 1993, 28ff.). Instead,

> *"An inefficient industrial structure was then built – oversized vis-à-vis the domestic market but with most of the plants below the international MES (minimum efficient scale, JMS) – heavily dependent on permanent protection, even though most of the heavy industry sectors were either led or totally dominated by the most efficient producers of the world."* (Moreira 1993, 31)

2.2.3   The "Economic Miracle", 1964-73

This model was not transformed fundamentally after the military coup of 1964; it was instead modified and "deepened" (Hurtienne 1984, 248). The new regime's liberal rhetoric soon gave way to a pragmatic eclecticism that found expression in a sustained high level of state intervention in the economy.

The reforms undertaken by the new government affected fiscal and foreign-trade policy. The system of taxation was reformed with an eye to improving the revenue situation. The prices of the state-owned firms were adjusted. The creation of a central bank brought with it, as a pioneering innovation, the introduction of indexed government bonds; from then on these served as a means of providing a continuous adjustment to inflation and made it possible to reinterpret the legal limit on interest rates, which was now read as a limitation on real interest rates. This also paved the way for private financial institutions to enter into the credit business; and this not only improved the financing potentials of firms, it also constituted the foundation on which consumer credit was introduced. The access of firms to foreign credit was also facilitated.

The foreign-trade policy pursued by the government provided for the gradual introduction of a uniform exchange rate that replaced the split exchange rates previously in effect for specific product groups as well as for imports and exports. Various nontariff trade barriers were reduced; the *similares* rule no longer banned imports per se, although it did prohibit state incentives for the import of goods that were also produced domestically. Moreover, the average tariff rate was cut from 99 to 66 %, although, as early as 1968, problems with the current-accounts balance again moved the government to raise tariff rates (Moreira 1993, 36). Exports were stimulated with the aid of tax breaks, direct subsidies, subsidized export credits, and the introduction of a drawback system (Peñalver et al. 1983, 53ff.; Pinheiro et al. 1993, 475ff.).

On the institutional side, the state attempted to safeguard the coherence of its industrial policy by creating a Council for Industrial Development (*Conselho de Desenvolvimento Industrial*, CDI). CDI was supposed to bring together the competent state authorities and integrate the *grupos executivos*. In fact, however, CDI did not succeed in assuming the coordinating role conceived for it and failed to impose clear-cut criteria for the allocation of financial resources. *"CDI's incentives were distributed at random, without any clear criteria, but to increase investments."*[3] The reason for this was, among other things, that CDI was given both a regulatory function and a promotion function (Frischtak and Atiyas 1990, 26). An additional factor was that there were, apart from CDI, at least a dozen other regional or sector-specific agencies over which CDI had no control. These included institutions as powerful as the development agencies for the northeastern region

(SUDENE) and the Amazon region (SUDAM) as well as for the Free Production Zone in Manaus (SUFRAMA).

This institutional diversity mirrored on the one hand regional interests that frequently were at odds with any national logic. SUFRAMA, for instance, led to the emergence of isolated domestic-market oriented srewdriver factories, typically manufacturing for foreign electronics firms whose products had to be transported thousands of kilometers on bad roads to consumers in the south and southeast. On the other hand, it reflected a structural flaw of Brazil's civil service, whose main function, even today, is to create income opportunities for the clientele of politicians. This is the reason why in many authorities very few posts were filled on criteria such as personal competence and terms of employment were brief. True, even under the dictator Getúlio Vargas there were efforts to build a modern civil service (hiring on the basis of qualification, political autonomy, freedom from party-political influences); but these initial steps were quickly rescinded after 1945, and various attempts at a reform of the civil service undertaken between 1945 and 1964 came to nothing (Holanda 1993, 166f.).

In was only in the phase of the military dictatorship that these initiatives were taken up again. But this often meant little more than that structures were created on top of the traditional authorities, though these structures were organized in keeping with modern criteria (e.g. meritocratic recruitment, stability of post) and had the appearance of *"pockets of efficiency"* (Evans 1989a, 577). And it was for this reason that no systematic nexus of relations developed between the state and the economy that displayed at least a certain measure of transparency and clear-cut rules; instead, these relations were often personalistic, linked to the presence of particular persons in particular agencies. This structure was, to be sure, neither conducive to a systematic, horizontally articulated formulation of industrial policy nor did it establish reliable, communication channels between administration and firms (Evans 1989a, 579). Yet the latter would have constituted the sine qua non for clarifying the risk of longer-term commitments by private firms. The short-term orientation of a large part of the local private sector was, in this sense, rational. Exceptions of intensive and durable relationships of the type documented for the steel, paper and food industries and mechanical engineering confirm this rule (Soto 1993 and Diniz 1989, 113f.); the case was such in these sectors that representatives of the specific industrial organizations worked closely together with representatives of government agencies in order, for instance, to establish what imports were to be admitted or what preferential import tariffs might be granted.

The efforts directed at creating technology institutions were more successful.[4] The newly established System for Scientific-Technological Development (SNDCT) was given the task of formulating and coordinating R&D policy. Universities were expanded and a special institution for the control of technology imports was created with an eye to limiting the costs of technology acquisition and ensuring that technology was distributed throughout the country's industry.

The model at times appeared extraordinarily successful; the high growth rates between 1965 and 1973 (a yearly average of 10 % of GDP, 11 % of industrial output) were indicators of a dynamic industrial development. Furthermore, between 1964 and 1970 inflation dropped from 90 % to 16 %, and more and more exports and capital flows eased the country's current-accounts problems.

Yet industrialization failed to raise the incomes of broad segments of the population, and instead reinforced the tendency toward income concentration; *"the 'miracle' was very much built on the indebtedness of a tiny middle class"* (Moreira 1993, 44). Internally, growth potentials were structurally restricted. Outward-oriented growth was to be had only on the basis of export subsidies, for otherwise Brazilian industrial goods were unable to compete in the world market. The country's dependence on imports remained great, as did its vulnerability to external shocks. The latter case made itself felt in 1973 when the oil price crisis began.

2.2.4   Intensified Import Substitution, 1974-79

The military government responded to this state of affairs not by initiating measures geared to redistributing income and heightening competition and efficiency but by expanding public investment aimed at deepening import substitution in the raw-materials and energy sectors (Second National Development Plan /PND II), increasing state consumption, and forging ahead with programs of export subsidization (in particular the 1972 BEFIEX program which coupled government support to year-long export commitments). This did not entail any change in the basic orientation of an *"exaggerated and permanent protectionism"* (Suzigan 1988, 10); on the contrary, the roots of the economic problems were sought in an insufficient level of import substitution.

Tariffs were again hiked as a means of intensifying import substitution, and various new nontariff trade barriers were introduced. These measures impeded the import not only of consumer goods but of investment goods as well, the intention being to stimulate direct investments of foreign producers of capital goods.

The export subsidies were needed in particular to compensate in certain sectors for the anti-export bias of Brazil's development policy (Suzigan 1988, 1). The exporters of metals and metal products, processed foods, and electrical appliances profited greatly from the export subsidies (Baumann and Braga 1988). The total (direct and indirect) subsidies reached a high level, some 60 % of the value of manufactured exports (Figure 2). The costs of this export promotion for the state budget were even further increased due to the fact that export credits were granted at strongly negative real interest rates (8 % nominal in the face of an average inflation rate of 41 %) (Moreira 1993, 49).

The manner in which domestic investments were financed, namely, for the most part via BNDE credits, constituted a similar burden. The losses were very high, above all in 1976, when the nominal interest rates were between 0 and 2 % and adjustment for inflation was limited to a maximum of 20 % – in view of an annual inflation rate of 37 % the subsidy component thus incurred amounted to some 88 % of the credit

Figure 2:

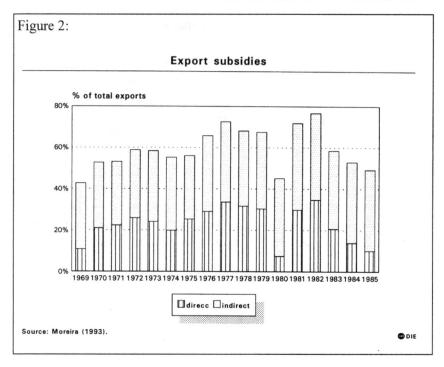

Export subsidies

% of total exports

Source: Moreira (1993).

volume. BNDE's share of gross capital formation in the private sector rose in 1976 to 18.7 % (1973: 5.9 %, 1979-87: between 5.7 and 11.6 %) (Frischtak and Atiyas 1990, 63ff.).

Industrial policy in the narrower sense was marked by a situation in which various agencies pursued different, indeed often conflicting and even contradictory, conceptions and strategies. In certain sectors – petrochemicals, telecommunication equipment, computers – the activities of foreign firms were restricted (joint ventures only) or ruled out entirely, in most other sectors the regulations applied to the local content prescribed. As a means of strengthening the country's technological base - the bottleneck in this area had been recognized in the meantime – financing programs were devised that were geared to expanding the university system and strengthening the country's scientific base (among other things via programs for post-graduates and scholarships for study abroad). Furthermore, technology import licenses were tied more strongly to the absorption capacity of the technology recipient concerned, and a special BNDE credit line was created to promote the technological development of local private firms. Another significant factor was the support provided by big state-owned firms for the technological upgrading of private firms, in particular by Petrobás.

The strategy was highly dependent on capital flows from abroad, for Brazil's balance of trade, in any case deficit-ridden, went deeper and deeper into the red on account of the oil price shock and the import needs of newly emerging branches of industry.[5] The flow of direct investment, averaging 1.1 billion US-$ per year, was higher than in the phase of the economic miracle (0.2 billion), and the foreign debt tripled to some 50 billion US-$. PND II thus even exacerbated the country's external vulnerability. The rise in oil prices and the explosion of real interest rates thus, toward the end of the 1970s, led directly into the debt trap.

Moreira's scathing résumé on PND II:

> *"Under total protection, largely market-led credit allocation, lax investment and FDI licensing, fragmented and inefficient industrial structures continued to survive and proliferated as IS moved upstream. On the financial side, the key issue of long term financing for LPFs (local private firms, JMS) was only precariously solved. In this sort of environment, the LPFs' growth was bound to be hampered and macroeconomic imbalances were inevitable, regardless of any 'macroeconomic failure'."* (Moreira 1993, 61)

This diagnosis is somewhat exaggerated, for in fact the dynamic was increasingly borne by national private firms, and it was selectively stimulated and tied into the capacity-building process in key industries such as metal production, petrochemicals, and investment goods; the share of private firms in BNDES credits, an indicator relevant in this context, had been 65.4 % in 1970 and rose to 81.1 % by 1976 (Frischtak and Atiyas 1990, 65). And there was one additional factor: the industrial dynamic that unfolded until 1979 was doubtless impressive, both for Brazilian and for foreign observers (Tyler 1981, 1). Their "impressed" state explains the sharp divergence in the way they judge industrial import substitution: it was impressive with regard to the technical achievement of building, within a relatively short period of time, a highly diversified industrial base. But it was far less impressive when the costs, the efficiency level, and the macroeconomic and social consequences were included in the analysis.[6] Moreira's assessment is right to the extent that he points to continuing structural deficits that are essential to any understanding of the causes of the economic crisis underway since 1979.

2.3   Stagnation Without Adjustment: Brazil's Industry in the 1980s

There are two reasons why the 1979 oil-price and interest-rate shock led the way into economic crisis: unlike, say, South Korea (which was at the same time able to avert a critical development of its debt situation), a large share of Brazil's foreign credits went into projects which (like, for example, the capital goods industry) could not be turned to direct advantage to boost exports or (like, for instance, dam projects) contributed only indirectly and over the medium term to an improvement of the country' competitive position. The anti-export bias continued, and there were very few firms that were competitive enough to achieve rapid growth in exports without massive subsidies. True, the growth in manufactured exports in the PND II period averaged 16 % per year, but this mirrored the high subsidies and – particularly for foreign firms closer to the international efficiency level – the possibility of pocketing rents. In 1980 only eight of 108 branches of industry for which figures are available had an export share of more than 20 %, while the figure for 57 of them was below 5 % (Frischtak and Atiyas 1990, 21).

The second reason: Once, in the wake of the oil shock, beginning in 1974, success seemed to have been achieved in "growing out" of the crisis, so that the proponents of an austerity-oriented adjustment policy were in a bad position in 1979; the guiding principle of the country's adjustment strategy was, at first, debt-financed expansion, but the limits of this strategy became clear prior to the onset of the debt crisis. In Brazil the 1980s turned into a phase of crisis management. Rehabilitation concepts of different economic provenance followed one another in rapid succession: *"There were eight stabilization programs, four different currencies, eleven different indices for calculating inflation, five wage and price freezes, 14 different wage policies, 18 changes in exchange regulations, 54 modifications in the rules governing price controls, 21 proposals for renegotiating the foreign debts, and 19 government decrees on fiscal austerity."* (Fiori 1992, 184)

Brazil's economic policy was not merely erratic, though. Measures designed to solve acute problems had a purely ad hoc character; they were not backed by concepts keyed to the longer term. For it was only toward the end of the 1980s that the insight gained currency that the crisis was not was not merely a spell of bad wheather which had to be gone through before it was possible to sail on in the accustomed fashion, and that the ship had in fact run aground and it was high time to overhaul it from the keel up and to set sail in a new direction. Brazil was one of the last countries in Latin America to take leave of the conventional import-substitution strategy.

2.3.1   Deterioration of Competitiveness in the 1980s

Only at first glance is it surprising that industry not only survived in the hyperturbulent setting of the 1980s but even, at least in financial terms, strengthened its position. It regularly succeeded in making profits, and the average annual rate of return in the 1980s declined only slightly in comparison with the previous period. (Figure 3) The reason for this must be sought in the circumstance that firms had little difficulty in commanding higher prices in this highly inflationary environment. More than ever, investments were financed from returns; the debt-equity ratio sank from 55–60 % in the 1970s to 41–43 % in the period between 1986-89 (Exame, Melhores e Maiores, annual publication). The reverse die of the coin was accelerating inflation and a competitiveness deteriorating due to a lack of adequate adjustment measures.

Figure 3:

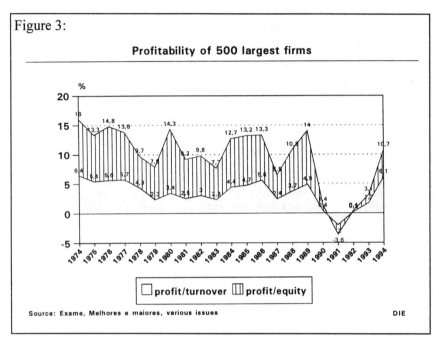

Profitability of 500 largest firms

profit/turnover　profit/equity

Source: Exame, Melhores e maiores, various issues　　　　　　　DIE

This is true even though the level of investment long remained high; in 1988 the nominal investment rate was 23.2 %. And the composition of overall economic investment had changed: the state investment share of GDP fell from 4 % (1970s) to below 1 %, and the share of state-owned firms declined from 6 % to 2.7–2.8 %. A closer look at the investment rate, however, illustrates a further critical point in addition to the shift of investment activity from the public to the private sector, namely, a decline in investments in fixed assets (Figure 4). These data alone indicate that the 1980s were not a phase in which industry undertook efforts aimed at structural adjustment, i.e. improvement of its competitiveness in a changing environment. In fact, any attitude of this sort would, to be sure, have called for an extreme measure of strategic behavioral disposition, for an unpredictable economic policy and uncertain economic development prospects left little scope for a serious assessment of long-term trends.

Figure 4:

Public and Private Investment in Brazil, 1950-1993

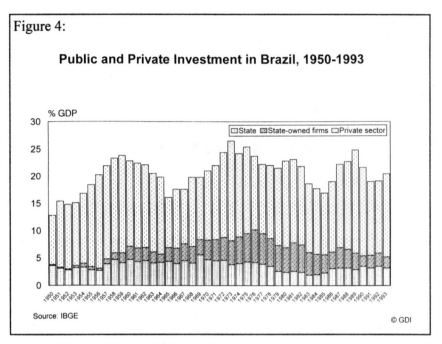

Source: IBGE

© GDI

While between 1980 and 1989 GDP grew by an annual average rate of 3 %, industrial output increased by only 2.2 %; the number of jobs in industry dropped by 10 % (UNIDO 1992a, 3). Industry's competitiveness was on the decline. One indicator of this is provided by studies which focused on the differences between the national and international price level. One of these studies found for the period between 1983/85 that in 45 % of industries the national prices were below world market prices, whereas 7 % showed figures up to 10 % above international levels (Araujo et al. 1990). Another study *"shows that in 1988 only 15 % of the subsectors were clearly competitive, while in 12 % of the cases competitiveness was marginal."* (H. Kume 1988, quoted after Frischtak and Atiays 1990, 7) *"These studies thus suggest that the proportion of fully or marginally competitive segments fell by nearly half (from 52 % to 27 % between 1983/85 and 1988)."* (Frischtak and Atiyas 1990, 7) The authors who make this comparison do, however, at the same time point to the methodological problems connected with it: *"International price comparisons tend to present well-known problems of choice of an appropriate exchange rate comparability of products differentiated by quality and performance, etc. Yet such price data can be suggestive of broad trends in a country's competitive position in world markets, as in the case just discussed.*" (Frischtak and Atiyas 1990, 7, note 4) The latter assessment is understandable; yet an additional qualifying reference is also appropriate: the study first cited also collected data on the export shares in the individual industries concerned, and there is no clearly perceptible linkage between price level and export performance. This reflects factors such as quality and access to international marketing channels, though it also underlines the problems involved in the price comparison itself. A further question is how the prices came about, since a great number of distortions of relative prices emerged in cartelized markets and due to state interventions, i.e. subsidies and tax breaks. Comparisons of this kind must thus be viewed with the greatest caution; to cite them alone as an indicator of deteriorated competitiveness would be methodologically questionable.

An alternative approach to the issue of competitiveness is made possible by studies that instead of comparing prices focus on other factors indicative of the efficiency of firms (but for a given date, and not as an intertemporal comparison). These studies likewise arrive at pessimistic assessments of the competitiveness of Brazilian firms. A study conducted in 1989/90 (Sequeira 1990) shows that even leading firms, often even firms active in exporting, display on the average very poor efficiency indicators (Figure 5). What is conspicuous here is the poor record for indicators pointing beyond traditional cost accounting, i.e. the dismal values for the indicators for quality and responsiveness.

A wide-ranging study conducted by SEBRAE and Fundação Getúlio Vargas which, in October of 1987, polled industrial firms on their self-evaluation of the proportion of technologically up-to-date products in their product pallet showed two different things. First: roughly one half of the firms in the consumer and investment goods industry were aware of a technological lag. Second: the extent of heterogeneity among industries was great (Figure 6).

Figure 5:

Indicators of competitiveness of leading Brazilian firms

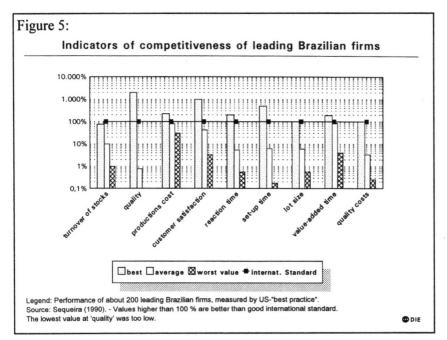

Legend: Performance of about 200 leading Brazilian firms, measured by US-"best practice".
Source: Sequeira (1990). - Values higher than 100 % are better than good international standard.
The lowest value at 'quality' was too low.   ⊕ DIE

Figure 6:

State of the art of technology in industry

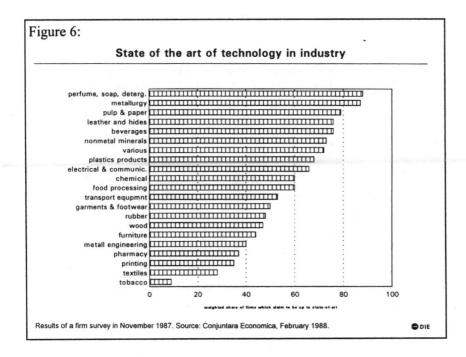

Results of a firm survey in November 1987. Source: Conjuntara Economica, February 1988.   ⊕ DIE

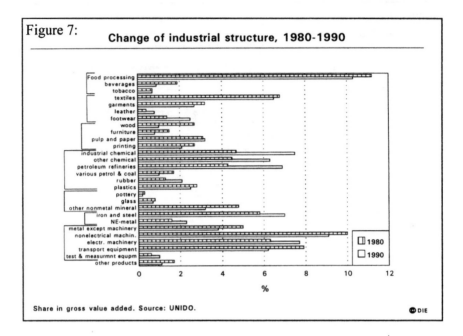

Figure 7: Change of industrial structure, 1980-1990

Share in gross value added. Source: UNIDO.

A glance at the changes that emerged in the industrial structure in the 1980s shows clear-cut tendencies, but also some surprising individual findings. Figure 7 shows the share of individual industries in value added in two years in which value added was nearly identical; declining shares thus reflect an output volume declining in absolute terms as well. What is clear is the dynamic in many resource-based sectors, particularly metal production and petrochemicals (in this period both sectors took up production in industrial complexes that had been planned and launched in the 1970s), and in the shoe industry. On the other hand, there are slumps in metal products, in nonelectrical machine-building (which was suffering from a drastic decline in state investment and drops in private fixed capital investment) and in transportation equipment. It must be noted that the slump was due on the one hand to a decline in production in the automobile industry and on the other hand to a major slump in the shipbuilding industry. But it was not only these "modern" industries that suffered losses. Branches of industries that, in the discussion on Brazil, are often regarded as comparatively dynamic, or appear to possess great potential on account of their factor endowments, either had declining output figures (e.g. clothing, furniture,or minerals, including the tile industry, an important exporter) or were caught up in stagnation (e.g. the pulp and paper industry).

2.3.2   Factors Behind the Export Success

The dynamics of industrial exports, which in the 1980s gave rise to the impression that an efficient industrial base had emerged in Brazil, are only apparently inconsistent with the diagnosis of declining competitiveness. In fact, three reasons can be cited to explain why industrial exports grew in spite of an overall decrease in competitiveness.

– One of the consequences of Brazil's erratic economic policy was abrupt fluctuations in domestic demand. Many firms attempted successfully to compensate for sluggish domestic demand by harnessing their existing capacities to step up exports; economic growth and growth in exports correlated negatively between 1981 and 1989 (Figure 8).[7] This path did, however, not lead to continuous export activity; the country's export performance, showing growth in tendency while fluctuating sharply from year to year, conceals a large measure of sporadic and random exports.

– In other branches of industry, e.g. automobiles, the Brazilian government from the 1970s on sought to boost exports by paying large subsidies to multinational corporations whose affiliates supplied the sheltered domestic market. An attempt between 1979/80 to cut the subsidies led to a sharp decline in exports, and the subsidies were then quickly restored to their old level.

– Finally, firms from some industries succeeded in achieving international competitiveness thanks to high investments financed by the national development bank, and continuous learning processes. These include industries whose static locational advantages are quite considerable, e.g. paper and cellulose production.[8] These were joined by other industries, such as producers of concentrated orange juice or frozen poultry, that included dynamic firms which

Figure 8:

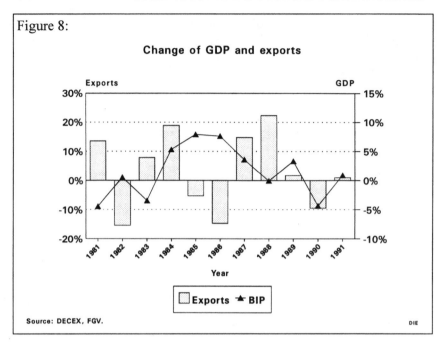

Change of GDP and exports

Source: DECEX, FGV.

succeeded in linking high efficiency and quality with rapid progress in learning in the field of marketing know-how, or the shoe industry, where the factors contributing to the development of competitiveness included extremely low wage levels and technological learning processes that were stimulated by foreign trading firms (Schmitz 1993).

A detailed analysis of Brazilian exports shows a clear-cut deterioration in performance. Whereas in the first half of the 1980s the majority of industries succeeded in expanding their market shares (although the better part of this was in markets with below-average dynamism (Figure 9a), the situation was reversed in the second half of the decade (Figure 9b), i.e. the Brazilian economy failed to utilize its chances in this period, which was marked by high growth in world trade (6.1 % as opposed to 2.1 % in the first half of the 1980s) (GATT 1992, 77). If Brazilian exporters had held their shares in foreign markets in the second half of the 1980s, the country's exports would have amounted to

Figure 9:

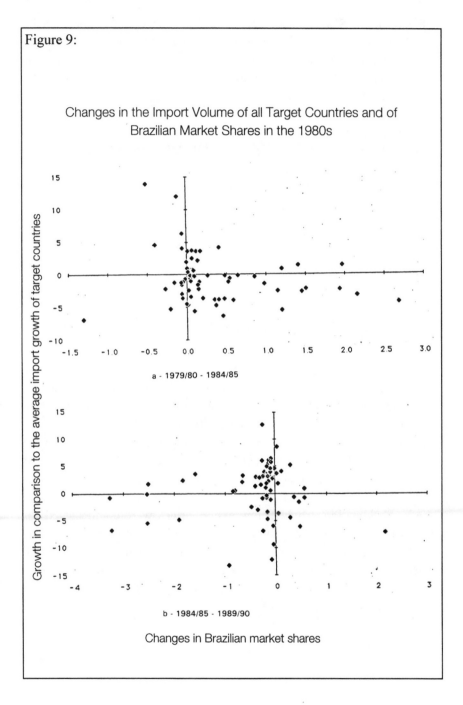

Changes in the Import Volume of all Target Countries and of Brazilian Market Shares in the 1980s

a - 1979/80 - 1984/85

b - 1984/85 - 1989/90

Changes in Brazilian market shares

Growth in comparison to the average import growth of target countries

48.5 billion US-$ in 1990, i.e. some 50 % above the value actually reached in this year. In fact, however, the gains in market shares made in the first half of the 1980s were lost in the second half of the decade (Batista and Fritsch 1993, 8). Figure 9b shows that only 14 of the total of 70 industries covered were able to expand their share of the world market in the second half of the 1980s. These industries were: tobacco, iron ore, iron and steel, nonferrous metals, ceramics, unprocessed minerals, trucks, aircraft, fertilizer, agricultural machines, construction machines, special machines, optics, and large electrical machines (Batista and Fritsch 1993, 12ff.). In many cases the driving force behind these figures was individual national or multinational firms, e.g. Embraer for aircraft, Mercedes-Benz for trucks (in the 1980s Brazil was scheduled to be built up into an export platform for the whole continent), Maxion for agricultural machines, or Siemens for hydroelectric turbines.

2.3.3   Distorted Incentive Structures

The insufficient state of competitiveness reflects an incentive structure that failed to reward improvements in efficiency, quality, or innovativeness - the competitive pressure that could have brought this about was low in the domestic market; and in the export market many Brazilian firms were in competition in the low-price, low-quality market segment. Other firms which delivered good quality (e.g. leading car part suppliers) often achieved this at the expense of efficiency; it was not only in this case that the firms introduced a system of internal cross-subsidization in which low export prices were compensated for by excessive prices in the domestic market. Government price controls neither generated efficiency pressure on firms nor did they lower the price level; *"since firms in price-controlled sectors have to justify price increases on the basis of costs, the price control system at best prevents excessive price increases."* (Baer 1987, 1022)

The market constellation typical for Brazil can be illustrated with two examples:

- Price formation was in precise contradiction to what economics textbooks would lead one to expect: when quantities declined, a new equilibrium price formed not at a low level but at a high level. The firms responded to sales slumps by raising their prices with an eye to stabilizing their returns. In most cases this worked because the firms themselves had market power enough or because they were operating in oligopolistic markets in which there was either no struggle for market shares or competition was regulated not by price but, for instance, with the aid of costly advertising campaigns.

- Firms were very reticent in making product innovations – which are a key competitive instrument in the developed industrialized countries. Between 1983 and 1992, for example, only one really new car model was introduced: the Chevrolet Kadett, that is, the Kadett E developed by Opel. It was produced in Germany from 1983 to 1991 and introduced in Brazil in 1987; a slightly modified version of the Kadett C (produced in Germany from 1973-79) was offered until the end of 1993 as the Chevrolet Chevette besides the Chevrolet Kadett.

It was not only such that Brazil had no competition policy and no agency to control effectively the abuse of market power – economic concentration was for a protracted period even an explicit political goal (Fritsch and Franco 1989). Key industrial-policy instruments were used accordingly: firms that received incentives from the Council for Industrial Development or the BEFIEX Program were eight or ten times as large as the average firm in their industry. 67 % of all BEFIEX contracts were concluded with firms belonging to conglomerates. And even BNDES lending was largely concentrated among a small number of big customers (Frischtak and Atiyas 1990, 63ff.). Despite the dynamic growth process, the degree of industrial concentration thus increased between 1950 and 1980; Gini indices of 0.5896 and 0.8075 have been calculated for these two years on the basis of industry census figures (Bastos 1992, 264).

The measures promoting concentration were at least understandable in the 1970s in the context of the import-substitution logic and in a phase in which the concern was to expand capacities. Yet protection was not at all reduced to the same degree to which firms grew more mature, on the contrary: *"As the industrial sector matured, protective barriers solidified, and firms became increasingly secure of their market positions"* (Frischtak and Atiyas 1990, 7) On the one hand, there were a variety of barriers to entry; *"formal regulatory constraints and limited access to investment incentives deterred entry and helped incumbents reinforce their market positions. Fiscal and financial incentives were granted mostly to dominant firms for capacity expansion in mature subsectors."* (Frischtak and Atiyas 1990, 8) In the 1980s some 55 % of manufacturing value addet accrued to industries with pronounced barriers to entry. These were in part the result of the authorization required for investment (in petrochemicals, fine chemicals, and fertilizers); in the period between 1979-86 over 40 % of all applications for investment were rejected (Frischtak and Atiyas 1990, 29). In other industries it was the selective granting of tax incentives, import licenses or customs facilities, and BNDES credits that made for a situation in which the market entry costs were prohibitively high for nonfavored firms (which thus, for instance, had no access whatever to investment credits). On the other hand, there were also exit barriers; *"... fiscal and financial incentives have allowed producers to postpone exit"* (Frisctak and Atiyas 1990, 8) One factor of considerable significance here was BNDES rescue actions aimed at saving ailing firms from bankruptcy.[9]

In the industries targeted by industrial policy, firms were subjected to very little pressure. The policy-makers concentrated their efforts on a limited number of firms – in the expectation of advantages to scale and with an eye to avoiding the buildup of unneeded capacities; this minimized competitive pressure. The policy-makers could hardly permit their "pupils" to go under for lack of competitiveness; this de facto survival guaranty for firms minimized the pressure to perform.

At the same time price distortions were not only perpetuated, in some industries they were even reinforced through discretionary interventions. On the other hand, there were a number of industries whose products commanded in the national market prices several times as high as the price in the world market. One particularly extreme case was consumer electronics (Araujo et al. 1990), where the prices were four times as high as world market prices. The reason was the low level of production efficiency and high transportation costs, for this industry was mainly located in the import production zone of Manaus; thus it was that the consumers provided their contributions to the creation of jobs in this remote region. On the other hand, there existed branches of industry that commanded prices less than half of those obtaining in the world market. This did not necessarily have anything to do with high efficiency and productivity or absolute cost advantages due to cheap inputs (e.g. energy). In the steel industry, for instance, the state forced the firms to remain below the inflation rate when they adjusted their prices so as to subsidize the competitiveness of downstream industries (Frischtak and Atiyas 1990, 45).

This is of course not to say that in general all firms were able to rake in goods profits without making any efforts of their own. For firms that had no secure access to the "BNDES hospital" (Mathieu 1991b, 23), the factor decisive for overall business results was the effectiveness of financial management. Owing to the highly inflationary environment and the government's erratic economic policy, this is the point at which it was decided whether a firm operated in the red or in the black. Poor financial management could not be compensated for by highly efficient production; but conversely, good financial management could provide for a positive result even in the face of moderate production efficiency. This constellation was a further reason why firms undertook only limited efforts directed at improving their competitiveness by raising production efficiency and innovativeness.

2.3.4   The Sarney Government's Incrementalism in Industrial Policy

The erratic economic policy, the futile attempts at stabilization, the unsound budgetary policy, and the lack of personnel stability in state institutions were important reasons why relations between private firms and the state, which were disturbed since the 1970s on account of the preferential treatment accorded to state firms (Diniz 1989, 115ff.; and Lamounier 1991), failed to improve in the 1980s. Moreover, toward the end of the 1980s the political signals regarding the country's industrialization strategy were particularly inconsistent. The most important effect of these signals was a deterioration of the investment climate as a result of growing uncertainty. The government, for its part, announced in 1988 a new industrial policy that aimed for partial liberalization and underlined the need to improve competitiveness. The constituent assembly, on the other hand, adopted in October of 1988 a constitution that displayed pronounced nationalist tendencies in the economic domain.

The industrial policy announced at the end of May 1988, set its sights on six areas:[10]

- individual sectors of industry were to be modernized on the basis of integrated sectoral programs;

- programs geared to the development of industrial technology were to provide firms in different sectors with the possibility of writing off their R&D investments at an early point of time and of availing themselves of low-tariff imports of technology and capital goods;

- import restrictions were also scheduled to be reduced, above all by lowering tariffs and striking numerous products from the list of goods whose import was either banned or subject to authorization;

- exports were to be promoted;

- state industrial holdings were to be reduced;

- conditions governing the investment of foreign firms were to be improved; export production zones (EPZ) were to be set up, among other places in the northern and northeastern states. Firms operating there were not to be subject to restrictions on their imports. They were to be permitted to market 10 % of their production domestically.[11]

The policy did in fact result in some perceptible changes. The average import tariff sank from 56.2 % to 38.1 %,[12] and the share of products not subject to nontariff barriers dropped from 55.6 % (1985) to 21.8 % (Frischtak and Atiya 1990, 16, note 9). But the foreign-exchange regime was not liberalized; the rationing of foreign exchange implied a given upper limit on imports. And the similarity rule continued in effect, so that little was changed as far as nontariff barriers were concerned (Marcovitch 1990, 97). The local content regulations were eased. But not much was done to change the existing entry and exit barriers: in certain industries investment licenses continued to be required, and the discretionary approach to tax breaks and BNDES credits was not modified (Frischtak and Atiyas 1990, 31). Furthermore, additional sectors were given access to tax breaks, so that any effective implementation of the new industrial policy would have meant additional financial burdens for central government (Frischtak and Atiyas 1990, 61).

In effect, the impacts of the new industrial policy remained small – also for the reason that the central government's control capacity was headed toward zero in the final phase of the Sarney Government. One of the central goals of economic policy, which was, however, not achieved, was limitation of inflation, which grew to nearly 100 % per month toward the end of the government's term of office. In response, building investments increased while investment in machinery and equipment declined. It was for this reason that tax breaks on depreciation were unable to develop much impact, and the significance of selected import tariff reductions sank owing to the general tariff reductions.

Furthermore, the Sarney Government's clientelist orientation and the political-conceptual fragmentation of the government resulting from it prevented any implementation of the new industrial policy extending beyond initial patchy beginnings. Sectoral programs were never introduced because there were no funds available to pay for tax incentives; import barriers remained high in comparison with international levels; and no EPZs were set up. Moreover, the Sarney Government's industrial-policy practice was, in important projects, not consistent with its programs. One example was the launching of an additional petro-chemical complex in Rio de Janeiro (Mathieu 1991, 155) – a concept entirely in line with the traditional logic of import substitution.

The constituent assembly at the same time pushed through rules geared wholly to the import-substitution strategy. This became manifest, for instance, in the regulations reserving given activities (in particular mining) to national firms; and here the criterion of nationality was formulated just about as restrictively as it was in the computer sector. The practical effectiveness of these rules was low; but they were an indicator for the continuing effectiveness of conventional thought patterns. Insight into the fact that the potentials of import substitution were exhausted was slow to gain ground. New concepts (e.g. the concept of a competition-oriented integration with the world economy, presented by BNDES in 1988) (BNDES 1988) at first encountered a lack of understanding and outright rejection.

2.3.5   Import Substitution vs. Competitiveness

The industrial development of the 1980s did not reflect any – even partial – process of adjustment to new framework conditions and instead mirrored – primarily for lack of an adequate adjustment policy – the continuation of traditional behavioral attitudes, at least as long as this was possible. Brazil's industrial policy continued, until the end of the 1980s, to operate with the same incentives that had been introduced in the previous decades as a means of building new industries, namely, tax breaks, favorable credits, investment licenses, import facilities, and export-promotion programs – only that now the goal was no longer to build up new industries but to make it possible for existing industries to acquire rents, for the discretionary policy measures entailed a variety of market entry and exit barriers and therefore generated effects not conducive to competitiveness.

It was therefore only in exceptional cases that a constellation emerged that could have permitted functioning competition and thus led systematically to an efficiency close to the internationally usual level. In many sectors every producer along the value-added chain could reject criticism of his lack of competitiveness by pointing to the inefficiencies of the production stages upstream from him. In fact, however, the case was such that inefficiencies accumulated along the value-added chain and the possibility of shifting the blame to others provided for a situation in which no link in the chain felt responsible for undertaking efforts to improve its own competitiveness.

In some sectors the firms were inefficient because they were far removed from the minimum-efficient plant size once the low level of selectivity shown by industrialization policy had led to the emergence of a number of firms too large for the narrow domestic market (e.g. in the capital goods industry) (Fritsch and Franco 1989). In other sectors (above all the heavy industry) highly concentrated supplier structures were prevalent and prices were formed not in markets but between monopolist suppliers or between a cartel and state price-control agencies.

A continuing structural aspect of Brazil's industry is its high degree of heterogeneity as concerns firm size, technology levels, productivity, and competitiveness (Ferraz 1989). There are in many industries individual firms that are close to the international best practice. Their existence indicates that import protection, monopolization, and deterrent framework conditions have not completely discouraged dynamic entrepreneurship. The decline of competitiveness does, however, indicate that this state of affairs will not last forever: in an environment inimical to innovation and competition, firms can go through learning processes that pave their way to international competitiveness. But the closer they come to the top international level, the thinner the air becomes – to be specific: all the more difficult it will be to be competitive in view of a lack of suitable suppliers and, accordingly, with a high level of vertical integration; all the more costly will be the efforts required to acquire a sufficiently qualified workforce; all the more expensive will be R&D, which, for lack of any technological network, has to be operated on an inhouse basis.

Industry's lack of competitiveness is in the end the outcome of a number of deficits plaguing Brazil's variant of the import-substitution strategy:

- there was no long-term strategy, but also no five-year plan à la East Asia (exception: *Plano de Metas*, which, however, was not very differentiated and established few clear-cut industrial priorities);

- there were no clear-cut priorities and very little selectivity in decisions relating to industrial policy, for which reason no specialization profiles developed;

- there was hardly any coordination between sectoral policies, so that the linkages provided for in the ISI concept frequently failed to materialize;

- for national firms there were no performance criteria, policy's only instrument was the carrot, but not the stick (the only exceptions being the procurement policy of Petrobrás, the state oil company, which subjected its suppliers to quality controls, and the BEFIEX program, which was based on quantitative export obligations) (UNIDO 1992b, 14);

- there were a variety of barriers to market entry and exit, so that the competitive pressure and the risk of entrepreneurial failure were low in many industries, especially capital-intensive ones (above all basic materials, capital goods, and durable consumer goods);

- there was no systematic pressure to achieve international competitiveness;

- the stop-and-go economic policy discouraged at the company level any strategic orientation and sustained export activity;

- industrialization was for the most part not financed via domestic savings (exception: compulsory saving to finance BNDES) but funded directly over the state budget (inflation tax as a variant of compulsory saving; the use of government bonds to attract savings) and through foreign savings;

-   there were – depending on the market power and the price policies of the state firms – a variety of distortions of relative prices.

The deficiencies of the import-substitution strategy can not be interpreted as the outcome of technical errors made in situations in which contingent decisions were possible; they resulted instead from the political economy of this model. A feature characteristic of the industrialization process consisted in the fact that collusion arose between civil servants and entrepreneurs in the wake of the government-forced, -stimulated, and -financed development of industry. The possibility of state-level actors to exert systematic performance pressure on the firms, thus compensating for the lack of competitive pressure (as was the case, say, in South Korea), was slight:

-   In the first place, their personal success depended on the success of their "pupils", and the collapse of one of the firms receiving support would have cast a bad light on their earlier promotion decisions. The firms enjoying support could therefore be comparatively certain that the risk of involuntary market exit on account of insufficient competitiveness was low; the frequent BNDES rescue actions for ailing firms illustrate this phenomenon.

-   Second, the decisions on promotion and geographic dislocation of new industries were made not on the basis of any "objective" technical and/or economic rationale but in the context of intensive pressuring and bargaining on the part of regional interests, and the newly emerging firms often subsequently allied themselves with these interests. The firms were in any case not compelled to face state actors without any support, they were able to rely on allies in the political sphere – who in turn – and here the wheel comes full circle – could see to it that new entries were prevented which might have meant undesirable competition, and that in times of difficulties state funds were provided for rescue purposes.

This structure of the market and competition was one of the reasons why the industrialization process was accompanied (with the exception of the phase between 1964-72) by a high level of inflation; it was in fact the real cause of the inflation. The other reason was that it was seldom that orderly social redistribution mechanisms were successfully organized to finance the industrialization project. *"Chronic inflation has always been caused by the political difficulties in allocating the sectoral costs of structural adjustment, that is, difficulties of defining 'who pays the bill' of growth."* (Schwarz 1990, 17) Instead of a sound financial policy, the state created money; this was the monetary cause of inflation.

2.4   Technology and Industrialization in Brazil

2.4.1   Development of a Science and Technology Policy

Sectoral technological initiatives started out in the 1950s, when the National Research Council (CNPq, 1951) and the Technology Institute for Aeronautics (CTA, 1950) were founded. These measures were flanked by the establishment of a program designed to promote top qualifications (CAPES, 1951). The objective of CNPq was to promote scientific research in all disciplines, although the actual impetus must be sought in the ambitions of the military to create an independent scientific base in nuclear research (Dahlman and Frischtak 1993, 417). The creation of CTA likewise followed military interests. The time that followed saw the emergence within CTA of several training and research institutes for aeronautics and an institute for aerospace research (INPE 1961), and CTA came to constitute the core around which an aerospace cluster developed that included the aircraft firm Embraer and a number of specialized suppliers (Marcovitch 1990, 112f.).

This science and technology policy was, in its initial phase, characterized by two guiding principles: on the one hand, orientation in terms of concretely identified bottlenecks, on the other confidence in the science-push effect. In the field of nuclear research the latter was – in view of as yet fresh memories of the US efforts in the Manhattan Project with a relative nearness of basic research and application – a phenomenon of obvious interest.

Beyond the promotion of militarily significant projects, formulation of a policy geared to strengthening technological competence was for a long time not a priority target within the framework of Brazil's import-substitution strategy. The lack of science and technology (S+T) institutions appeared (with the exceptions named) to be a low-priority problem; development planners were convinced that access to technological know-how would be ensured via technology transfer from abroad and foreign direct investment.

This view first changed during the military dictatorship; its ideological superstructure, the *"doctrine of national security"* (Branco 1983), implied among other things a strengthening of the country's S+T base. In 1964 two new S+T-oriented funding lines were created within BNDE: the financing fund for the training of technical personnel for universities (FUNTEC) and the financing fund for the acquisition of machinery and equipment (FINAME). In addition, an agency was established to finance studies and research projects (FINEP, 1965) (Dahlman and Frischtak 1993, 447, note 10).

Toward the end of the 1960s the military government began to consider longer-term strategies, and this led to the identification of bottlenecks in the areas of technology and human capital which seemed to pose a threat to import substitution and a challenge to national security. Apart from this there were doubts concerning the country's pronounced dependence on foreign firms in key sectors. The outcome of these considerations was the formulation of the First National Development Plan (PND I, 1972-74) and the subsequent formulation of the First Plan on the Development of Science and Technology (PBDCT I, 1973-74). The National Institute for Industrial Property Rights (INPI) was founded in 1970, and this phase saw the creation of additional institutional structures: the National System for the Development of Science and Technology (SNDCT), the Secretariat for Industrial Technology (STI, under the Industry Ministry), and the National System for Science and Technology Information (SNIST). Two new funding instruments were created: the National Development Fund for Science and Technology (FNDCT, 1969) and the Program for the Support of Technological Development in National Firms (ADTEN, 1973). The FNDCT subsequently became the central instrument for the institutional promotion of newly emerging research institutes and postgraduate facilities at universities (Nussenzveig 1992, 139). A reform aimed at improving the quality of the universities was also launched (Bastos 1993, 16f.). The year 1972 saw the establishment of an advisory service for small and medium-sized firms (Gonçalves 1992, 15). In 1973 a bill was adopted that created a national MSTQ system (Ramos 1990, 24). This was accompanied by intensified efforts to strengthen the country's scientific-technological base in militarily significant fields such as informatics, telecommunications, the arms industry, aeronautics, and nuclear energy (Dahlman and Frischtak 1993, 419).

These initiatives did not lead to the emergence of a national innovation system; they instead followed the traditional pattern of additive creation of agencies. What emerged were clusters of science and technology institutions; Bastos (Bastos 1993, 17) distinguishes between the "planning cluster" around the Secretariat for Planning (to which CNPq, BNDE/ FUNTEC, FINEP, FNSCT, and ADTEN reported from 1974 on), the "industry cluster" (INPI, STI), and the "training · cluster" (CAPES, Federal Education Council), each of which enjoyed a great measure of independence in the formulation of policies. The institutions' relative competence varied, in part as a function of recruitment practice; *"recruitment ... was dominantly meritocratic in BNDE and FINEP, mixed with political appointments in CAPES, STI, INPI, and CNPq, and dominantly political in the ministry of education."* (Bastos 1993, 18) In none of these institutions was the principle of peer review introduced with any consistency,[13] nor was any control mechanism in evidence, which led to a situation in which the promotion agencies were able to take discretionary decisions on the allocation of funds. The effectiveness of these decisions depended on such factors as competence, commitment, *esprit de corps*, and direct political influence.

There was little articulation between state and society when these S+T institutions were established. This applied both for relations with the private sector and, above all, with the scientists themselves. Following the 1964 coup, politically dissident scientists were subjected to a great variety of means of repression (down to and including dismissal from universities, jail terms, and exile); the relations of the scientists to the ruling military were marked by mutual antipathy and mistrust. Scientists had little to say in the formulation of PBDCT I.

Spending for S+T purposes was expanded in the course of the 1970s; in the second half of the decade this spending reached its hitherto highest relative level, 0.7 % of GDP (Frischtak and Guimãres 1993, 7). The lion's share consisted of government spending, and with the arrival of the crisis of the 1980s the source of funding became more and more unreliable; after 1982 the main concern was no longer development strategy but crisis management, and technology policy enjoyed no more than low priority in this context. One of the direct effects was that FNDCT's budget declined by some 80 % between the end of the 1970s and the beginning of the 1980s (Nussenzveig 1992, 139).

The *Nova República* for the first time experienced the establishment of a ministry for research and technology (MCT). In the 1987 fiscal year the ministry succeeded in having its funds and the funds of the institutions below it increased to roughly 750 million US-$, which was twice the amount it received in 1984 (Figure 10). Even outside MCT's sphere of influence the collapse of funding for research and development suggested by some authors (Bastos 1993, 15) is difficult to go along with on the basis of the data available (Figure 11). True, after 1986/87 the hoped-for and anticipated further increases proved unrealizable due to the deterioration of the public budget situation. The perception of crisis thus likely stems from three sources:

–   The anticipated fund increases failed to materialize – MCT had set out with the goal of increasing R&D spending to 1 % of GDP.

–   Funds were shifted within the budget, and this was done at the expense of programs like FINEP and FNDCT, which represented a central source of revenue for many research institutions. Moreover, the efficiency with which funds were used seems to have decreased in the course of the 1980s (Schwartzmann 1993, 16f.).

Figure 10:

R&D expenditure of Union, States, and industry

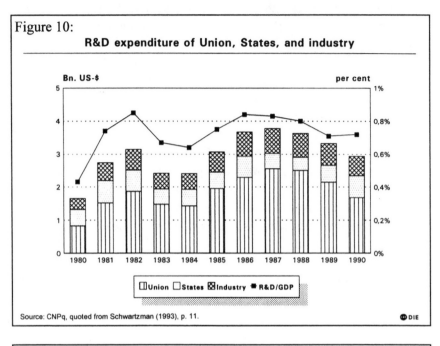

Source: CNPq, quoted from Schwartzman (1993), p. 11.   ⊕ DIE

Figure 11:

Science and technology expenditure

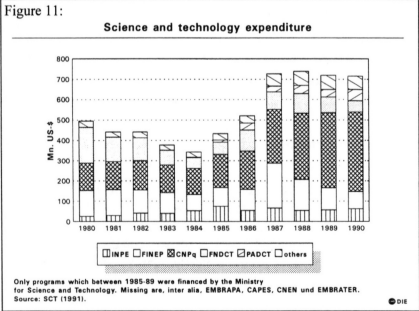

Only programs which between 1985-89 were financed by the Ministry
for Science and Technology. Missing are, inter alia, EMBRAPA, CAPES, CNEN und EMBRATER.
Source: SCT (1991).   ⊕ DIE

- The scientific community regarded the creation of MCT as the solution of many problems whose causes were sought in the lack of articulation between state and society; the 15 years prior to its establishment were characterized by a struggle among scientists for more influence in the granting of state funds (which, they hoped, would lead to a more rational decision-making process) (Guimarães 1993 25; and Nussenzveig 1992, 140). In fact, however, this area itself was not spared by the declining effectiveness of state interventions; nor was this changed by the rights of code-termination that scientists enjoyed in panels active in S+T policy.the first real decline in financial resources came only at the end of Sarney's term of office. MCT's declining influence became clear in 1989, when, in the wake of the *Plano Verão* stabilization program, it was demoted to the status of a secretariat reporting directly to the president (Bastos 1993, 23). Under the Collor Government the ambitious technology-policy goals were not expressed in adequate funding; in 1990 federal R&D spending were one third below the 1988 figure, and in 1991/92 the situation evidently failed to improve (Schwartzmann 1993, 16).

2.4.2   Technology Transfer Policy

Control over technology transfer was a central instrument in Brazil's technology policy. Unlike the case of East Asian developing countries, Brazil did not stimulate the transfer of technology via direct investment, licensing and patents, and the import of capital goods; it instead consciously impeded it. For some time now this point has been distorted in the Brazilian discussion: because the country was comparatively open to foreign investors, and foreign investment was seen as constituting a large share of technology transfer, it was postulated that what was stimulated was not autonomous technology development but technology import. In truth, however, neither the one nor the other was stimulated. The technology import regime was not primarily geared to strengthening, in the most efficient and effective ways possible, the country's technological competence but was more interested in saving foreign exchange and stifling an exploitative behavior on the part of foreign technology donors and investors. Important instruments to this end included the following (Dahlman and Frischtak 1993, 428-434):

- Payment of license fees to foreign licensers was restricted to 5 % of net sales.[14] The payment of license fees was prohibited outright for investments with a 50 % or higher share of foreign capital (since the foreign investment bill of 1962 was adopted).

- Technology transfer agreements were subject to authorization, first by the central bank, since 1970 by INPI. One factor characteristic of the decision criteria was that they gave INPI a large measure of discretionary decision-making power. The general terms included a limitation of the duration of such agreements to five years (with one possible extension of five years), the obligation of the technology donor to pass on improvements made since the agreement was concluded, and disclosure of all technical information.

- The import of capital goods was impeded, especially since PND II, as a means of stimulating the development of a domestic capital goods industry.

- Process and product know-how were not patentable in the fields of chemicals, pharmaceuticals, and metal alloys.

These regulations discriminated against national firms as opposed to foreign firms in that the former, in acquiring technology abroad, were subjected to fussy and, in the last analysis, unpredictable transactions with INPI. At the same time the regulations provided foreign investors with no more incentive than foreign technology donors to use their newest process know-how in Brazil – the one group was unable to utilize this to its own financial benefit, and both groups had to fear (above all in the chemical, pharmaceutical, and metal industries) that their confidential know-how might be passed on.

The result was that in the 1980s – a period in which, among other things, large capacities were built up in the petrochemical and pulp and paper industries – only small payments for technology flows could be observed (Figure 12). One striking fact is in particular the very unequal relationship between the purchase of technological services and other

Figure 12:

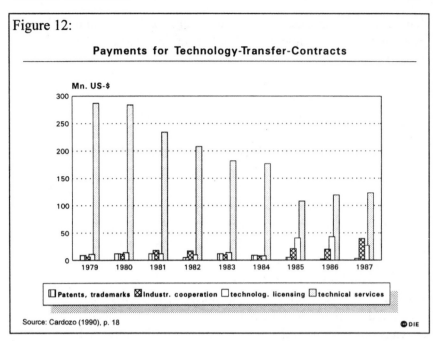

Payments for Technology-Transfer-Contracts

Source: Cardozo (1990), p. 18   ⊕DIE

forms or technology transfer; while this ratio was nearly 4 : 1 in Brazil in the period between 1982-86, it was, for instance, roughly 1 : 3.5 in South Korea.[15] The decline of payments over the course of the 1980s was due to a more restrictive authorization practice on the part of INPI (the percentage of authorized technology transfer applications sank between 1979 and 1987 from 97.3 % to 66.8 %) and erratic economic development (Cardozo 1990, 14, 18).

In some cases the prohibitive framework conditions for technology transfer were compensated for through intelligent bargaining strategies vis-à-vis foreign firms. This was especially the case in the petrochemical industry, which in many areas featured a combination of mature technology and tacit knowledge – the role played here by patent protection being small in comparison with the technical know-how of the experts of foreign joint venture partners. Some of the potential technology suppliers were not prepared to transfer essential know-how. But the Brazilian side did manage to capitalize on the sharp competition in the international petrochemical industry (fueled, among others, by

Japanese firms just entering the market) and exchange technical know-how for access to its highly profitable domestic market (Mathieu 1991, 147ff.).

2.4.3 Company-Level R&D and Technological Learning

Systematic technological efforts in firms – measurable in terms of the separate earmarking of R&D expenditures or the setting up of R&D labs – were limited in the past. The number of firms claiming for R&D expenditures in their tax statements was 1,050 in 1976/77, sank to 780 in 1981/83, at the end of the recession, and then picked up to 1,090 in 1985. This figure is not negligible, but in the last year named the R&D-to-sales ratio of these firms was a mere 0.4 % (Dahlman and Frischtak 1993, 425). Moreover, state-owned firms made up a share of not less than 62.5 % of overall R&D expenditures, and eight of these firms accounted for more than the half of the total amount spent. This weak attachment to R&D on the part of industry is also reflected in the distribution of R&D personnel: in 1986 the greater majority of the 52,863 persons statistically recorded were working for the state – 62 % at universities, 20 % in technology institutes, 3.4 % in state-owned firms, and 6.1 % in other state institutions. 6.5 % of the remaining 8.4 % were employed by private universities (Dahlman and Frischtak 1993, 426). These figures demonstrate that the number of firms really undertaking efforts in R&D is far less than one thousand. In fact, Brazilian observers assume figures somewhere between 200 (Marcovitch 1990, 106) and 366 (Dahlman and Frischtak 1993, 426). There is in fact reason to believe that the R&D-to-sales ratio is less than the figure named above would lead one to expect; it may have been as low as 0.16 % at the beginning of the 1990s.[16]

One possible hypothesis that might at least in part explain this low figure might be sought in the sectoral structure: the share of industries that generally have a low R&D quota is large. Yet this hypothesis does not lead far: in a developed industrial country with a sectoral composition equivalent to that of Brazil's industry, the R&D-to-sales ratio would be 2.14 %.[17] The discrepancy remains large. Nor can it be ex-

plained by the fact that transnational corporations are strongly represented in those industries that have a medium or high R&D intensity
(automotive, chemicals, pharmaceuticals, electronics, and electrical
equipment), and that these firms are responsible for only a small part
R&D in Brazil, since the sectors named account for only 29.5 % of all
foreign direct investments and reinvestments, while their figure for
value added is 34.6 %.[18] Furthermore, these are sectors in which there
are an above-average number of firms active in R&D in Brazil.[19] Only
one possibility remains: the level of R&D activities has, on the whole,
simply been low in Brazil. The firms have been able to prosper even
with low expenditures for R&D.

Technological efforts nonetheless undertaken by firms can be described under three key headings: unavoidable capacity building in
sectors involved in import substitution and industries without any international counterparts, capacity building in world-market-oriented
niches, and entrepreneurship.

Unavoidable capacity building. Various authors concerned with the
issue of technological learning have noted learning effects in Brazilian
firms in different industries. In sectors such as the steel industry, these
effects have resulted from the need to stretch existing capacities and
from the constraint to restrict technology transfers from abroad
(Dahlman and Fonseca 1987). One of the reasons why such effects
have occurred in the capital goods industry is that nowhere else were
plants manufactured to produce alcohol-blended fuels; and in areas like
the distillation of fuel from sugarcane the process know-how also had,
at least in part, to be developed from scratch, since this process is not
in use anywhere else (Sercovitch 1984). Learning effects from this
subsector were then transferred to other, technically related subsectors
(Teubal 1984).

Technological competence in world-market niches. Technological
competence has also been built up to develop and produce technically
complex products, at first for domestic consumption, then for specific
niches of the world market; the most prominent examples are aircraft
manufacturer Embraer (civilian and military producers) and the arms

industry. Most of these firms were established in the phase of military dictatorship, and the military support for them continued under the New Republic. They do, however, have characteristics typical of firms geared to military needs and, with an eye to Embraer, they can be summarized as follows: *"an overemphasis on the performance side of the price-performance equation, and a tendency to respond with 'engineer-driven' solutions to market requirements."* (Frischtak 1992, 2) The viability of these firms was dependent on the ability of the military to mobilize public funds in periods marked by sluggish demand. This ability was not very pronounced at the beginning of the 1990s. Since at this point the world market for weapons entered a crisis, the firms were faced with a struggle for survival. Embraer is heavily indebted, and at the beginning of 1994 the biggest arms producer, Engesa, was in the process of liquidation.

Evidently there was no spinoff from the military to the civilian branch of industrial and technological development. Military research and production had the character of an enclave (even in firms active in both the civilian and the military sphere). If there were any linkages at all, they tended in the opposite direction; Conca (Conca 1992, 147) speaks of a *spin-in* in that *"several of the most successful weapons-system exports of the late 1970s and early 1980s were based on technologies initially developed for civilian applications in the automotive, aerospace, and other industries."*

Entrepreneurship. There are in many industries individual firms that have long attached great significance to strengthening their technological competence and developing innovative products and processes.[20] This was typically the outcome of an owner decision to swim against the tide of the prevailing incentive structure. A stimulus that may have played a role here is the great social prestige enjoyed for some time now by such entrepreneurs; one indicator of this is the way they are presented in the media.

2.4.4 Development and Decline of a Top-Heavy Educational System

An effective educational system is a sine qua non for any development of technological capability. Brazil's educational systems is organized as follows:

−   primary school (eight years); graduation from a primary school is seen as evidence of an acceptable level of professionally useful general education;

−   secondary school (four years); qualification for university enrollment;

−   university (roughly four years); offers a diploma equivalent to the US bachelor degree;

−   postgraduate courses (*pós-graduação*), which offer masters (*mestrado*) or doctoral (*doutorado*) degrees.

Beside this system there is also a vocational-training system, for the most part organized on a private basis: industrial vocational training (Serviço Nacional de Aprendizagem Industrial, SENAI) is run by the state-level *Federação das Indústrias*, and training for the service sector is organized by the *Federação do Comércio* (Serviço Nacional de Aprendizagem Comercial, SENAC). SENAI/SENAC offer courses lasting up to two years; they are in demand in the industrial and service sectors. Cooperation between training organizations and firms is often very close.[21] There is in addition a network of government-run technical schools, and their quality is (at least in the more financially strong states) good.

Notwithstanding the political confrontation between intellectuals and the military, the phase of military dictatorship was marked by a perceptible expansion of the system of higher education (Table 3); the planners recognized that the existing capacity was not sufficient to cover national requirements for highly qualified personnel.

Table 3: Changes in Brazil's Education System			
	Post-Graduate		
	1967	1985	change (%)
Courses	52	1,162	2134.6
Teachers	863	19,106	2113.9
Immatriculations	2,440	34,476	1313.0
Graduates	1,080	4,513	317.9
	Graduate		
	1967	1988	change (%)
Courses	1,449	4288	195.9
Teachers (thousand)	38.7	137.8	256.1
Immatriculations (thousand)	212.9	1,503.6	606.2
Graduates (thousand)	30.1	224.8	646.8
	Primary and secondary education		
	1967	1988	change (%)
Courses (thousand)	134.5	211.7	57.4
Teachers (thousand)	564.8	1,349.1	138.9
Immatriculations (thousand)	14,071.0	29,048.0	106.4
Source: IBGE, quoted from Frischtak and Guimarães (1993), p. 9.			

This expansion was, however, achieved at the expense of primary and secondary education. In the 1980s, as funds became scarce, the structure of government spending for education took on a highly distorted aspect. Since the universities were forced to economize less than the schools, nearly 60 % of the 1985 federal education budget went into this sector (World Bank 1991, 225).

Primary education. It is today an undisputed fact that primary education is in the midst of a deep crisis. The extent of the crisis is made plain by several statistical indicators: only 34 % complete primary school, i.e. eight years of schooling (Fogaça and Eichenberg 1993, 99);

Figure 13:

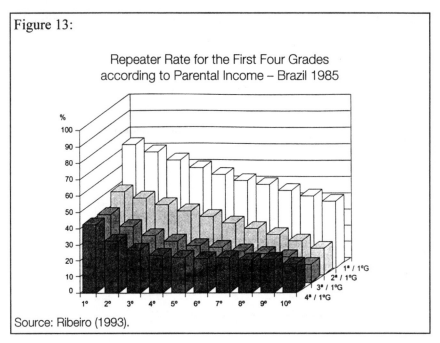

Repeater Rate for the First Four Grades
according to Parental Income – Brazil 1985

Source: Ribeiro (1993).

the average time needed to complete primary school is 11.8 years
(Ribeiro 1993, 151). The repeater rates are extremely high (Figure 13).

The extremely high repeater rate for the first grade can be explained in
part by the fact that preschool education in Brazil is severely underdeveloped and, the first time around, the first grade in a way serves the
function of preschool education (Castro 1989, 271). It is particularly
striking that the repeater rate – especially in the second to fourth grades
– does not decline rapidly as a function of increasing parental income.
If this rate is taken as an indicator of the quality of primary schooling,
one thing is clear: quality is generally low, not only in schools in socially weak environments.

One of the reasons for the low performance levels of primary schools
was that the qualifications required of teachers was lowered in the
wake of the reform and expansion of primary education in 1971; in
1987 23 % of the teachers in the Northeast and Southeast had themselves completed no more than four grades of schooling (Fogaça and

Eichenberg 1993, 103). Levels of qualification and pay were mutually reinforcing; in 1987 the average teacher pay was 286.33 US-$ (Fogaça and Eichenberg 1993, 112), about three times the minimum wage.

One of the effects was the expansion of the private primary school system, which is seen by middle-class parents as offering superior quality. In fact, however, this assessment cannot be proven.[22]

The low quality of primary education results in an overall low level of formal basic qualification of the employees (Table 4), in particular in industry where only 13.1 % of the employees had a formal secondary or university graduation.

Table 4: Qualification of Employees		
	total	industry
Fourth grade graduated	38.0%	49.7%
Eighth grade not graduated	13.5%	19.2%
Eighth grade graduated	12.2%	11.4%
Secondary not graduated	7.1%	6.1%
Secondary graduated	15.4%	7.4%
Tertiary (with and without graduation)	12.7%	5.7%
Source: calculated from Carvalho (1993), p. 67.		

Secondary education. The main problem facing secondary schools is that their role is inadequately defined. Preparation for college is the goal of only a part of students of secondary schools, because the number of graduates is twice as high as the number of university places available. The attempt initiated in 1970 to introduce in secondary schools a vocational-training component was doomed to failure; the reasons include lack of acceptance and the fuzziness of the qualifications to be imparted. The attempt was abandoned in 1981, without being succeeded by a new project (Castro 1989, 278ff.). The result is that the students are relatively reluctant to identify with this stage of training. Castro describes as follows one key phenomenon in secondary schools; *"It seems as if those who are fortunate enough to enter secondary schools believe that they have succeeded in overcoming the most* *difficult stages, and that from now on everything will be smooth sailing."* (Castro 1989, 278)

Universities. In Brazil universities are a relatively new phenomenon; the university in Rio de Janeiro was founded in 1920, the one in São Paulo in 1934 (Castro 1989, 282). Previously there were individual colleges specialized in one discipline (mining school in Ouro Preto, founded in 1875; agricultural research station in Campinas, 1887) (Dahlman and Frischtak 1993, 41). Such existing institutions often provided the core around which, later, universities were developed; this approach was, to be sure, not conducive to the cohesion of the emerging institutions (Castro 1989, 282) – not university but diversity would be the better term for many, even leading, Brazilian institutions of higher education.

The quality differences between universities are great. Castro (Castro 1989, 283f.) differentiates, ironically, four types of university to illustrate these differences: the model of the research university in which there is a diversity of incentives to produce first-rate research and teaching is seen as a necessary evil; the model of the teaching university in which the professors' prestige correlates with the professional success of his students; the model of the diploma factory in which teachers and students proceed from a tacit agreement stating that the goal is a degree utilizable in the labor market, and not any profound grappling with subject matter; and the country-club model – *"by frequenting their premises, but not necessarily their classes, one can find congenial company, spouses and future business connections."*

The sharp expansion of *graduação* training at universities in the 1970s was accomplished at the expense of quality (Dahlman and Frischtak 1993, 441). This situation was exacerbated by the financial problems that emerged in the 1980s; between 1980 and 1984 the funds appropriated to federal universities declined by nearly 60 % (Castro 1989, 286). The bottlenecks were dealt with in particularly via cuts in real wages; efficiency remained low.[23] Private universities, which accommodate some two thirds of the students enrolled, were hardly in a position to compensate for this development, since they are primarily adherents of

Table 5: Leading Brazilian University Courses by Type of University[24]		
	graduação	*pós-graduação*
Federal universities	181	74
Universities of the State of São Paulo	93	70
Other public universities	11	1
Catholic universities	39	20
Other private universities	23	6

the "diploma factory" model; institutions like the Catholic University in Rio are the exception that confirms the rule (Table 5). A limited number of small, more local universities constitute a special case; they are for the most part funded privately and offer a good price-to-benefit ratio; Castro sees them in analogy to the American-style community colleges, which, aside from providing higher education, also offer extension services (Castro 1989, 298f.).

Integration between the first (undergraduate) stage and the second (*pós-graduação*) stage, which was also strongly expanded beginning at the end of the 1960s, has remained insufficient. *"Young PhD's returned home imbued with research ideals, but with little inclination for the drudgery of undergraduate teaching. Copying the model of graduate education they had experienced abroad was a very natural path to follow."* (Castro 1989, 300) The division went so far that the graduate schools not only resided in separate buildings, they even developed administrative structures of their own; one factor that facilitated this was that they were expanded with the aid of additional funds (CNPq, FNDCT) and thus constituted no burden on the normal university budgets. In fact, money was not what was most lacking in the 1970s; *"it seemed that there was more money available than bona fide research could use."* (Castro 1989, 30) This phase saw the development of a dense network between the funding institutions, whose commitment in developing an efficient postgraduate training system (including research capacities) was undisputed, and the faculties themselves: Thanks to a high level of communication density, this was very effective, although it at the same time implied – owing to ambitious targets and efficiency-mindedness – a performance control as well. But in the 1980s, when funds became relatively scarce, this situation marked by trust and rivalry changed into a situation of distrust, envy, and enmity (Castro 1989, 304f.).

2.4.5   Science – System or Fragmented Landscape?

One aspect characteristic of the Brazilian discussion on the alleged national innovation system is that it takes over, sight unseen, categories from the discussion relating to the industrialized countries. A widespread misconception is illustrated by the following quotation: *"Schools, universities, and technological institutes are the only places where a country can develop enough skilled labor, and university-based, academically oriented research is becoming the main source of competence to support long-term national policies of technological choice, adaptation, and (eventually) innovation."* (Schwartzman 1989, 219) The first half of this statement is indisputable. The second half, on the other hand, describes – if "academically oriented research" translates out as university research – the problem prevalent in countries like Brazil, and not the solution: academic research has little to do with technological development in firms and can in fact contribute very little to it, since the great majority of firms move in "mature" industries whose essential problems have been researched academically and set down in textbooks. The concern of these firms is to build the capacities needed to optimize production processes and product innovations; the key factor here is training institutions that provide the engineers and technicians needed. When these firms are faced with a technical problem they are unable to solve with the means available to them, an academically oriented university researcher is unlikely to be able to help them out. What they need is an experienced consultant. Such consultants may come from a consulting firm, an industry association, or a purchaser of their products. University research has a direct connection to industry chiefly when the industry concerned is a science-based one that either relies on continuous inputs deriving from new scientific knowledge or is just in the process of emerging. It is, however, an elementary misunderstanding to confuse an industry new to a country, one that is mature in international terms, with an industry new in international terms.

A further misunderstanding stems from the fact that everything done at universities is regarded as research. Universities also engage in technical activities that have little to do with original research. If, for example, a metal-manufacturing firm regularly works together with a university because the firm is unwilling to operate an advanced metallurgy lab of its own and prefers instead to make use of the equipment and personnel available at a university, this is, to be sure, a form of cooperation between science and industry. But what is at stake here is a technical service that is not necessarily part of the field of activity of a university.

The lack of networking between technology institutions and firms and the specifics of research programming in institutes reflect an incentive pattern that can be summed up in the following points:

– an academic orientation of university research which is often keyed to research trends in industrialized countries; the central success criterion for ambitious researchers is the outcome of peer review, not the social or economic relevance of the results achieved;

– low incentives for systematic inhouse R&D as a result of the low requirements in a sheltered domestic market;

– low incentives for systematic quality assurance in firms, which for this reason place very low demands on the national MSTQ system; this in turn generates little efficiency pressure on the MSTQ system, and it remains underdeveloped (Ramos 1990, 23ff.);

– inadequate networking between universities/technology institutes and firms because of a lack of problem-formulation and recipient structures in the firms and the academic orientation of the research;

– impediments to the transfer of technology from abroad, which triggers a process of import substitution for simple services (e.g. metrology).

2.4.6 Conclusions: the Futile Search for a National Innovation System

As yet there exists in Brazil – even if this is suggested by some authors (Dahlman and Frischtak 1993; Frischtak and Guimarães 1993; Castilhos 1992; and Villaschi 1992a) – no national system of innovation; there are at best elements of such a system, and these elements are without any systemic character. There are policies that are, if at all, loosely linked, activities and institutions in different sectors that have, in various historical phases, emerged for very specific reasons. There were in the past efforts, but there has been no continuous practice of a systematic, cross-sectoral technology policy. There has been little coordination, cooperation, and synergy effects between institutions in different sectors, and redundancies are widespread. Isolation vis-à-vis external influences has increased the prospects of success for a sectoral or subsectoral agency, and the establishment of a new agency has often made it appear unnecessary to reform an existing agency with its well-established structure of political supporters. The constellation of actors tips heavily in the direction of the state; technological activities in the private sector, above all in industry, are few in number, because, within the framework of import substitution, the incentives for technological efforts in firms have been low. As far as the state is concerned, the constellation is weighted in favor of science; activities regarded as basic research predominate over activities dealing with applied research and technology development. Technological cooperation between firms on the one hand and universities and research institution on the other is quite uncommon. The transfer of technology from abroad has in this way been deterred.

There is not only no national innovation system. The existing elements that could give rise to one (firms, technology institutes, training institutions) differ sharply in quality. Moreover, the crisis of the 1980s and 1990s has exposed the existing state institutions to a constant process of erosion; frustration, resignation, cynicism, and mutual accusations of incompetence are not rare. Even if the existing universities, research institutes, and firms were intensively networked, an effective innovation system would not be likely to emerge. There is, in other words, great need for profound reforms, as far as both existing institutions and the degree of networking between them are concerned. A new technology policy for industrial competitiveness cannot be restricted to reprogramming existing institutions by introducing new incentives, it must be conceived on a much broader basis.

2.5   The Informatics Policy – the Last Try in Traditional Industrial and Technology Policy

In the era of import-substituting industrialization, the year 1974 marked a change in Brazil's development policy. Responding to the oil crisis which had exposed Brazil's external vulnerability, the Geisel government initiated a new phase of import substitution. Its "Second National Development Plan" aimed at an extension of the energy and basic industries and intended to foster the machine industry. Beyond this, a completely new industry was to be inaugurated: an "informatics industry" producing microelectronics components, computers and peripherals (Tigre 1983; Adler 1986; Ramamurti 1987; Botelho 1989; and Langer 1989).

Three groups of supporters – the technocracy aiming at extending import substitution, the military trying to reduce technological dependency, and a "technological guerrilla" of computer experts – immunized the policy against external pressure. Internally it was hardly disputed because it followed the traditional path of development policy. In 1984 this led to the almost unanimous passing of the "Informatics Law", which laid the foundation for the continuation of the policy until 1992.

The policy was implemented by an agency that until 1985 was closely linked with the military intelligence community: the Special Secretariat for Informatics (SEI). The SEI's most important instrument for promoting the domestic informatics industry was a market-reserve policy which tightly ruled the import of informatics products and technology.

2.5.1   Structural Problems of the Brazilian Informatics Industry

As a result of market-reserve policy Brazil a domestic informatics industry emerged which covered virtually the whole product spectrum. The only major gap was in the manufacture of advanced integrated circuits. The domestic industry's market share exceeded 50 % since 1984. This was mainly due to the sharp growth in the sale of microcomputers. By the late 1980s, the 350 or so domestic informatics equipment producers employed over 50,000 people, the computer hardware sector accounting for the largest proportion (SEI 1989).

The Industry's Economic Situation

The Brazilian informatics boom in the first half of the 1980s was mainly due to the "microcomputer revolution" and to demand in the service sector, especially banking. In the latter field, one of the objectives of introducing informatics was to increase corporate maneuverability, the accounting problems raised by three-digit rates of inflation also being a major factor in this context. The main aim, however, was to rationalize corporate procedures by means of automation (Cassiolato 1990; Frischtak 1991). At the same time, the banks were expanding, which further increased demand and also largely compensated for adverse effects on employment. As long as business continued to be highly profitable, the banks opened new branches in rapid succession, and they too had to be equipped with EDP facilities. Underlying this trend was the fact that the banks were among the principal beneficiaries of the high rate of inflation, since it encouraged speculative transactions and raised interest rates to astronomical levels.

The first anti-inflation shock program, the *"Plano Cruzado"*, put a temporary stop to the boom in 1986, since it halted inflation for the time being. Above all, however, it imposed a limit on interest rates, which greatly reduced the banks' profits and caused them to take stringent rationalization measures. Furthermore, the skepticism about the possible failure of the stabilization program and declining profit margins following the introduction of price controls led to a reduction in the investment funds of public and private enterprises. Foreign companies had been cautious in their attitude towards investment for some years.

Nominal growth rates in the EDP hardware segment of the informatics market fell sharply from 1986, after fluctuating between 23 and 27 % in the three previous years. The scale of the decline becomes even clearer when the real figures are considered (SEI 1989, 20-22). They also show that the market did not generally recover in 1987 and 1988, as the nominal figures might suggest. Of the eight leading enterprises, only three were able to increase their turnover appreciably in real terms. Some informatics companies went bankrupt. Some more dynamic manufacturers had difficulty meeting commitments to customers because the shortage of foreign exchange prevented them from buying components. These developments boosted the spiraling crisis in the informatics industry by causing uncertainty and, therefore, restraint among potential customers.

All that prevented more firms from collapsing was the success of the Ministry of Science and Technology in negotiating the opening of additional credit lines for informatics companies with the National Development Bank (BNDES), which had initially opposed the idea. The informatics industry's share of BNDES lending rose sharply. Credit was granted to any informatics firm applying for it, there being no sign of a selective approach ("picking the winners"). Although this capital increase solved some of the immediate problems, capital resources and liquidity in the informatics industry remained below the average for industry as a whole.[25] Because of this and the persistently low rate of growth in the informatics market, the economic situation of many EDP hardware manufacturers continued to be critical. At a time when the export-oriented computer industries of South Korea and Taiwan were undergoing considerable expansion, excessive dependence on the domestic market (exports were close to zero) is causing stagnation in the national Brazilian informatics industry.

Entrepreneurial Structure

By the late 1980s, the Brazilian hardware industry was composed of different types of enterprises. There was a strong, but not dominant, position of two financial conglomerates. More important is the observation that, even among the 50 largest hardware manufacturers, strategically oriented, financially strong companies accounted for only about a third of total turnover. When it is remembered that the industry consisted of some 350 enterprises, this is still to put the figure too high. Hence, the capability of the industry to act in a strategic manner was limited. There was good reason to be skeptical about its capacity to deal with major changes like an opening of the market.

A controversial issue at that time regarded the formation of complexes, i.e. a process of concentration. It was empirically questionable whether these processes could already be described as dominant trends, as Brazilian analysts used to do.[26] This is not to say that there were no diversified electronics enterprises. The inconsistency of the various subsectoral industrial policies did not prevent a few companies from beginning to pursue strategies of developing electronics complexes. This concept, however, was only valid within the reserved market regime. Within a new environment, having to deal with international competitors, the corporate strategies had to change. In the global arena the trend to a polarization of the industry – large, integrated enterprises with more than 10 bn US-$ annual turnover on the one side, specialized enterprises with up to 1 bn turnover on the other – was already clear at that time.[27] It is evident that even the largest Brazilian enterprises came under the second category. Hence a conglomeratization strategy like the one pursued by Itautec did not seem to make sense. Just the contrary: Even the larger firms would have to find their niche, their field of specialization.

Technological Situation of the EDP Hardware Industry

The dynamic development of the EDP hardware industry was due in no small measure to trends outside the sphere of influence of Brazilian policy-makers. The informatics policy was established at a time when there was no open architecture. In the field of closed architecture (i.e. manufacturer-specific architecture of the central processing unit and operating system of minicomputers) the informatics policy was only a partial success. A first round of technology transfer agreements with smaller foreign companies delivered the basic technology. Although domestic producers were at first able to take over this segment of the market and constantly increase their sales, they could not keep pace with the rapid technological changes in the international minicomputer industry. A second set of agreements was therefore concluded in 1984, this time with the world's leading suppliers (Evans and Tigre 1989). Brazilian observers doubt, however, that, having acquired this state-of-the-art technology, domestic manufacturers managed to improve on it.

The microcomputer sector rather than the minicomputer sector was therefore presented as the real success of the informatics policy, being by far the largest segment of the market. However, this was true of only the market in computers with open architecture, i.e. the so-called IBM-compatibles. Only around 1990 development in Brazil began to catch up the usual two to three years it lagged behind the world market.

The majority of Brazilian informatics manufacturers depended for their product know-how on "reverse engineering", i.e. the unlicensed manu-facture of products developed elsewhere (Erber 1985a, 122). Depend-ing on the firm's objective, this assumed two forms: some firms, whose sole interest was quick profits, manufactured equipment developed abroad without making any effort to modify it. Others regarded reverse engineering as a process of creative imitation, i.e. they optimized the products they copied and so acquired, through learning by doing, the know-how needed to develop products of their own (Hewitt 1988, 154; Soifer 1988). Some domestic computer manufacturers were for a long time more heavily involved in research and particularly development than the foreign companies operating in the country, as the proportion of R&D personnel in the total workforce reveals. National companies employed more graduates than foreign (7,912 vs. 3,763 in 1987), and they employed a much higher proportion of them in product develop-ment (25.3 % vs. 5.7 %) (SEI 1989, 25).

The Brazilian informatics industry was thus more than just a "pack of pirates who were stealing technology from the US and other countries". Unfortunately, however time series with data on R&D-expenditure do not exist. It has been estimated that in 1985 R&D expenditure in the industry amounted to US-$ 78m (Hewitt 1988, 150). Later on, the companies spent between US-$ 150,000 and 2m p.a on R&D, the proportion of turnover fluctuating between 2 and 9 % (Proença and Caulliraux 1989, 105). As a proportion of turnover, this is the normal level of expenditure, at least for microcomputer manufacturers. Even the world's leading PC manufacturers spent far less on R&D than firms in other subsectors. In absolute terms, however, the sums were modest at best.

Therefore it was never a question of how Brazilian informatics companies could enter the global technology race. It was more a question of how, in a protected market, it could be ensured that the gap between Brazilian manufacturers and the world's leading suppliers was kept within tolerable limits – tolerable in the eyes of the users, who were, of course, aware of international developments. Surveys showed the technology gap to be one of their main criticisms.[28] This applied to computers and even more so to peripherals. The development·of the informatics industry was instrumental in revealing how weak domestic know-how was in such sectors as precision engineering. The concentration on digital technology resulted in disastrous neglect of such "traditional" fields of technology. Weakness in these sectors was one of the main reasons why Brazilian manufacturers of hard disk drives and computer printers were far less competitive than the PC manufacturers.

Even in the core area of microelectronics, however, government activities to strengthen the technological base were largely unsuccessful (Mendes 1988). Activities in this sector were confined to assembly, i.e. the insertion of imported semiconductor devices into ceramic packages. Diffusion, technologically a far more demanding stage of production, in which the semi-conductor architecture is applied to a silicon wafer, was only undertaken for relative simple integrated circuits. In the field of chip design some know-how was available, since Brazilian informatics companies had designed integrated circuits to simplify their PC architecture and then had them manufactured abroad.[29]

Two further informatics areas appeared underdeveloped: industrial automation and software. In industrial automation, national companies mainly focused the only market being relatively dynamic in the 1980s, i.e. process industries like chemical and pulp and paper. *"Demand from process industries accounted for at least two thirds of the Brazilian market for industrial electronics equipment during the 1980's"* (Carvalho 1991, 184). However, even in this field the technological fragility of producers as well as users severely hampered the exploitation of the full potential of digital process control equipment. In fact, it seemed that industrial automation repeated the story of the minicomputers – licensing technology from abroad but having a limited capability of understanding the basic technology and improving on it (Carvalho 1991, 199-217). Regarding prices domestic products appeared to be two and half to four times more expensive than imported equipment (Carvalho 1991, 195).

In batch production the major obstacle to the spread of informatics was the high price of such domestically manufactured products as programmable controllers and NC equipment (1.8 to 2 and 2 to 3 times world market prices respectively). The price of NC machine tools manufactured in Brazil was two to four times the international norm (SEI 1988, 103; Fleury 1988, 39; Tauile 1988, 16). Among other factors, this was due to a vicious circle: users did not buy machines because they were too expensive, and domestic manufactures charged high prices because the small production volumes prevented them from achieving economies of scale. An additional factor was that, as most manufacturers of informatics products for manufacturing automation were newcomers to the informatics sector, their learning costs were higher than those of companies which had been manufacturing other informatics products for some time. The number of suppliers was also out of all proportion to the size of the market: the 5,274 programmable controllers produced in 1988, for example, came from twelve different plants (SEI 1989, 62).

Software accounted for a comparatively small part of the overall market – probably because, unlike the hardware sector, the Brazilian software market had never been reserved for domestic producers. The considerable importance of software was recognized at an early stage, and here again an attempt was made to achieve a degree of independence. Thus firms wanting to manufacture microcomputers were required to use an operating system developed in the country. By and large, however, resources were concentrated on the hardware sector (Gaio 1989; Lucena no year/a). Furthermore, the software-law which was passed in response to pressure of the US government in 1988 facilitated imports (and for no obvious reason gave a monopoly to importers). Therefore the market was largely dominated by imports.

Where domestic production was concerned, the SEI's data showed that just seven hardware manufacturers accounted for some 75 % of the software sold. They were the multinationals IBM and Unisys (52 %) and the domestic companies Edisa, Medidata, ABC-Bull, Sisco and Cobra (22.5 %) (SEI 1989, 86). They operated predominantly in the minicomputer and mainframe segment. The dynamic growth of the microcomputer hardware market can only be ascribed to the easy availability of software, most of it copied illegally. Although some experts argued that a reasonable level of technological capacity building had been achieved (e.g. Lucena no year/b), the Brazilian software sector appeared to be underdeveloped. The formal software market was estimated to have amounted to US-$ 262m in 1988,[30] this being a particularly low relation between hardware and software sales. Obviously users themselves had developed a great deal of software in-house, i.e. a considerable proportion of demand was not met in the market. In the banking sector this appears to have led to innovative products. However, attempts to achieve mastery of the basic software in core areas of industry were in an incipient stage (Carvalho 1991).

We may conclude that the effort to achieve technological capacity building had a limited success. There existed the capacity for creative imitation but neither an innovative capacity nor the mastery of the technological core, i.e. microelectronics.

The Informatics Industry's Price Problems

The high price of microcomputers in Brazil was one of the criticisms most commonly leveled at the informatics policy (e.g. Frischtak 1990; Cline 1987; Corsepius and Schipke 1989). The usual approach was to compare Brazilian PC prices and those of equipment with identical features in the USA. The price ratio, calculated at the parallel exchange rate, was then about 2 to 1 (Corsepius and Schipke 1989, 147). If, however, Brazilian prices were compared with prices in, say, the Federal Republic of Germany,[31] the result was far less unfavorable, Brazilian products being 15 to 25 % more expensive. The difference was due to the fact that PCs in the USA were far cheaper than in other industrialized countries. Far more meaningful than a price comparison with the USA would be a comparison of Brazil and such countries as Mexico, where IBM manufactured PCs locally,[32] and Chile, where a liberal attitude was taken towards imports. It should also be remembered that, at 30 to 50 %, the margin of Brazilian PC manufacturers did not exceed the international norm.[33] Furthermore the defenders of the industry point at the fact that the price-performance ratio did improve time.

The industry attributed the glaring price problems that undeniably existed, especially in a comparison with East Asian low-price suppliers, to the cost structure: according to an empirical study of 14 manufacturers, while labor costs and depreciation accounted for 10 % of total costs, inputs consumed 50 %, the remaining 40 % consisted of financing costs (Proença and Caulliraux 1989, 39). Another study has domestic inputs accounting for 45 % of total costs, labor costs for 35 % and imported inputs for 15 %.[34] Some of the inputs manufactured in Brazil by transnational companies were clearly very expensive. The price of certain non-digital electronic components was said to be two to five times the world market price (Tigre 1988).

The informatics industry also argued that, as the high tariffs had made certain supplies – such as the high-grade copper and chemical compounds needed for printed circuits – extremely expensive, the prices of domestic informatics products could not be reduced.[35] This is supported by the observation that the prices charged by foreign computer firms for some of the products they manufactured in Brazil were far higher than the prices of the same products in their respective home countries (Botelho 1987, 44; and Piragibe and Tigre 1990, 20).

A further cause of the price problems was said to be the size structure of the firms (Frischtak 1990). The "pulverisação" of the industry prevented most manufacturers from achieving production volumes that permitted economies of scale (Tauile 1988, 23; and Hewitt 1988, 114). In 1989 the leading Brazilian manufacturers produced up to 20,000 PCs.[36] By comparison, the largest Taiwanese manufacturer (Acer) produced 400,000 PCs in 1988.[37] The disparity was similar in the case of manufacturers of peripherals. The productivity of the Brazilian firms was correspondingly low. While some leading PC manufacturers in the USA achieved a turnover per employee several times higher than IBM's (worldwide), none of the Brazilian manufacturers equaled IBM do Brasil.

Another problem is the high degree of vertical integration. A network of specialized suppliers began to evolve only a few years ago (Cassiolato, Hewitt and Schmitz 1991, 406-7).

Another quite important reason seems to be the distortion between the industry's preoccupations with *product* and with *process* innovativeness. In terms of product innovativeness, Brazilian companies had been increasingly able to turn out new products in certain areas, e.g. microcomputers based on new types of commodity microprocessors. The innovativeness in other areas (some of which regarded as areas with the highest level of technological capacity building) seemed to be somewhat lower, e.g. in banking automation where Brazilian vendors continued to offer machines with 8-bit-technology. Nevertheless, in all these areas there was one core problem called *scale*. Hardly any enterprise or hardly any product line capable seemed to be able to reap scale economies. The small batch sizes in the informatics industry permitted no more than a low level of division of labor and automation (Caulliraux 1989). Automation, however, was the key to quality in electronics assembly. In fact, the organization of work in the informatics industry was pre-Fordist. As a matter of fact, the larger part of informatics production processes in Brazil employed basically artesanal modes of organization. For instance, the degree of automation in the insertion of printing circuit boards was very low, and SMD-technology was virtually non-existing. This is the main reason for the price- and quality-problems of the industry. The restructuring of the organization of production designed to increase the depth of the division of labor which Caulliraux observed in isolated cases must be seen as an attempt to initiate the transition to Fordist mass production.

Two main reasons for this deficiency can be identified. The informatics policy has never been occupied with process efficiency and scale economies. Enterprises always had to apply to government if they wanted to launch a new product. However, the SEI officials' main criterion for passing new projects was never the size of the market and the scale and efficiency of production but the technological nationality of the project. Any project that incorporated a reasonable content of national technological effort and capacity building was passed.

The second factor is much less obvious and much more controversial. The political and economic environment did not stimulate Brazilian informatics enterprises to gain process efficiency. This, however, applied to for Brazilian industry as a whole. Nevertheless, a significant number of national enterprises existed which were highly efficient and competitive in the world market for car parts, certain types of construction and agricultural machinery or electrical motors. No doubt, they were oases of modernity in a desert of inefficiency. Nevertheless, not a single oasis in the informatics sector could be spotted. This was somewhat strange since the defenders of the sector had always emphasized that Schumpeterian entrepreneurship existed in the sector. This may hold true for some product development departments. However, the Schumpeterianism did not reach the shop-floor. Due to unknown reasons the "technological guerilleiros" of the industry did not deal with the technological and organizational challenges of organizing factories. This failure was one of the keys to the understanding of the problems of the industry and hence for the frustration of the users who finally have been successful in their pressure for a major reorientation of the policy.

2.5.2   The Changing Political Base of the Informatics Policy

Controversies about Informatics and Industrial Policy

When the military passed political power into the hand of civilian politicians in March 1985, most analysts expected the informatics policy to
get into calm waters. What actually happened was the opposite. External pressure increased; the US government for some time threatened to
retaliate against Brazilian exports unless Brazil opened its informatics
market (Evans 1989; Ventura-Dias 1989; and Bastos 1991). This conflict could be solved by opening the Brazilian software market. Surprisingly, however, as well in domestic politics the informatics policy became a focal point of conflict in the most heterogeneous Sarney cabinet.

Behind these conflicts there were divergent interests and rivalries between left- and right-wing-factions of the governing PMDB/PFL-
coalition (see Meyer-Stamer 1990), which prevented the Brazilian state
from pursuing an active industrial policy (beyond the limitations of the
market-reserve policy) for the informatics sector. The subsidies for
which the informatics law provided played no more than a limited role
because of the tight budgetary situation, and there was consequently
little in the way of active steering of the informatics sector (through
financial incentives to establish enterprises in strategically important
product sectors, for example). Far more important was the continuing
need for the SEI's approval before informatics products could be imported or manufactured. Control of the informatics sector (through
refusal to grant licenses) was thus predominantly passive.

In the broader field of the electronics complex, i.e. the informatics,
telecommunications equipment and consumer electronics industries
and the upstream manufacture of components (see Erber 1985b), an
integrated industrial policy was virtually impossible. The institutions in
charge (SEI, the Communications Ministry, and SUFRAMA, affiliated
with the Ministry of the Interior and responsible for the Manaus free
production zone [ZFM]) were pursuing adverse policies:

- SEI favored a market-reserve policy for national enterprises and a restrictive policy towards technology transfer in order to build up a national technological base. Politically, SEI had been attached to the newly-created Ministry for Science and Technology (MST) which was linked to the center/left-wing of PMDB.

- The Ministry for Communications was able to exploit the tough competition on the world market for telecommunications equipment and was therefore less restrictive as regards foreign participation (Hobday 1985). Politically, this ministry was linked to conservative factions of the ruling coalition.

- The ZFM has housed for some time the major part of the Brazilian consumer electronics industry. National and foreign enterprises investing there received tax exemptions and were allowed to import freely. Although their products tended to have a low domestic content they were classified as 100 % national (Possas et al. 1987). Politically, the Ministry of the Interior was also linked to conservative factions. More importantly, if fought any attempts, particularly those of the MST, to interfere in the ZFM.

The available evidence shows that none of these strategies were particularly successful. The informatics industry was plagued by technological and economic problems; the telecommunications industry was highly dependent from foreign know-how; and the consumer electronics industry turned out technologically outdated products with elevated prices (Frischtak 1990).

In spite of this unsatisfying performance there was (at least until the Collor government took office in early 1990) no revision of industrial policy. This reflects the tough controversies in the political arena. On the one hand, the so-called "New Industrial Policy" announced by the Sarney-government in 1988 was geared to (albeit limited) liberalization. On the other hand, the constitution adopted by the constituent assembly in October 1988 has pronounced nationalist tendencies in the economic sphere.

As a result of increasing political pressure conceptual reorientation had been discernible in the SEI since 1988. To place this reorientation on a sounder basis in the longer term, various commissions were set up to consider the prospects for informatics in various spheres of application (industry, transport, health, etc.) or to discuss certain problems of the sector (e.g. prices, quality). They were composed of representatives of various government institutions, academics, trade association officials and employees of public and domestic private enterprises. There were, however, no signs that this enhanced the articulation between different sectoral policies or succeeded in re-establishing the political base of the informatics policy.

The longer term efforts of the SEI at that time concerned four issues:

– the quality of Brazilian informatics products was considered inadequate and was to be improved;

– the cost structure was to be examined (the assumption being that excessively high prices of non-electronic inputs were primarily to blame for the high level of retail prices);

– the market was to be consolidated, meaning specifically that the market was to be extended beyond the areas of industrial concentration in the south-east;

– exports were to be increased to 20 % of total output.

However, even though SEI tried to deal with some core problems of the informatics industry, its legitimacy was not reconstituted ; in fact, the defenders of the national informatics industry, who used to have a politically very strong position, severely lost ground. This was to some extent due to a very ironical fact. Though not the worst Brazilian industrial sector in terms of quality, price and innovativeness the informatics industry attracted the heaviest critique. The quality of the products increased and the price distortions decreased significantly over the years as the producers went down the learning curve. The distortions were not larger than in other Brazilian industries. Finally, the innovativeness in terms of products was certainly much higher than that of, for instance, the Brazilian affiliates of multinational car manufacturers which were still producing some models in the early 1990s that had been developed in the seventies.

Paradise Lost: Fundamental Changes in the Political Environment

In the first year of the Collor government the most profound change was the dismantling of the Special Secretariat for Informatics, SEI. Responsible for planning as well as implementing the informatics policy, SEI had been the aim of severe criticism for quite some time. Initially most pressure came from foreign enterprises – informatics multinationals in Brazil which were not allowed to enter certain markets and saw their imports restricted; informatics multinationals outside Brazil which could not sell their products on the Brazilian market; and most of all multinationals in other branches of industry that had to rely on deficient national products for many of their automation projects. Nevertheless, what appeared as a national consensus at the passing of the informatics law in 1984 soon began to crumble. National enterprises increasingly became frustrated with high-price/low-quality informatics-products and started to blame them for their low competitiveness. This probably was true for national non-electrical-machinery producers; electronic equipment counts up to 28 percent in the value of a numerically controlled machine tool (Wogart 1989, 59), and with the NC-equipment costing two to five times the world market price an enterprise could hardly compete on the international market. However, there was, as pointed out before, a high level of inefficiency of the Brazilian economy as a whole – from the macro-level of state regulation and intervention to the micro-level of organization of factories.[38] Hence, it can be assumed that in the majority of industrial branches costly informatics equipment was only a minor factor in explaining poor efficiency levels.

Nevertheless, during the second half of the eighties it became increasingly fashionable to blame informatics. Undoubtedly SEI helped its critics. SEI approved on a case-by-case-basis each and every application for import of certain components, start of production or technology-transfer from abroad; and its criteria of decision were often not transparent. Worse, with the growth of the informatics sector the time horizon for getting SEI's approval grew up to several months. Moreover, SEI held some quite idiosyncratic interpretations of certain parts of the informatics law. Particularly regarding deals with foreign enterprises (technology transfer or product acquisition) it always took a very restrictive position. Hence, even when SEI rationalized its operations in 1988/89 this did not calm its clients. Their pressure was one of the determining factors in the extinction of SEI – not necessarily in the sense of direct lobbying but in the sense of a general feeling that the time was ripe.

The second – and essential – factor was the general reorientation of industrial policy. The changes began to manifest themselves in June 1990, when the government announced "General Guidelines for Industrial Policy and Foreign Trade" ("Diretrizes Gerais para a Política Industrial e o Comércio Exterior"). They emphasized the necessity of abandoning general protection via market-reserves. A new system based on tariffs was designed to open the market and put competitive pressure upon national industries in order to force them to achieve efficiency.

The opening-up had a dramatic impact on the domestic informatics industry (Table 6). Turnover, investment and employment decreased substantially. Imports rouse as firms started to import components, including major parts like PC motherboards. In fact, some of them terminated production altogether and started to market products manufactured abroad under their brand name (Baptista, Fajnzylber and Pondé 1993).

2.5.3   Conclusions: The Last Failure of Import Substitution

There is a sharp contrast between the emergence of the Brazilian informatics industry and the creation of microelectronics and computer industries in countries like Korea, Taiwan, or Singapore. Without doubt there were various windows of opportunity (Perez and Soete

Table 6: Informatics Firms: Performance 1989 and 1992		
	1989	1992
Turnover of domestic firms	2774	2061
Turnover of foreign-owned firms	2025	2691
Imports	882	1498
Investment of domestic firms	848	238
Investment of foreign-owned firms	1597	374
Employees with higher education	24113	13343
Overall employees	74930	30919
Data in line 1 to 5 in million US-$.		
Source: Doria Porto (1993), p. 10.		

1988) open in different fields of the informatics sector during the 1980s, yet Brazil did not use any of them. This was due to the fact that the informatics policy in the end followed the usual ISI logic, emphasizing in particular the issue of securing technological sovereignty. The ultimate goal of the informatics policy was not to create a competitive computer industry but to reduce technological dependency. Underlying the informatics policy was the export pessimism of the classical ISI doctrine, something that was hard to understand as Brazilian manufactured exports increased substantially in this period.

Informatics policy and industry reflect various typical features of import-substituting industrialization:

- there was no coordination between sectoral agencies in related areas, but rather a strong rivalry, and agencies were pursuing different and incompatible policies;

- there were neither priorities nor selectivity but undiscriminate protection for all firms;

- there were no performance criteria so that firms could appropriate protection-related rents;

- there was no long-term strategy, policy adjustment was often delayed and mostly ad-hoc;

- the aim was not to achieve international competitiveness but to create 'national technology';

- there was little entrepreneurship and rather a lot of horizontal diversification of firms sensing an opportunity to appropriate rents or a risk-free application of available funds;

- factories were below minimum efficient scale, which was not penalized as there was no price or quality-based competition, not even in subsectors with a large number of incumbents;

- as competition was low, productivity increases were low as well, and technological learning on the whole occurred at a slow rate;

- there was no articulation between firms and R&D institutes.

Just like there is a classical ISI paradox, there is an informatics policy paradox. The ISI paradox lies in the fact that increased efforts to substitute imports lead to increased dependency on imports. The informatics policy paradox means that an effort to decrease technological dependency in the end resulted in increased technological dependency. As domestic firms were shielded from the fierce competition which emerged on the international informatics market during the 1980s and were dependent on a small domestic market, they had neither incentives nor the sufficient size to pursue a massive innovation effort, and accordingly lagged in technological terms. Due to both issues, incentives and size, it makes little sense to speculate about policy failures of SEI. There was something profoundly wrong with the policy.

A completely different policy would have been necessary to create a sustainable informatics industry. This would have been a policy which did not aim at reducing import dependence in as many fields as possible but rather at concentrating the efforts of firms on few, selected fields were competitive advantages might have been built. Yet, after the passing of the informatics law such an approach was no longer possible.

3   Crisis of Import-Substituting Industrialization and the Political System in Brazil

The problems of technology policy in Brazil cannot be understood adequately without reference to the structures of the country's overall political-administrative system:

–   Firms, one of the main target groups of technology policy, do not respond solely, indeed often not even primarily, to instruments of technology policy; instead, they are receptive to the incentive structure shaped by the state (in particular economic and foreign-trade policy). What is meant here is not merely the framework conditions, which in the past were not very conducive to innovation, but also mechanisms such as the ad hoc introduction of taxes to close fiscal gaps, which often burden interfirm transactions, thus discouraging the formation of networks, or the likelihood of shocklike stabilization programs which discourage the formation of long-term strategies in firms and, as far as implementation is concerned, lead to an every-man-for-himself situation in which each firm seeks to shift the costs of adjustment to the next firm. This leads to an atmosphere of mutual distrust that likewise impedes the formation of interfirm networks.

–   Most science and technology institutions, the other main target group, are public institutions themselves and they have to operate in an often chaotic and – especially in financial terms – unpredictable setting; to this extent an understanding of the processes behind the formulation of the government budget is no less important to understanding the scopes open to such institutions than are research-policy initiatives in the narrower sense of the term.

What follows will demonstrate that the Brazilian state's limited governance capacity is not due merely to poor political management (though this is a factor, as will discussed below) but is grounded in particular in the structure of Brazil's political-administrative system. The analysis will focus especially on the blockade situation in the relations between the three powers of state; it is this constellation that restricts the scope open to thoroughgoing reform projects.

**3.1   The Legacy of the 1980s: Impending State Bankruptcy,
        Abortive Stabilization, and Lack of Structural Adjustment**

In Brazil the 1980s were a period marked by profound political change
and persistent economic structural crisis. Toward the end of the 1970s
the ruling military had initiated a process of *abertura*, i.e. opening and
democratization. In 1985, after 21 years of military rule, a civilian
president was elected. The election was in the hands of an electoral
college; this construct the military hoped to use to ensure the election
of a tractable candidate. A political campaign aimed at pushing through
direct elections led to a mass mobilization, but not the outcome desired.
But the military's strategy also failed as the electoral college turned
down its candidate, electing instead the candidate proposed by the opposition. But this politician, Tancredo Neves, who enjoyed broad political support, died immediately before his inauguration, and his
lower-profile and politically weak deputy José Sarney assumed the
presidency. This constellation cast a shadow over the "New Republic,"
for it implied a low level of autonomy on the part of the president and a
never-ending search for political allies, who often made their support
contingent on material benefits (Skidmore 1988, 257ff.). This was one
reason for the growing financial bottlenecks faced by the state in the
1980s.

The government's economic performance was on the whole weak.
From 1987 on, the country's per capita GNP was on the decline (Figure
14). Four economic stabilization plans failed, and at the end of the
president's term of office the monthly inflation rate had reached almost
100 percent. The Brazilian state was on the road leading to insolvency
(Mathieu 1990, 154ff.). This was in part the result of the framework
defined by the world economy; the debt crisis ruled out any improvement of the budget deficit and the inadequate mobilization of domestic
savings by attracting foreign savings; as the terms of trade deteriorated,
Brazil lost any possibility of achieving rent incomes by exporting raw
materials, which, in turn, could have been used to subsidize an industrial apparatus only marginally efficient; and recession and an erratic
economic policy at the same time scared off foreign investors. This
blocked the escape routes that had, since the 1950s, made it unneces-

Figure 14:

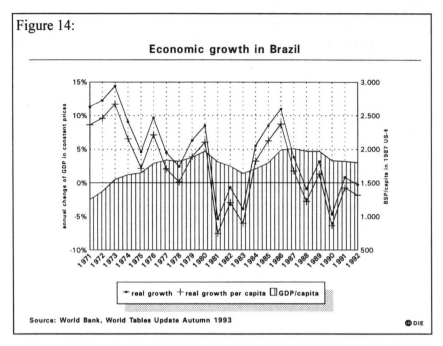

Economic growth in Brazil

Source: World Bank, World Tables Update Autumn 1993

sary for Brazilian governments to demand sacrifices from segments of
the agrarian oligarchy or the industrial bourgeoisie.

On account of the domestic political constellation described above, the
Sarney government was too weak to push through the required adjustment measures – improvement of the revenue situation, a realistic price
policy on the part of state-owned firms, and a reduction of the high
levels of subsidization – and compel industry to work for a perceptible
increase of its competitiveness. Even in the last phase of military dictatorship the government had failed to actually implement the austerity
policy it had aimed at (Baer 1987, 1023). Price controls and devaluation were counteracted by an expansive financial policy. The expansion
of clientelism and corruption associated with *abertura* burdened both
the spending and the revenue side of public budgets. The chronic public budget deficits were initially balanced by printing new money; the
fact that this state of affairs was ignored was one of the most important
reasons why the *Plano Cruzado* failed. By replacing the heterodox
economists with orthodox ones, the finance ministry signaled its pref-

erence for a different inflationary method of balancing accounts: the issue of government bonds. Aside from the fact that the interest on these bonds was funded via new debt, they also inflated the money supply by themselves assuming the character of liquidity, for they could be sold at short notice ("overnight") and their sale entailed very low transaction costs in that the central bank was obliged to repurchase at any time the bonds it had issued. In addition, these bonds yielded (as a risk premium) high interest and often had very short times to maturity (in the final phase of the Sarney government less than one month). The financing of the deficit via credit thus created very high-yield investment opportunities for private owners of capital (i.e., aside from the upper class, above all businesses); often the gains accruing to firms from financial investments were higher than the profits stemming from their productive activities, or they masked low levels of production efficiency. The seemingly sound financial position of private industry was thus inseparably linked with an escalation of the government debt; and the latter drove inflation to new heights. To this extent the disruption of the macroeconomic framework and the sound financial state of businesses were two sides of one and the same coin.

3.2   The Collor Government: Confrontation Between Executive and Legislative

In 1989 it was evident that the election could be won only by a candidate not linked with the Sarney government. So it was not surprising that the second round of the election saw Fernando Collor de Mello pitted against Luis Inácio Lula da Silva. These two candidates did, however, stand for fundamentally different political patterns. Collor ran a pronouncedly populist election campaign in which he skillfully denounced the abuses of the Sarney era, including clientelism, self-enrichment, and corruption; Lula could point out that his party, the Workers' Party, which has emerged only the 1980s, had remained outside the oligarchic structures and proven its character as a comparatively modern party with a broad social base (Sader 1987). Although Collor's style of campaigning was geared to putting distance between his party and the existing establishment, he was nonetheless – particularly with regard to his personality structure – a representative of the archaic northeastern faction of the establishment.

The policy package put together by the Collor administration had two goals: on the one hand short-term measures aimed at combating inflation; on the other hand medium- and long-term structural reforms intended to redefine the key framework data for economic development. The most important element of the structural reforms was the abolition of nontariff import barriers and the establishment of a timetable for a drastic reduction of customs duties; this was intended to increase the pressure on industry and force it to modernize. This policy was practiced consistently; its outcome was radical change in the business environment and incentive structure.

Short-term stabilization, on the other hand, basically proved a failure. Its aim was to eliminate inflation with the aid of three instruments:

– a freeze of savings accounts and securities in order to put an end to the overexpansion of the money supply, and a wage and price freeze;

– a balanced state budget (to be balanced by doing away with government agencies, dismissing government employees, privatizing state-owned firms, etc.) as a means of eliminating the fundamental cause of inflation;

– a strengthening of market mechanisms (e.g. gradual opening of markets, establishment of an antitrust agency, and introduction of a consumer protection agency) in order to heighten the competitive pressure on businesses and diminish the abuse of market power.

The main impact of this antiinflationary policy was a temporary paralysis of economic activity, a state which abated only gradually. But the policy missed its mark. Neither was the "inertial" element of inflation curbed nor were government finances successfully reorganized; seeming successes were achieved with the aid of tricks such as delayed financial appropriations or a certain laxity in paying bills. Nor did it prove possible to eliminate monopolies across a broad front (due to, for instance, the gradual opening process), while other measures (e.g. the abolition of price controls) took effect immediately. The outcome of this economic policy was thus hyperstagflation – a high and rapidly accelerating inflation accompanied by levels of economic activity that were sluggish, or even markedly retrogressive.

The ad hoc response was – ten months into Collar's term of office – a wage and price freeze, which at least succeeded in slowing down inflation. This admission that the first program had failed at the same time undermined the administration's legitimation; the president had always emphasized that all that was available was "one shot" (i.e. only one chance to combat inflation).

As a consequence senior heads rolled in the economics ministry in May of 1991. The new leadership determined to try its hand at a semi-orthodox stabilization (restrictive monetary policy, reduction of the budget deficit with the aid of fiscal tricks), which at least stabilized the level of inflation (Figure 15).

Domestic policy following Collor's accession to office was marked by a confrontational style. Collor's political model was essentially authoritarian, and it soon called forth resistance: once the initial surprise effect had diminished, congress recalled the increase of power with which the constitution endowed it; among other things, congress torpedoed the president's decrees (*medias provisórias*) by not voting on them within the required period of 30 days. The inclination to do so was fueled by the extent to which the executive documented its limited competence by frequently changing its course and committing various formal and technical errors (Moura 1993, 14). The outcome was a political standoff and – in consequence – failure of the government's antiinflation policy.

The technocrats who in the initial phase formulated the government's economic policy attempted to push through a new model against the resistance of most organized social groups:

Figure 15:

Monthly inflation and stabilisation plans - 1985-1993

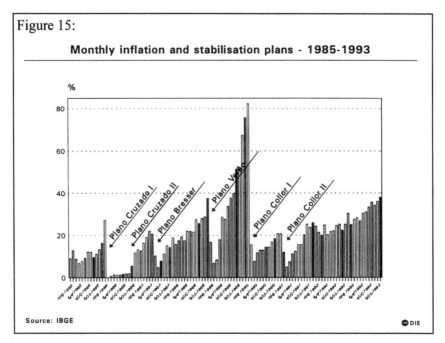

Source: IBGE

- the majority of businessmen, who wanted to see the protected domestic market retained and were reluctant to see the cozy arrangement abolished that the closed market had brought them. In the Sarney era representatives of business organizations often, in their speechifying, called for denationalization, and the next day went to Brasilia to demand protection of subsidies;

- the labor unions, which wished to continue to enjoy the material blessings of oligopoly;

- the big landowners, who fought against any interference with their privileges (e.g. their tax exemptions);

- the rich upper class, which rejected any attempts to reform taxation (the highest tax rate: 25 %);

- the civil servants, who were determined to hold on to their prerogatives (e.g. job security);

- the military, for budget cuts would have affected them as well.

Moreover, the government managed to discredit itself with all conceivable segments of society; and Collor – unlike his opponent in the second round of voting – had no political base of his own. The first Collor Plan not only paralyzed the economy, it also hit the entire middle class; this meant alienating a segment of society which might have been a useful ally against the country's oligarchy.

In Brazil, voluntarism was at the helm – embodied in a troop of technocrats, chiefly economists, who were entirely familiar with the concepts for stepping up economic performance that were then under international debate. The new government, however, sought to harmonize a new economic orientation with conventional political and social structures. This was an attempt to resuscitate technocratic rule of the type that had emerged under the military dictatorship; and it was not such that this technocracy included any modernization of social structures in its overall modernization efforts. Otherwise it would be difficult to understand why the technocrats invested the greater share of their energy in the development of conceptual projects, but without bothering to look for political allies in society. For them, denationalization was not democratization, it was privatization of state-owned firms and dissolution of isolated, particularly inefficient state institutions; the target of modernization was the production apparatus, not, however, the apparatus of state.

The government invested little effort in the coordination and – in the actual sense of the word – political (as opposed to technical) preparation of policy projects (Shapiro 1991, 12ff.). The government's dealings with congress were confrontational in style; the new president issued more decrees within a few months than his predecessor had during his entire term of office. He attempted to rule not with but against congress. The latter was quick to erect its defenses; discussions over the possibility of impeaching the president got underway as early as the summer of 1991. This constellation explains the unusual initiative and dynamism developed by congress in connection with the impeachment procedure it initiated. Faced with impeachment for financial irregularities, Collor resigned in December of 1992; as early as September he had handed his official functions over to his deputy, Itamar Franco.

That congress – in spite of urgent problems – failed to formulate any reform project on its own accord can be explained as a result of the structure of Brazilian parliamentary practice (Chapter 3.5). Furthermore, however, the government made hardly any effort to find social allies who might have exerted pressure on congress. Even within the government coordination was inadequate, although one factor at work here was that Brazil has no tradition of cabinet meetings involving a regular exchange of information and discussions of pressing problems.

3.3   The Political Economy of the Budget Deficit

The confrontation between government and congress not only slowed down various or prevented reform projects of the Collor and Franco governments, e.g. the *Projetão*, a project for structural economic and social reform launched in February 1991. It in particular undermined any attempts to combat inflation.

The federal budget is basically written in red ink. In practice it consists of two parts. The one part contains the existing debt. When Sarney left office, the debt was roughly 140 billion US-$, higher than the country's foreign debt, but under Collor stabilization policy (including privatization of state-owned firms) led to a reduction; in mid-1992 the debt, some 45 billion US-$, reached its lowest level and has been slowly climbing again since then.[1] A good part of the debt is the result of acute budget gaps (which are also in part closed by creating money); part of it is a legacy of earlier governments that is constantly rolled over. The interest on the debt is covered by additional credit.

The other part is the budget in the narrower sense, and it is marked by a structural deficit (Table 7). One of the main reasons for this is the 1988 constitution, which introduced four important new elements, all of which entail spending:

–   Extensive rights of codetermination for the parliament in framing the federal budget, but without infringing on the ultimate responsibility of the president or the executive for the budget. Congress'

Table 7: Central Government Budget Deficit (bn. US-$)			
	1990	1991	1992
Receipts	111	78	68
Spending	144	113	108
Deficit	33	35	40
Source: Cardoso (1993), p. 2.			

dealings with its budgetary competence did not develop in the direction of responsibility. It had more a clientelist, populist, indeed even criminal character.

- A perceptible increase of the federal government's appropriations of funds to the states and municipalities, but without any reapportionment of tasks and spending obligations (Nóbrega 1993, 92f.). The uses to which these funds are put by the states and municipalities is highly contingent; the scope is sometimes used for effective development programs, but more often it finds expression in clientelist or criminal activities.

- Various amendments to the laws covering employment and salaries in government service; federal employees are tenured once they have worked for five years. Regulations were also introduced on *isonomia*, i.e. increases of real wages are transferred automatically from one group of employees to another (R.W. dos Reis Velloso 1993, 125); rising military pay is automatically transferred to civilian employees, rises in the emoluments of congressmen are automatically extended to state legislators and city councilors, and so on.

- The expansion of social security payments (pensions and health insurance, welfare, and unemployment benefits) and the number of persons entitled to such benefits, and the establishment of minimum rates that apply in all cases (J.P. dos Reis Velloso 1993, 109). Furthermore, in 1992 a constitutional amendment was adopted which specifies that the benefits of pensioners and retired federal workers (who, aside from employees and judges, include former parliamentarians and government ministers; parliamentarians who have served for eight years are entitled to a full pension) be paid out of the current budget, and not out of the general social security fund. These benefits amount to 1.5 % of GDP.[2]

The result of these regulations is under discussion in Brazil as the *rigidez orçamentária*, i.e. the minimization of the budget funds available; in 1992 this was on the order of 0.8 % of GDP (in the face of tax revenues, without social security contributions, of 7.2 %). This 0.8 % must suffice for all expenditures not covered by fixed appropriations defined by law (e.g. for the training system). This includes the current costs of federal administration, infrastructure investments, spending for maintenance and repairs, upkeep and procurement of military hardware, subsidies for firms, and so on. In practice, however, these expenditures make up at least 1–1.5 % of GDP (J.P. dos Reis Velloso 1993, 101), and this implies public-sector borrowing.

The parliament's budget policy has thus far followed the principle of pork-barrel politics: the voters have been far more interested in immediate benefits – a newly paved road here, a little irrigation or drainage there – than in a fiscal discipline that would, at best over the medium term, have diminished inflation. Allotments of funds directly benefiting the congressmen's electoral consituencies have been one, if not the central, instrument of legitimation for the latter. Any responsible approach to budgetary competence would thus have directly undermined this legitimation, and could therefore not be in the direct interest of the congressmen.

One factor that exacerbated the problem was that this mechanism frequently operated in the same way at the state and municipal levels; this was the background for the pronounced interest in the automatic apportionments of funds provided for in the constitution. Yet despite this approach fiscal behavior has not changed decisively. Until recently governors compelled their state banks to grant credits that were then not repaid, which often, in the end, meant that the banks concerned became insolvent and had to be bailed out. The last major rescue action involving state and municipal finances took place in 1990, when the federal government assumed roughly half of debts amounting to more than 10 billion US-$. Three years later the debt had again reached a level of some 12.5 billion US-$.[3]

Another cause of problems is that the federal budget is not indexed. The result is that in periods of high inflation fiscal practice is quick to lose sight of the original budget. Inflation leads to nominally rising revenues, and these are used by congress to finance real additional spending. At the same time, however, the financial requirements for originally earmarked budget titles also rises. This mechanism is a further reason for the notorious budget deficit (Franco 1993, 32f.). In order to lower the deficit, the executive has taken refuge to three measures. Payments to state institutions, e.g. for physical resources, are held back until the nominal budget items have been largely eaten up by inflation; payments to private contractors and suppliers are made belatedly and without adjustment for inflation; and appropriations, for instance, to the social insurance agencies are held back – especially toward the end of the year.

Many of these problems would be less dramatic if the revenue situation were more favorable. In fact, however, there are serious problems here too which can be summed up in a paradox: tax revenues are inadequate, and the tax burden is relatively low in overall economic terms; but the complaints of taxpayers about heavy tax burdens are at the same time entirely understandable.

The solution of this paradox is that the number of taxpayers is on the whole low. It is, for instance, estimated that only some 30 % of wage earners actually pay taxes (World Bank 1991, 129); and even the business world has a large number of persons who operate in the tax-free realm of the informal sector. Self-employed persons hardly pay taxes at all, and even farming incomes are scarcely taxed. Still, the income tax makes up some 50 % of the federal tax revenues;[4] this implies a heavy burden for those who actually pay income tax. To be sure, there are two significant taxes on sales, IPI and ICMS, the latter taken in by the states; it is for that reason not included here. For firms, on the other hand, the issue of who takes in the tax on transactions is of secondary significance. For them the decisive aspect is the great tax burden that results from the two taxes and other taxes and levies and leads to a situation in which interfirm transactions are often unprofitable. If the make-or-buy decision often turns out in favor of the make, this is because a supplier is compelled to offer a price advantage on the order of 30–40 % in order to compensate for the tax burden.

3.4   Blockades in the Struggle Against Inflation

The circumstance that some of the central reasons for the budget deficit are created by the constitution greatly restricts the government's scope of action. Unlike the case in other countries, the necessary thoroughgoing reforms cannot be introduced by presidential decree or a simple majority in parliament; they require a constitutional amendment, which needs a congressional majority of two thirds. This is why any sustained antiinflationary policy can begin only when it proves possible to organize a broad-based alliance in congress.

There are also other reasons why the outlook for a comprehensive antiinflation initiative is not particularly good: even in the past the lack of success in combating inflation was not only due to dilettantism in matters of economic policy, it was also the result of the manifest interests of a number inflation profiteers (Kane and Morisett 1993). One example are the private banks, for inflation is – in view of the nonexistence of credit for investment or consumption – their most important source of revenue: thanks to the fees on transactions, which are much higher than in other countries; and due to the difference between interest on deposits and investments in government bonds.

Inflation is furthermore an important mechanism in the social struggle for the distribution of wealth, for it leads to a redistribution from the bottom to the top: bigger earners minimize the cash assets they hold and can protect themselves against inflation by investing their liquid assets in short-term, high-yield bonds, while the poor majority is exposed to rapid devaluation of the money they hold.[5]

There is another, economic reason for the problems involved in fighting inflation. While the 1980s discourse on inflation often ignored the government budget deficit (Singer 1988), it has more recently come to be seen as the sole cause of inflation. This means overlooking the fact that inflation is fueled by a number of factors; and the "inertial" component of it has been lost sight of no less than the real component, i.e. the oligopolistic or monopolistic formation of prices in many commodity markets. It is a feature of the inflation discussion in Brazil that it tends to focus on one single cause, ignoring the actual complex nexus of causes (that complicates any attempt at therapy).

3.5   Blocked Decision-Making Processes as a Constitutive Feature of the Political System

Brazil's political system is the outcome of historical learning processes and continuities. More precisely: it is the result of isolated structural decisions which sought to avoid individual, evidently inadequate elements of earlier Brazilian governance systems, but without an eye to ensuring that these decisions were compatible with one another; and it is also the result of the continuity of political institutions that have developed in specific historical contexts. What has emerged in this way is a system that is difficult to reduce to one conceptual denominator. It contains corporativist, neocorporativist, clientelist, pluralist, and plebiscitary elements, but without any clear-cut dominance of one of these elements over the functional logic of the system as a whole. The outcome is a system marked by a very low capacity to reach positive decisions that reflect anything more than particular interests. Indeed, it is even questionable whether this system has a clear functional logic at all – or whether the situation is not one marked by competition among several incompatible functional logics. The latter consideration could explain the problems facing both analysts (in journalism as in scholarship) and actors in describing the system.

The political system is characterized by horizontal blockades and weak or dysfunctional vertical procedures of representation and the mediation of interests. In order to disentangle the mess we will take a look at each of the three powers.

The legislative. One factor characteristic of the parliament is that the structure of the parties represented in it is fluid and party discipline is extremely low (Kinzo 1993). The fluctuation among the parties is (with the exception of the PT) high;[6] a congressman's personal reputation is not tarnished by a switch to another party. The parties' tickets are open, i.e. the voters pick their personal favorites (Mainwearing 1992, 686 and 703). Since they are not compelled to set up clear-cut slates, the parties have little incentive to organize fixed party structures. This furthermore implies a lack of classical "party careers," and for that reason there are no negative sanctions against switching parties. The parties have (with three exceptions) no countrywide structures ("machines"). The exceptions are the PT, which in many parts of the country can rely on the support of the CUT labor unions or grassroots initiatives, and the two parties that emerged from the duopoly in the phase of military dictatorship (ARENA, the governing party, and MDB, the opposition): the PMBD which developed from the MDB, and the PFL, which split off from ARENA's successor party, the PDS (today PPR). The senior politicians of all other parties have, in cases of doubt, left these two parties to organize new ones or to join parties revived when the dictatorship came to an end; many of these parties have local or regional strongholds (Ames 1994), but these are the result of historical contingencies and do not gel to form a nationwide structure.

Another reason why the number of parties is large is that in the past the costs of founding a new party were low – thanks to the loose structure involved and the general lack of grassroots organizations. An additional factor was that in times of election campaining access to cost-free commercials on television did not differ as to the significance and age of a party; this regulation was just recently introduced. There is in practical fact no minimum number of votes required to enter parliament, for candidates whose party fails to reach the required 3 % mark can switch to another party within 60 days, thus saving their seats (Mainwearing 1992, 704).

Table 8: Representation of Regions in the House of Representatives		
Region	% of representatives	% of population
up to 1988		
North	10.0	5.8
Northeast	31.5	28.7
Southeast	35.4	43.6
South	16.1	15.2
Central west	7.1	6.8
since 1988		
North	12.9	6.5
Northeast	30.0	28.5
Southeast	33.6	43.6
South	15.3	15.1
Central west	8.2	6.2
Definition of regions: North = Amapá, Roraima, Amazonas, Pará, Rondônia, Acre, Tocantins; Northeast = Maranhão, Piauí, Ceará, Rio Grande do Norte, Paraíba, Pernambuco, Alagoas, Bahia; Southeast = Minas Gerais, Espírito Santo, Rio de Janeiro, São Paulo; South = Paraná, Santa Catarina, Rio Grande do Sul; Central west = Goias, Distrito Federal, Mato Grosso, Mato Grosso do Sul. Source: Rosenblatt and Novaes (1993).		

The structure of representation is distorted, i.e. directly reflects neither population nor economic potency. This is particularly evident in the senate, to which each state delegates three senators; this means that here the low-population and/or structurally weak states of the central west, north, and, in part, northeast of the country are overrepresented. Nor is there much quantitative representativeness to be seen in the house of representatives. The distortions even augmented when new states were created (on the basis of the 1988 constitution) (Table 8).

The link between parliamentarians and parties is weak, whereas that between parliamentarians and their local/regional constituencies is strong. O'Donnell vividly illustrates this when he refers to it as the *"... old style of politics. Essentially, this is a style based on patronage and clientelism, typical of an oligarchic republic in a primarily agrarian society, in which capitalist relations are relatively underdeveloped and the lower classes are neither organized nor mobilized. In such con-*

texts, politics tends to consist of 'conversations among gentlemen' subject to very little party discipline. Politicians have basically clientelistic relationships with their constituencies; among themselves, the politicians barter power and exchange favors for the regional interests they represent. And the state apparatus is essentially a patronage system. This oligarchic style dominated Brazilian politics until the 1964 coup. Afterward, the authoritarian regime, by allowing existing local legislatures to remain in place and by accommodating the members of the political class whose orientations and connections were more parochial and archaic, greatly contributed to preserving that political style. " (O'Donnell 1988, 290)

The significance of the local constituency is an outcome of features specific to Brazil's electoral system. There are neither electoral wards nor party tickets; elections are conducted at the state level. But to garner the votes required a politician need not campaign throughout a state, he can concentrate on a given, limited region. His legitimation in this region is based on the fact that he represents its interests, and this in practice means that he will manage to direct federal funds into the region. He will furthermore often be at pains to represent the interests of his state or the governor in office, for state funds are a second important source of finances for a given locality, and the governor can sanction disagreeable parliamentarians by blocking appropriations. The strong link to the local constituency often leads to a situation in which for parliamentarians common regional interests assume more significance than party loyalties; *"when it comes to ensuring that their states and regions get a fair share of the pie, they put aside party commitments and join hands. "* (Mainwearing 1992, 700)

Politicians' strong links to their local constituency and weak commitment to any party identity become evident when the 1989/90 election results are looked into (Table 9) (Kinzo 1993, 144f.). The two parties that initially made up the ruling coalition of the "New Republic" (PMDB and PFL) did very poorly in the presidential elections of 1989. This reflected the extremely low popularity of the Sarney government at the end of its term of office. In the 1990 gubernatorial and parliamentary elections, however, candidates of these parties were the winners; but it would not be correct to characterize the two parties as the winners of the elections.

Table 9: Shares of PMDB and PFL in the 1989/90 Elections			
	Presidential elections 1989	Governor elections 1990	Elections to Senat 1990	Parliamentary elections 1990
PMDB	4.4	25.9	33.3	21.5
PFL	0.8	33.3	18.5	17.3
Source: Kinzo (1993), p. 145.			

The parliament's ability to come to grips with the tasks that should actually be its chief concern – control over the executive, solution of urgent societal problems – is limited. Congress' most important instrument vis-à-vis the executive is right not to consider legislation, since the executive has no legal means to compel the legislative to vote on bills. The executive is therefore forced to rely on lobbying, bargaining and deal-striking. This is particularly true in connection with *medidas provisórias* (MPs), i.e. the presidential decrees used by the executive to enact directly legally binding policy decisions. While in earlier times an MP came into effect permanently if was not rejected by parliament within 30 days, since the new constitution was adopted in 1988 the case has been such that an MP becomes null and void if congress fails to approve it within this same period of time; and then the MP cannot simply be reissued (i.e. without substantial changes). In this way the weight of decision-making was shifted toward the legislative, while the right to prepare decisions has remained entirely with the executive.

The parliament seldom assumes an initiative function, for this would presuppose an extremely complex process of consensus formation within the parliamentary groups and the formation of alliances between them, while particularist interests can best be served on the basis of the simple principle of reciprocity. But the system operates on an additive logic, i.e. on the basis of an implicit agreement not to interfere in the decisions of other actors in matters of financial appropriations as long as the other side refrains from interfering with one's own decisions; accordingly, legislative control would amount to either-or decisions, or even neither-nor decisions. This is facilitated by the fact that any congressman can propose *emendas*, i.e. spending-related amendments to the budget,[7] and that there is no rule prescribing a balanced budget, i.e. the congressmen can vote whatever expenditures they see fit, and do so independently of the revenue situation.

There are, beyond clientelism, cases not only of corruption but of criminal activities on the part of congressmen intent on lining their own pockets, and this is the outcome of the additive logic in operation here. That this logic – as happened between 1993/94 when a congressional investigation committee uncovered cases of self-enrichment on the part of congressmen – is at times contravened by the investigation of such illegal doings, some newly rich congressmen being called to account, indicates that even in congress there is a growing awareness that this type of parliamentary practice on the whole undermines the legitimacy of the democratic political system.

Structural changes, however, are faced with severe handicaps, for the amorphous character of the country's party structure cannot be regarded simply as an accident. It reflects the widespread opinion that a diversified party structure is preferable to a two-party system of the type established by the military after 1964 and typical also of the "Old Republic" prior to 1930. There is also a historical explanation for the distorted structure of representation: the concern is to prevent any dominance by the large and powerful states of the type experienced in the "Old Republic," *where São Paulo and Minas Gerais played this role"* (Lamounier 1993, 123). The parliament is basically an instrument serving to balance out regional differences. Decisions keyed to the public interest, or indeed structural reforms, exceed the bounds of its functional logic.

The executive. The president assumes the central position in Brazil's political system; this is at least the normative view that was reflected in the 1993 campaign over the issue of presidentialism vs. parliamentarism. The victory of presidentialism in the ensuing referendum mirrors the widespread hope that a strong president, legitimated by a broad majority,[8] might, vis-à-vis a fragmented parliament, prove able to push through a more or less coherent policy, including in particular structural change. This is underlined by the fact that the percentage of un-marked and void ballots was much lower in the 1989 presidential elections than in congressional elections (Moisés 1993, 582); voters thus displayed a large measure of confidence in the presidency. In fact, however, there is little reason for the hopes placed in a strong president, for the president's position has, since the Vargas era, inevitably been more or less weak. Lamounier points out that the president's ability to sway the nomination of his successor is a good indicator of his strength; the only president to succeed in this in the last 50 years was, as Lamounier sees it, Ernesto Geisel (Lamounier 1993, 132). In other words: even in the phase of military dictatorship the president's position was not altogether too strong (which in this phase was a matter not of the countervailing power of congress but of the rivalries between factions of the military leadership; a further factor was that the central government was successively forced to cede powers that it had initially arrogated to itself to regional politicians whose cooperation it needed) (Skidmore 1988).

The president's position is furthermore weakened by the provision stating that he may not be reelected following his five-year term of office. Historically, this rule is on the one hand the reaction to the long presidency of Getúlio Vargas (1930-45). It on the other hand mirrors a basic structural feature of Brazil's traditional political system, which was not representative democracy but the alternating rule of individual factions of the oligarchy; and there was implicit consent that no one faction should be given the possibility of self-enrichment for more than five or six years (in the "Old Republic" this was the main function involved in the filling of political posts).

In Brazil's system the strength, i.e. the governance capacity, of the president rests above all on the availability of the control medium money. Financial appropriations made to benefit particular sectoral, but also and above all regional, interests are the means used to forge a parliamentary constituency.

This mechanism operates directly, but also indirectly. The latter is linked with the manner in which government ministers are appointed.

It is above all senators and representatives who come in for these posts. For them attaining a ministerial office presents an opportunity to serve their clientele most generously. The president's rationale in selecting ministers is also to bind to himself a given group within congress – the one to which the ministerial candidate belongs. This mechanism does, to be sure, not work very well, because there is little cohesion even in groups below the parliamentary fraction level.

An alternative logic operative in the appointment of ministers is the attempt to win the loyalty of social groups by nominating functionaries of social organizations or persons with a good reputation within a given community (e.g. the scientific community). Frequently neither of these two logics is operative in the finance ministry, for a widespread view held in Brazil's political-administrative system is that the finance minister ought to be a professional economist.

One feature of the executive is that it displays, in certain areas only, e.g. diplomatic service, established meritorcratic recruiting and career patterns. The efforts, begun under the military, to reform the civil service have not been pursued in the "New Republic;" administrative reforms have become the dependent variable of attempts at economic stabilization (Holanda 1993, 170). There is a high degree of personnel rotation, stimulated in particular by changes in senior political posts;[9] new officials typically replace up to 500 staff members, not only in elevated positions ("Dança de 26 000 cadeiras," Veja, May 26, 1993), and fill the posts, in part, with personnel without administrative experience. The lack of clear career prospects for public servants leads to a situation in which they have no incentives to identify with their agency's mission, and are instead motivated to develop individual utility-maximizing strategies (Evans 1989, 578).

The situation was exacerbated by the so-called administrative reform undertaken by the Collor government; it consisted in fact in nothing further than the dissolution of a number of offices and the (failed) attempt to cut drastically the number of federal employees; *"in the end* [the Collor government, JMS] *demolished the administrative machinery, recentralized the decision-making process, and destroyed the deli-*

cate balance between administrative arrangements and informal rela-
tionships which – in a chaotic setting – kept the government going."
(Holanda 1993, 165) The government also cut the real salaries of civil
servants, which led to a mass exodus in particular among the better
qualified civil servants, thus permanently impairing the substance of
the federal administration (as well as related agencies, e.g. the economics and sociology think tank, IPEA) (Holanda 1993, 174f.).

The judiciary also contributes its part to stabilizing the constellation
of blockade. Brazil has been piling one law on another for over 170
years now, without paying much attention to the aspect of legal consistency. The consequence of this is that there are several legal solutions
for any one problem that occurs, and this in turn implies – in particular
with more recent experiences in mind – that any decision made by
congress or president can be blocked at least for a time, if not declared
outright null and void. The fact that the legal system is not especially
effective and law does not apply equally to all people (discrimination
of the poor population) should not lead to the conclusion that the judiciary is generally dependent on political structures or incapable of rendering decisions.

The **mediation of the interests** of executive and legislative on the one
hand and society on the other is achieved in three different structural
contexts: corporativist structures, pressure-group structures, and clientelist structures.

The fact is often overlooked that the corporativist structures introduced
beginning in the 1930s and then, beginning in 1937, regularized as a
core element of the *Estado Novo,*[10] were cut back in their function
during the phase of military dictatorship,[11] but never abolished. Even
today the central element is representation through *sindicatos* of respectively firms and workers; these organizations have a regional monopoly, are licensed and financed by the state via compulsory levies.
The "new labor unions" that have emerged since the end of the 1970s
have adapted to this system in the 1980s – in particular on account of
the financial benefits it offers them. On the business side, the continuing existence of the *sindicatos* has discouraged the formation of inde-

pendent business associations defined along the lines not of industry affiliation but in terms of shared political interests – e.g. market liberalization and elimination of the anti-export bias. The costs involved in founding such associations were faced by uncertain benefits: the infrastructure required to found a new association would lead to direct costs. The levies used to fund the *sindicatos* are compulsory levies, i.e. continue to fall due even when a firm is no longer active in a *sindicato*. Indirect costs come about in that such firms can then no longer participate in the social benefits provided by the peak organization, the *federação*. Furthermore, until 1990 a *federação* had many possibilities to wield influence, e.g. in defining exemptions for imports; it is unclear to what extent these exemptions are still in effect.

Organized pressure groups exist in particular in the sectors not covered by the corporativist system. These include the science system, which hardly existed in the 1930s; the Brazilian Society for Progress in Science (Sociedade Brasileira para o Progresso na Sciência, SBPC) acts as a lobby vis-à-vis the political-administrative system, its goal being to expand spending for R&D. Furthermore, single-issue movements arise on a case-by-case basis, as, for instance, the Brazilian Informatics Movement (Movimento Brasileiro para a Informática, MBI) in 1983/84 on the occasion of discussion on a controversial legislation covering informatics.

The clientelist relations between political office-holders and their constituency are at times difficult to separate from the relations between politicians in power and pressure groups. These relations find expression, for instance, in the fact that after elections as many as several thousand public servants are replaced or new posts are created, because the clientele of elected politicians expects to be supplied with sources of income. Another mechanism is the clientele-oriented allocation of funds to carry out either given public-works projects that serve in the short term to improve morale among the constituency (which explains, for instance, intensive but qualitatively inferior road-tarring jobs just before elections) or projects whose means is their end, i.e. in which work creation is far more important than the ultimate finished structure (or – frequently – skeleton). In the 1990 election campaign the governor of the state of São Paulo spent nearly 1 billion US-$ for such public works to ensure the election of his successor (Shapiro 1991, 11), and his successor drove the state into bankruptcy four years later.

The role played by the "fourth power" in Brazil's political system is controversial. That the media exercise their control function is obvious; and there is no question that they influence political events. But the experiences of the recent past are too contradictory to permit any clear-cut statements. There is on the one hand the experience that Collor's 1989 candidacy would have been far less hopeful had he not enjoyed the support of TV Globo, by far the country's largest TV broadcaster. The direct support occured through intensive reporting on Collor's election campaign, which contributed to raising his popularity level and disseminating his populists slogans, being supplemented by the direct demolition of his opponent in the second round of voting, Lula; without the Globo campaign, which attacked Lula's credibility, the election result might have turned out differently (Castañeda 1993, 380).

It is on the other hand striking how, in relative terms, moderate the effects have been of the investigative journalism of the major daily papers and the two big weekly magazines Veja and Isto é. That they succeed in using massive reporting (i.e. a number of large-scale reports in successive issues plus presentation of the core issues in ads) to force politicians to resign (e.g. Orestes Quercia and Eliseu Resende in 1993) has thus far been the exception. In particular, the regularly successful exposure of cases of corruption evidently does not lead to a situation in which the corrupters and the corrupt are more reticent, or at least more cautious. The deterrent value of public exposure is low, doubtless not least because its impact is very limited, the number of readers of print media being low. More significant are the electronic media, though a good number of them are controlled by politicians (in 1990 some 20 % of the senators and representatives had a radio or television station of their own) (Power 1991, 94); and outside the urban centers it is not only the media but also, and above all, the local politicians who effectively influence public opinion (Ames 1994, 106).

3.6   Conclusions

The limitation of state-level scopes of action in the course of import substitution is easily grasped in the case of Brazil. Central elements of the political structure of import substitution are reencountered here – increasing governance requirements in the face of decreasing governance capacity, inability to establish a solid financing of the country's industrialization process, accumulation of conflict structures, overlapping clientelist, corporativist, and pluralist structures, inability to tackle political reforms.

In view of the problems outlined, the widespread expectation on the part of Brazilians that a new government could in a brief period of time bring about economic stabilization and the basic reform of the political-administrative system required for the purpose have proven largely unfounded. It is doubtless helpful that discussion on an economic-political goal corridor has got underway, i.e. that ideas are being developed on what constellation might emerge at the end of a reform process.[12] This is the *sine qua non* if reforms are not to be slapdash attempts, possibly even conflicting ones, to solve isolated problems but rather approaches that complement one another. Still, it must be emphasized that a long sequence of reform measures will be needed to overcome the dysfunctionalities responsible for the blockade constellation in the country's political system. Nor will it prove possible, in view of the qualification problems noted above, to thoroughly and successfully reform public administration in the short run.

The executive can push through rapid, effective reforms only where it can disregard the legislative. This would include in particular the field of foreign trade, in which fundamental reforms have been initiated since 1990, and the state-owned firms, whose privatization is making gradual progress. In other areas required to create an environment that stimulates technological learning and industrial competitiveness, the government will have to enter into complex negotiations with the legislative and come to terms with the resistance put up by social actors. This includes both an economic macropolicy that depends for its scopes of action on limitation of the budget deficit and an active industrial policy operating with financial instruments, or indeed an educational policy calling for coordination with states and municipalities.

Reform processes initiated by the government are reciprocally linked to processes of change that occur in society independently of them. Some of the latter will be looked into in Part II of the present study. They include in particular changes in the structures of the mediation of interests beyond traditionally corporativist or clientelist channels as well as changes in some regional polities. An analysis of some of these processes of change would go beyond the scope of this study. This would include, for instance, an analysis of changes in the structures of recruitment and legitimation, which, it would appear, might lead to a reduction of the dominance of pork-barreling.

Part II Technology, Innovation and Industrial Competitiveness: The Discussion in the OECD-Countries – Prospects for Brazil

1 Technology, Innovation, and Industrial Competitiveness

Now that the primarily inward-looking industrialization model has failed, many DCs are launching a reorientation in the direction of market economy and active world-market integration. With this new orientation, the firms in these countries are facing incentive structures similar to those existing for firms in developed industrial countries. For them, too, the features of their environment mean that efficiency, quality, flexibility, and innovativeness are rewarded, or that any lack of them is penalized. In order to be able to respond adequately to these incentives, firms in these DCs will place demands on their environment that have, for the most part, already been met in the industrialized countries. The shaping of the environment will become a central political task the solution of which may differ from the logic pursued in the industrialized countries in terms of specific orientation, though not fundamentally. Technology policy, i.e. the shaping of the technology-related setting, is a key element in the design of a new environment. It is here that the technology-policy discussion underway in the industrial countries assumes direct relevance for developing countries.

This is all the more the case as the lessons to be extracted from the experiences of the successful first-generation export-oriented NICs are limited. These countries were generally able to gear their development of a national innovation system to the model presented by the industrialized countries; and they were able – in that the industries concerned were chiefly mature ones – to count on gaining nearly unrestricted access to technology. But today the industrialized societies are themselves caught up in a process of structural transformation in which organizational and behavioral patterns and regulatory mechanisms are being questioned radically at all levels of society; for some years now a search process has been underway to find new patterns of organization and regulation. And furthermore, new technologies are being developed that place great demands on the capability of firms and the support environment available (training, research, and technology institutions). Technology is becoming a central competitive factor, i.e. firms are using exclusive know-how to build up competitive advantages. In this setting the access to know-how is more complicated for newcomers.

The causes for the process of social structural change in the ICs are to be sought in the exhaustion of the growth model that lead, following the Second World War, to the emergence of welfare societies. The model rested on a new form of the organization of industrial production which had emerged in the late 19th century and was rooted in an intensified division of labor; its most prominent proponent (although he was nevertheless no pioneer) gave the phase its name ("Fordism").[1] This organizational pattern permitted high productivity growth and a distinct reduction of the gap between wages and prices for durable consumer goods. It at the same time created the material base for redistribution mechanisms that made it possible to blunt frictions (e.g. temporary unemployment) and negative concomitant phenomena (e.g. the dissolution of traditional solidarity structures).

This model reached its limits when growth in productivity began to decline steadily, the state's control capacity (e.g. in the face of cyclical fluctuations) turned out to be less strong than anticipated, and the welfare state ran up against financial boundaries.[2] Since the end of the 1970s those liberal-conservative politicians have assumed government power who have long since opposed the social-democratic model of global control over government demand policy and found in monetarism and/or supply-side economics the normative-theoretical foundations of an alternative model. The 1980s did, however, show that this alternative model is unable to keep the promises it has made (Krugman 1994). It became clear in Great Britain in particular that any consistent implementation of it (not – as in the US – countered by deficit-financed "armaments Keynesianism") may lead to far-reaching social change, but not to a substantial improvement of international competitiveness.[3]

This is not surprising in view of the recent discussion on the link between technology and industrial competitiveness.[4] Two things become evident here. First: the economic doctrine on which the "neoliberal revolution" is based is without any concept of technology and technological change (Nadal Egea 1990); and assumptions made on the basis of common sense are often empirically wrong (Hofmann 1993). Second: there is a close interaction between government activities and technological change, although this cannot be regarded as a one-sided cause-and-effect relationship (in whatever direction). Leaving the process of technological change to the anarchy of the market thus misses its specific points.

The following presentation of central elements of the industry-related technology discussion in the OECD countries pulls together various strands of the research on the complex of technology and innovation. This is done at two levels:

– **Firms and interfirm networks**. The central locus for innovations is the firm. It is here that innovations are implemented in more efficient processes and improved products. Well-functioning, cooperative interfirm structures can provide an important contribution to this end. An understanding of this level is a central presupposition for effective and efficient interventions at the second level:

– **The technology-related mesospace**. State-level industry-related technology policy has a strong influence on the innovative ability and behavior of firms. An effective structure of science and technology institutions supports firms in their efforts to achieve innovativeness. Regulation and other control instruments mark out the direction in which the process of technological change will move.

Far-reaching processes of change can currently be observed at both levels. It would therefore – to emphasize this once again – be wrong to attempt to develop from the experiences made in the OECD countries a clear-cut requirement profile that would have to be met by developing countries. And it would be just as wrong to set up the first-generation NICs as a model, since their recipes for success in the 1960s and 1970s were in many respects context-specific; and they too are today faced with the challenge of developing a new model of growth and finding governance patterns adequate to it. The concern is thus to illuminate the direction of the search processes currently underway in developed industrial countries and possibly to develop from them a new model for the technological dimension of industrial competitiveness.

1.1   Innovation and Competitiveness: Logic and Patterns of Innovation Behavior

The discussion on technology, innovation, and industrial competitiveness is marked in the OECD's economic debate by the controversy between the neoliberals and their critics. Neoliberal economics regards innovation as a black box, as events with exogenous causes ("manna from heaven")[5] that sometime disrupt an economic equilibrium before a new state of economic equilibrium has been reached at a higher production level. This view is questioned by economists of various schools of thought, who direct their gaze to the interior of the black box; they pick up on some thoughts of Schumpeter's (creative destruction by means of pioneering inventions) (Freeman 1982), on Nelson and Winter's evolutionary theory (Nelson and Winter 1982), or approaches from industrial economics (Scherer and Ross 1990, 613ff.). Their first question is how, i.e. what mechanisms are concealed behind the phenomenon of technological change? Proceeding from there, they attempt to develop tentative propositions on why, which thus far have constituted attempts at medium-level theory formation. The main level of investigation is the firm or a branch of industry. This is the place where most innovation takes place. Analysis of the economic factors of innovatory entrepreneurial behavior is the main strength of these approaches, and their most important findings can be summed up in the following ten points:

- four innovation types can be distinguished;

- four sector-specific types of innovation behavior can be identified;

- an innovation is not an event but a process;

- an innovation is the result of cumulative learning;

- technological development trajectories emerge to master technological uncertainty;

- firms have a core technological competence;

- the significance of inhouse R&D increases over the course of time;

- imitation and inhouse R&D constitute not alternatives but complementary activities;

- two types of technology diffusion can be distinguished;

- innovation behavior differs as a function of context.

These experiences constitute important framework data for technology-
policy initiatives. Whenever, in what follows, the present study reflects
on the arguments for and points of departure of technology policy, it
will often refer back to the points discussed below.

1.1.1   Types of Innovation

Four types of innovation can be distinguished (Freeman 1987, 60ff.):

- everyday, *"incremental" technological change* in small steps – an
  improvement in a production process, an improved product, a new
  service. It is this type of innovation that ensures that the productivity of firms will grow. Yet it does have inherent limits: even
  continuous improvements were, for instance, unable to prevent the
  replacement of sailing ships by steam ships;

- *technological breaks* due to radical innovations, which alter the
  course of development of an entire industry – the introduction of

the zipper, nuclear technology, or electronic word-processing systems would be examples;

- *upheavals in a technological system* that affect more than one industry; one example would be the success of plastics;

- *upheavals in a techno-economic paradigm* – new technologies prevail throughout entire societies, new industries emerge, old industries lose significance, conventional organizational patterns are invalidated.[6] This type proceeds from the long-wave theory.

1.1.2   Four Sector-Specific Types of Technological Change

The relative significance of inhouse R&D and technology transfer, of formal and informal technological efforts, varies sharply among different industries. According to Pavitt (Pavitt 1984, 354ff.; Dosi 1988, 1148f.), four types of industries can be distinguished (Table 10):

- **Supplier-dominated industries**. These include traditional consumer-goods industries (textiles and clothing, leather, wood, printing, simple metal products). Technological impulses stem from upstream industries. They manifest themselves in nontechnical mechanisms, i.e. trade marks, advertising, or special designs. Process innovations outweigh product innovations.

- **Scale-intensive industries**. These include certain process industries (steel, glass) and the mass production of durable consumer goods. Technological impulses stem on the one hand from production engineering, i.e. the department systematically involved in optimizing the production process; they derive on the other hand from upstream industries. They manifest themselves in the accumulation of nontangible and confidential know-how, in patents, and in the building of technical leads. Here too, process innovations outweigh product innovations.

Table 10: Sectoral Technological Trajectories: Determinants, Directions, and Measured Characteristics

Category of firm		Typical core sectors	Determinants of the technological path of development		
			Sources of technology	Type of user	Means of appropriation
Supplier-dominated		agriculture, housing; private services, traditional manufact.	Suppliers' research, extension services, big users	price-sensitive	non-technological (e.g. trade marks), marketing, advertising, design
Production-intensive	Scale-intensive	bulk materials (steel, glass); assembly (consumer durables, cars)	production engineering, suppliers, R&D	price-sensitive	process secrecy and know-how, technological lags, patents, dynamic learning economies, design know-how, knowledge of users'
	specialized suppliers	machines, instruments	design and development, user	performance-sensitive	
Science-based		electronis / electrical; chemical	R&D, public science, production engineering	mixed	R&D know-how, patents, process secrecy and know-how, dynamic learning economies
Source: Pavitt (1984).					

–　**Specialized suppliers**. These include the manufacturers of machines and measuring and control equipment. Technological impulses stem on the one hand from the development department, on the other from the users. They manifest themselves in the accumulation of design know-how and in patents. Product innovations predominate process innovations in this area.

–　**Science-based industries**. These include the electrical, electronics, and chemical industries. Technological impulses stem from inhouse R&D, from the science system, and from production engineering. They manifest themselves in R&D and process know-how

(Table 10 continued)				
Technological trajectories	Measured characteristics			
	Source of process technology	Relative balance between product and process innovation	Relative size of innovating firms	Intensity and direction of technological diversification
cost-cutting	suppliers	process	small	low, vertical
cost-cutting (product design)	in-house, suppliers	process	large	high, vertical
product design	in-house, customers	product	small	low, concentric
mixed	in-house; suppliers	mixed	large	low vertical high concentric

as well as in patents. Process and product innovations are of equal significance.

Pavitt's typology moves at a high level of abstraction, and to this extent it is possible to find individual examples of branches of industries that are wrongly categorized here; in the food industry, for instance, it is without doubt possible to find branches that are science-based (because they are built on methods deriving from biotechnology/genetic engineering). The typology's value is, first, that it systematically works out the big differences in the innovation patterns in different branches of industry and, second, that it points to what is in all probability (with a few exceptions) the innovation pattern in a given industry.

1.1.3   The Process Character of Innovation

Innovations are in general not sporadic sensations; instead, they have process character. Incremental innovations – at least in developed capitalist industrial societies – are part and parcel of the essence of industrial production. Firms do not simply remain at a productivity level once achieved, they engage in constant efforts to optimize their production processes and products. The most important incentive is provided by economic competition, for if a firm neglects to innovate or fails to innovate sufficiently, it will be unable assert itself against its competitors.

Insight into the process character of innovation puts to the question the conventional distinction of invention, innovation, and diffusion that goes back to Schumpeter. Schumpeter underlined discontinuous *"recombination"* (Schumpeter 1964, 100) (i.e., in Freeman's diction: radical innovation) by the dynamic entrepreneur as the dynamic factor, but

> *"most of the productivity gains associated with the diffusion of new technology do not come as an immediate consequence of the first radical innovation. On the contrary, they usually are only achieved as a result of a fairly prolonged process of learning, of improving, scaling up and altering the new products and processes. This involves many follow-through inventions and innovations throughout the commercial life of the product or system."* (Freeman 1991, S. 305)

Innovations usually turn out to be the result of an interactive process. There exists in firms an interactive process between R&D personnel, engineers, technicians and production workers, and marketing and service people. Beyond the firm itself, customers, competing or cooperating firms, and technology institutions and other research facilities may be tied into this interactive learning process.

1.1.4   Innovation as a Learning Process

An innovation is the outcome of a cumulative process – it rests on the accumulation of know-how, i.e. it is based on learning processes. Often a concrete innovation is a visible intermediate product of a continuing learning process. Elements of this learning process are (OECD/TEP 1992, 38; Rosenberg 1982, 120ff.):

- *learning by doing,* i.e. continuous improvement of a production process based on an increasing understanding of single components; this learning process occurs with the manufacturer of a product and points back to the production process;

- *learning by using,* i.e. improvements in the application of a product; this learning process takes place with the user and points back to the product acquired;

- *learning by interacting,* in which both sides get together, i.e. learning processes that occur on the basis of the interaction between manufacturer and user;

- *learning by learning,* in that the ability to learn increases to the extent that knowledge is accumulated; this is especially true with regard to the ability to adapt innovations that have emerged elsewhere.

These learning processes are not something trivial that will take place in any case, but are stimulated and fostered in efficient firms. Technological learning is a complex, protracted process that cannot be substituted for by formalized training over a limited period of time. The reason for this is that technological know-how is never completely tangible and formalizable; it is tacit. Dosi illustrates the term as follows: *"tacitness refers to those elements of knowledge, insight and so on, that individuals have which are ill-defined, uncodified and unpublished, which they themselves cannot fully express and which differ from person to person, but which may to some significant degree be shared by collaborators and colleagues who have a common experience."* (Dosi 1988, 1126)

This leads to the recognition that the perfect information about technology assumed by neoliberal economics cannot, in practice, exist. What needs to be distinguished here is not merely public and proprietary knowledge. Even if all firms were prepared to hand over their know-how and provide a gigantic information system with data on their stocks of know-how, there would still remain the sphere of tacit knowledge that cannot simply be transferred and is thus not negotiable; and the significance of intangible know-how as opposed to formalizable and negotiable know-how is anything but marginal.

1.1.5 Uncertainty and the Limitation of Innovations in a Technological Trajectory

Technologies develop in corridors; Dosi (Dosi 1982) coined for this the term 'trajectory'. Technological trajectories are defined by shared views and shared search patterns.

There is an economic and a technological rationality for the emergence of technological trajectories. On the one hand, firms, owing to the costs associated with learning processes, are interested in preventing their accumulated technological know-how and their technical hardware from losing their value due to radical upheavals (Kemp and Soete 1992, 445). Moreover, the existence of a technological trajectory reduces uncertainty. Dosi argues that the uncertainty associated with innovation is much greater than is assumed in most economic models: *"It involves not only lack of knowledge of the precise cost and outcomes of different alternatives, but also often lack of knowledge of what the alternatives are."* (Dosi 1988, 1134)

On the other hand, there is a close link between the definition of a trajectory and successful innovation. The relative security of a technological trajectory stimulates incremental innovations that are essential to developing the productivity potential of a technology. The reason is the cumulative character of technology, i.e. the significance of the continuous accumulation of know-how.

Technological trajectories narrow down over the course of time, in that a canonization of approaches and views occurs (norms and standardization, textbook knowledge, sunk investment in firms). It is not seldom that a shared view includes shared prejudices on the part of the engineers concerned as to what the market requires (Dosi 1988, 112).

In contrast to widespread notions, decisions concerning a technological trajectory rarely follow a pure economic or technical rationality. Decisions in favor of a given technological line of development, and against others, are based on economic, technical, and political interests, and the outcome often has a chance character. Typically, such a decision is made long before the potential and the risks, the costs and benefits of a technology are clearly perceivable. *"In many cases, a technology is not chosen because it is efficient, but becomes efficient because it has been chosen"* (OECD/TEP 1992, 41; Nelson 1992b, 5ff.), i.e. it develops superior quality or productivity because development efforts are focused on it, thus generating cumulative learning effects.

The emergence of technological trajectories is associated with discrimination of technical alternatives and the development of resistances against pioneering technical innovations (OECD/TEP 1992, 40). It is not rare for a technological trajectory to turn out to be a dead-end street for the firms in it – at the latest when ever greater efforts generate no more than minimal improvements. If a technological break occurs in an industry – the conditions being favorable for it in a situation of this sort – the established firms often have great difficulties switching over to the new technology. The barriers to entry then sink drastically, i.e. the probability grows that firms with radical innovations will move into a market, forcing established firms out of it; the Swiss clock industry and the German typewriter industry are two instructive illustrations of this phenomenon in recent industrial history.

1.1.6   Innovation, Imitation, Core Competence

One feature of technological trajectories is that the firms involved have a core competence *"that is [defined], loosely speaking, by the scope of what 'they are good at' and the relevance of this specific knowledge to the activities of innovation, production and marketing of a certain commodity."* (Dosi 1988, 1133; Prahalad and Hamel 1991)

The emphasis of the aspect of core competence on the one hand and the criticism of the strict separation of innovation and imitation on the other furthermore has implications for any understanding of the efficiency and the prospects of success of newly established, innovation-minded firms. With early innovators, core competence is often found in product technology, whereas imitators frequently display it in the fields of production processes, marketing, or customer service. The latter factors are often more important for market success.

1.1.7   The Growing Significance of Inhouse R&D

Technological change is not merely a function of learning processes operative in the production and marketing departments of firms. Rather, it has, in the past hundred years, been marked increasingly by inhouse R&D efforts; in particular, England's loss of technological leadership and the assumption by Germany and the USA of the leading position is closely associated with the organizational innovation of inhouse research laboratories (Freeman 1992, 170ff.). Targeted innovation efforts initiated by the identification of a potential market have since become a central factor in the emergence of innovations, particularly in the emergence of firm-specific innovations:

> *"... the modern industrial R&D laboratory, linked within the firm with production and often marketing, had a number of advantages over reliance on outside research and development laboratories, particularly when aspects of the relevant technologies were somewhat idiosyncratic and tacit, and R&D needed to be tailored to those idiosyncrasies and to particular firm strategies."* (Nelson, quoted after Dosi 1988, 1132)

The intensity of inhouse R&D efforts has even increased since economic and productivity growth began to decline in the 1970s. The outcome has been that in the OECD countries the firm share of overall
R&D expenditures has grown continuously; especially in the countries
that spend relatively little on military R&D, the percentage has mean-
while grown much larger than that spent by the state (1990: Japan
73.1 %, Germany 63.3 %) (OECD, Main Science and Technology Indicators, 2/1992, 22).

It should, however, be noted that the quantitative relationship between
formal activities (R&D, training/advanced training) on the one hand
and informal innovation activities (R&D without an R&D laboratory,
not covered by statistics) and learning processes on the other vary
sharply from industry to industry. Formal and informal innovation
efforts are in part substitutable, particularly when innovations in the
production process are concerned. The cogency of common indicators
of innovation behavior (R&D spending, patents) is therefore limited,
since an industry with a low R&D-to-sales ratio will not necessarily
display only marginal learning processes. Even with regard to products, a low R&D ratio, like that commonly encountered in the field of
machine-building, need not indicate weakness in innovation.

1.1.8 The Complementarity of Technology Transfer and Inhouse R&D

Inhouse R&D and the adoption of knowledge developed elsewhere are
in most industries not alternatives but complementary activities
(OECD/TEP 1992, 51f.). This is all the more true the higher an industry's R&D ratio is (OECD/TEP 1992, 61). It is often systematic R&D
that first places a firm in a position to survey and assess the technological knowledge potentially available, and then to make a decision on
what know-how to adopt. This adoption is, however, not a trivial activity:

*"... the economic exploitation of the discoveries, inventions
and innovations, developed in other countries or firms, is nei-*

ther cheap nor quick, but costly and time consuming. Technologies are always complex. Their operation can almost never be reduced to simple sets of blue-prints and operating instructions that can easily and quickly be put into practice. As with riding a bicycle, or putting together a good soccer team, an extensive period of trial, error and learning is a necessary part of imitation and improvement. " (Pavitt 1992, 120)

Technology transfer thus for the most part requires considerable efforts both to adapt borrowed knowledge and to adjust the organization concerned – an activity facilitated by inhouse R&D. The lower the investments a firms has made to accumulate know-how, the higher the costs of technology transfer.

The communities of scientists and engineers in which experience is exchanged and problems discussed constitute an important element in the exchange of information and experience between firms; this can be subsumed under the term interactive learning. These networks do not merely establish cumulative interfirm learning processes, they also serve an important function in defining technological trajectories; for scientists and in particular engineers play a central part in the formulation of standards and norms (e.g. in Germany in the DIN committees).

Such networks emerge neither by chance nor randomly. The actors involved generally make very conscious decisions on whether to join or participate in networks. Scientists and engineers from firms in particular are very selective in exchanging know-how, since the information concerned is often proprietary knowledge that is of commercial interest (OECD/TEP 1992, 70).

1.1.9   Two Types of Technology Diffusion

The observation that nontangible know-how is of great significance proceeds from a distinction between two very different types of technology diffusion: diffusion of knowledge and diffusion of embodied technology. And yet this distinction has primarily heuristic value: the diffusion of knowledge will often be linked with the transfer of embodied technology; and the transfer of embodied technology is hardly possible without a simultaneous transfer of knowledge.

Diffusion of knowledge, the first of the two types, occurs both within firms and outside firms. Internal diffusion is the result both of informal mechanisms and of targeted management activities. Diffusion of knowledge between firms is accomplished both via market-mediated mechanisms (patents and licenses) and in informal ways. Reverse engineering practices, evaluation of journals, catalogues, and patent applications, exchange of experience at seminars and conferences, personnel fluctuation between firms, and interfirm cooperation projects lay the groundwork for a rapid diffusion of knowledge about new and/or improved products and processes; this seldom takes more than 12 to 18 months (Table 11) (Mansfield, quoted after OECD/TEP 1992, 49). A firm's possibilities of acquiring exclusively the fruits of an innovation are therefore limited. It must, however, be noted:

> *"While one might consider knowledge spillovers as 'leaks' or as an unjust loss of profits for the innovator, in reality they are the sine qua non condition for the development of knowledge and of the economy. It is because innovations benefit more than just the originating firm and because they become widely diffused that knowledge can develop in a rapid and cumulative manner. (...) The existence of knowledge spillovers thus suggests that production of knowledge by a particular firm or industry depends not only on its own research efforts but also on outside efforts or, more generally, on the knowledge pool available to it."* (OECD/TEP 1992, 50f.)

Put differently: a rapid, often informal diffusion of knowledge can give rise to a positive-sum game for all the firms involved – any losses due to information "leaks" are more than made up for by the gains deriving from the transfer of knowledge from other firms.

Table 11: How Many Months do Competitors Need to Reconstruct Product or Process Innovations? Data from Ten US Industries					
	Less than 6	6 to 12	12 to 18	18 and more	Sum
Product innovations					
Chemicals	18	36	9	36	100
Pharmaceuticals	57	14	29	0	100
Oil	22	33	22	22	100
Metallurgy	40	20	0	40	100
Electrical equipment	38	50	12	0	100
Machine-building	31	31	31	8	100
Transport equipment	25	50	0	25	100
Measuring and control technology	50	38	12	0	100
Steine und Erden	40	60	0	0	100
Other (1)	31	15	15	38	100
Average	35	35	13	17	
Process innovations					
Chemicals	0	0	10	90	100
Pharmaceuticals	0	33	0	67	100
Oil	10	50	10	30	100
Metallurgy	40	40	0	20	100
Electrical equipment	14	14	57	14	100
Machine-building	10	20	30	40	100
Transport equipment	0	67	0	33	100
Measuring and control technology	33	33	33	0	100
Steine und Erden	0	20	20	60	100
Other(1)	27	0	36	36	100
Average		13	28	20	39
Note: The data are based on a sample of 100 US firms which spent more than 1 mill. $ for R&D in 1981 (or invested at least 1 % of their turnover in R&D, given a turnover of more than 85 mill. $). (1 includes among others food, caoutchouc processing, and paper industry.)					
Source: Mansfield (1985), p. 220.					

1.1.10   The Context Specificity of Innovation Behavior

Even if the above-named elements are universally valid, this does not mean that innovation processes and systems are everywhere identical. On the contrary:

> *"Technological bottlenecks and opportunities, experiences and skills embodied in people and organizations, capabilities and 'memories' overflowing from one economic activity to another, etc., tend to organize context conditions which (i) are country-specific, region-specific or even company-specific; (ii) are a fundamental ingredient in the innovative process, and (iii) as such, determine different incentives/stimuli/constraints to the innovation process for any given set of strictly economic signals."* (Cimoli and Dosi 1988, 126)

> *"Much of what is involved in mastering a technology is organization-specific investment and learning. Hands-on technological capability is more like a private good than a public good. For that reason, if the economic conditions and incentives facing firms in different countries differ significantly, then firms in one country will require technological capabilities very different from those in another country. This argument is far removed from the conventional distinction according to which firms simply 'choose' to employ different techniques (e.g., factor mixes) within a common underlying technology."* (Nelson and Wright 1992, 1961)

There thus exists a complex reciprocal relationship between economic and sociocultural environment and innovation behavior. This manifests itself in company-specific forms in which learning processes are organized, industry-specific approaches to defining technological trajectories, and specific national technology styles (the last point will be addressed in Part II, Chapter 2.3.1).

1.2   Technology and Competitiveness: New Logics in Product Development and Production Process

Certain categories of evolutionary economics are reflected in the ongoing discussion in management and industrial sociology. Against the background of growing competition, shorter and shorter product life cycles, and the globalization of markets, firms in all OECD countries are experimenting with new technologies (new technical hardware, new organizational concepts, new requirement profiles as regards workforce qualifications) in order to strengthen their specific competitive position. The efforts concentrate on two points:

- a radical reorganization of the production process designed to enhance workforce qualification potentials for new learning processes, thus creating new scopes for incremental innovations (for: *"personal contact and discussion amongst a well-educated work force are the most effective means of learning"*) (Pavitt and Patel 1991, 366);

- reorganization of the development process with an eye to reducing lead times for new products, increasing the responsiveness to changing market requirements, and cutting costs in downstream stages of the value-added chain. The above-described form of in-house R&D in separate departments has, for various reasons, not turned out to be the optimal solution.

1.2.1   New Organizational Concepts in Production

Far into the 1980s, one feature of the discussion on inhouse technology strategies was that, thanks to the development of information technology (here: microelectronics, computers, and electronic data transmission), an old engineer's dream seemed close to coming true: the "factory of the future"[7] in which computer-controlled machines and robots would largely supersede man as a source of error.

The basic idea of the "factory of the future" was integration of all sub-sectors of production within one single data-processing system using one database – "computer-integrated manufacturing" (CIM).

> *"The leitmotiv of engineers and managers is the fully auto-matic, flexible transfer line which, based on the planning projects of the engineers, manufactures different products in any desired sequence and lot size with the flexibility and pre-cision of a laboratory job shop – in short: the factory chip, a black box with 'design drawing' as its input and 'product', in any number required, as its output."* (Coy 1985, 61)

Today's reality is far removed from the "factory chip;" indeed, it has long ceased to approximate to this model (Dolata 1988). Thus far only certain islands of industrial production are computer-controlled. The first reason lies in technological problems, for firms banking on a pri-marily technology-oriented rationalization strategy have had to recog-nize how incomplete any such strategy is (Hoffman and Kaplinsky 1988, 184ff.; and Ebel 1989, 537). General Motors (GM), for instance, has, since the beginning of the 1980s, been banking quite massively on microelectronics-supported automation as a means of improving its competitive position. GM at the same time launched a joint venture with its Japanese competitor Toyota. This so-called NUMMI (New United Motor Manufacturing Inc.) joint venture manufactures in Cali-fornia middle-class automobiles which are highly competitive in terms of price and quality. But the reason for this is not the efficient use made of new technologies by NUMMI, quite the contrary: NUMMI's plant is, compared with GM on the whole, more obsolete than not; its superior productivity derives from the adoption of Japanese manage-ment techniques, in particular in the areas of logistics and personnel management.[8] This is not an isolated case; the MIT automobile study argues that there is no systematic link between degree of automation and productivity. The reason for this is that

> *"... high-tech plants that are improperly organized end up adding about as many indirect technical and service workers as they remove unskilled direct workers from manual assem-bly tasks.*

What's more, they have a hard time maintaining high yield, because breakdowns in the complex machinery reduce the fraction of the total operating time that a plant is actually producing vehicles. From observing advanced robotics technology in many plants, we've devised the simple axiom that lean organization must come before high-tech process automation if a company is to gain the full benefit." (Womack, Jones, and Roos 1990, 94)

This experience has induced GM to rethink its position of banking wholly on technologization as an instrument of rationalization and to link this strategy closely with organizational innovations. GM is not the only firm to have recognized this fact: according to the OECD, up to 85 % of productivity advances has resulted from training, enhanced skills, and alterations in the organization of labor (OECD/TEP 1992, 129).

The second reason for the paradigm change is the reception of Japanese experience. Not only for GM was it a glance to Japan that opened up access to an approach to rationalization oriented not merely to technology. The phase of the discussion on the "factory of the future" was at the same time (not only in the US) the phase in which US and Western European firms were forced to admit to a substantial gap in productivity, and thus also in competitiveness, vis-à-vis Japanese firms. The differences in the automobile industry (Table 12) were especially striking. Legions of managers and social scientists pilgrimaged to Japan in search of the secrets to success. It took a while before, in the tangle of hypotheses (Dohse, Jürgens, and Malsch 1984), a number of key factors were identified which explained the reasons for Japanese superiority over the established Fordist-Taylorist "best practice:" material flows were organized differently in and between factories, and, in connection with this, there was a different quality philosophy, less vertical integration, and more flexibility in production (Cusumano 1988, 32f.).

In the opinion of many authors, this sets up a new imperative for industry in other regions of the world, for with its methods,

Table 12: Efficiency Differences in the Automobile Industry - Vehicle Production per Employee and Year		
	GM, Ford, Chrysler	Nissan	Toyota
1965	4.7	4.3	6.9
1970	4.6	8.8	10.9
1975	5.3	9.0	13.7
1979	5.5	11.1	15.0
1983	5.7	11.0	12.7
Adjusted for vertical integration, capacity utilization and length of working year. Source: Cusumano, quoted from Hoffmann/Kaplinsky (1988), p. 117.		

"as it were, a new generation of 'worldwide best practices', Japanese industry – the argument goes – has succeeded in its race with American industry for the first place in efficiency." (Kern 1989, 265)

Accordingly, the way open to the Western industrialized countries (and for newly industrialized Third World countries) can, it is argued, only be to grasp and transfer the Japanese method; this, it is claimed, is not even all that difficult, because

"there are numerous 'how-to-do-it' recipe books that describe very practically and in depth how firms should introduce new practices." (Hoffman 1988, 54)

The most far-reaching advance in this direction is made by the authors of the MIT world automobile industry study (Womack, Jones, and Roos 1990), who see in Toyota's production system a new universal paradigm of "lean production."

The response emerging today in the Western industrialized countries both to the "Japanese challenge" and the failure of one-sidedly technology-oriented rationalization strategies is that the diffusion of microelectronics in industry and in certain areas of the service sector initiates painful and often costly organizational learning processes that give rise to a fundamental change in organization philosophy. The significance of the technical component here is great, for it is technical development in microelectronics and the information technology based on it that is rendering superfluous the necessity of splitting up production processes in order to render them accessible to human control. Any abandonment of an exaggerated division of labor is attractive to the extent that the rationalization strategies subscribed to until now have entailed severe drawbacks that might be referred to as "Taylor's information dilemma:" the more intensively the production process is broken down, pushing forward the division between manual and intellectual labor, the higher will be the costs of coordination, the more time individual workers will need for orientation in the course of processing an operation, the longer processing will take, the larger will become in-company warehousing needs; in short: the more inflexible will the firm become.

It is not the Babbage principle and Taylorization, with their benefits as regards specialization and safeguarding the lines of power within firms that constitute the main feature of the new thinking,[9] it is the reintegration of in-company operations and previously fragmented working processes. The "new organization type" (Altmann et al. 1986) of "systemic organization"[10] is initiating the "end of the division of labor"[11] – Taylorization, with its more and more far-reaching fragmentation of the production process, has, at least as a guiding model, had its day (Ebel 1989, Drucker 1988; Peters 1989; and Bullinger, Niemeier, and Huber 1989). The new production concepts break with the core aspect of in-company social relations, for the Taylorist concept of rationalization saw in

> *"the residue of living work ... above all the potentially disruptive factor that, to whatever extent possible, had to be channeled and controlled. This approach is today challenged not only from the perspective of the workers but also angle of capital interests. (...) The credo of the new production concepts is: a) autonomization of the production process vis-à-vis living work with the aid of technification is not a value per se. The most extensive compression of living work does not, per se, bring with it the economic optimum. b) Any restringent*

*grasp on labor throws away important productivity potentials.
What a more holistic definition of tasks entails is not risks but
chances; qualifications and skill-based sovereignty of workers
too are productive forces that ought to be harnessed."* (Kern
and Schumann 1984, 19)

The MIT automobile study examines this view and adds to it a second
aspect:

*"The truly lean plant has two key organizational features: It
transfers the maximum number of tasks and resonsibilities to
those workers actually adding value to the car on the line, and
it has in place a system for detecting defects that quickly
traces every problem, once discovered, to its ultimate cause."*
(Womack, Jones, and Roos 1990, 99)

Elements of Systemic Organization

Systemic organization of industrial production at the firm level is a
three-dimensional process (Figure 16). The first dimension is the introduction of organizational innovations:

–   new logistics concepts at the company level in which final assem-
    bly in accordance with orders and flow optimization in production
    (in-company logistics, internal just-in-time) are used to minimize
    warehouse stocks (reductions of costs due to tied-up capital) and
    improve response times;

–   new logistics concepts at the interfirm level, i.e. inclusion of sup-
    pliers and customers in in-company logistics (intra-firm logistics,
    external just-in-time) and – in connection with this – reduction of
    vertical integration and more permanent relations with suppliers;

–   restructuring of quality assurance, e.g. by introducing quality cir-
    cles or total quality control. *"In recent years it has been proved
    conclusively that the old idea of having quality inspectors examine
    products either part-way through or at the end of the line is an
    extremely inefficient one"* (Fisher 1992, 144);

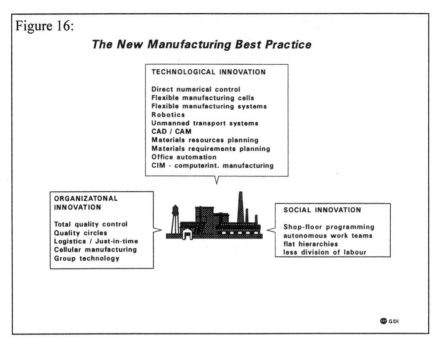

Figure 16:

The New Manufacturing Best Practice

TECHNOLOGICAL INNOVATION

Direct numerical control
Flexible manufacturing cells
Flexible manufacturing systems
Robotics
Unmanned transport systems
CAD / CAM
Materials resources planning
Materials requirements planning
Office automation
CIM - computerint. manufacturing

ORGANIZATONAL INNOVATION

Total quality control
Quality circles
Logistics / Just-in-time
Cellular manufacturing
Group technology

SOCIAL INNOVATION

Shop-floor programming
autonomous work teams
flat hierarchies
less division of labour

© GDI

- introduction of group technology, segmentation of production, and organization in manufacturing and assembly islands that make it possible to raise organizational flexibility and reduce administrative costs.

The second dimension includes social changes: on the one hand, concepts aimed at more flexibility in the deployment of labor in order to enhance the degree of utilization of costly computer-controlled machines; on the other hand, group work, shopfloor programming, reduction of hierarchic levels, and return of responsibilities to the shopfloor level – a restructuring of the work process that will often appear to be a reduction of the division of labor (Roth and Kohl 1988).

The third dimension is – once reorganization has created the conditions required for the purpose – the digitalization and electronic networking of machinery. This includes (Schneider 1986, 3; and Coy 1985, 62):

- computer-aided design (CAD); this – used in design departments – serves to rationalize technical drawing by doing away with the need to draw individually each new workpiece, instead making it possible to call up individual elements from a memory and display and manipulate them on a computer screen;

–   computer-aided planning (CAP) for direct production planning;

–   computer-aided manufacturing (CAM) is a catch-all term for various forms of computerized manufacturing, above all computer-controlled numerical machine tools (CNC machines) and flexible manufacturing systems (FMS, i.e. the coordination of several machine tools that automatically machine in sequence different workpieces);

–   CAD/CAM, as a rule taken to mean the coupling of CAD systems and CNC machines, the designed data being transmitted directly from the CAD terminal to a CNC machine, which then produces the desired workpiece;

–   Manufacturing requirements planning (MRP), *"with the main functions of production program planning, requirements planning, scheduling and capacity planning, job initiation and supervision."* (Schneider 1986, 3)

It should be emphasized that the essence of systemic organization consists in a comprehensive approach to the problem of organzing operational sequences – and not in the selective introduction of any of the single elements described above; "the issue is holistic concepts, i.e. concepts that are designed to grasp as a unit the levels of labor, operations, and the firm and that aim at restructuring production and the broad spectrum of research and development, manufacturing for internal or external needs, production planning and organization, down to and including sales." (Sauer and Wittke 1994, 46)

Problems and Consequences of the Implementation of Systemic Organization

In the view of many authors, the simultaneous approximation of firms to all three dimensions constitutes the groundwork of a new "best practice" of industrial production that is setting the standards for international competitiveness (Hoffman 1988; and Kaplinsky 1988). This view has, to be sure, come in for some criticism. Though organizational patterns are not per se culture-specific and can thus be transferred, they are of course nonetheless shaped both by economic, political, and social framework conditions and by historical specifics. And this, argue various authors (e.g. Jürgens 1992; Humphrey 1989), rules out any schematic transfer of experiences, e.g. from Japan; lessons learned from other countries or regions of the world should rather provide an impetus to reflect on established procedures, approaches, and views. The American Taylorist-Fordist model of mass production in an earlier phase of industrialization was not the model adapted for Japanese needs,[12] nor is it possible to transfer the Japanese model without further ado to other countries. Any such recommendation would negate the cultural, historical, and political specifics of the Japanese path to development (Kern 1989, 265; and Deutschmann 1989a). It would also overlook the fact that a central presupposition for the "clan model"[13] of corporate management was the historical defeat suffered by the independent Japanese labor movement in the 1950s (Halberstam 1988).

One further controversial issue in the literature is the issue of what precise implications socio-organizational innovations have in particular for workers. The point of departure of this discussion is that on the one hand these innovations meet some traditional demands for humanization (extended scope of tasks, less hierarchy, more responsibility for workers). On the other hand, there are the direct effects of rationalization processes in the form of layoffs and heavier burdens. Employees confronted with new organizational concepts often experience them as a compression of work sequences, as a closing of the "pores of the working day," and workers may lose scopes of action that were theirs in the past. There is no point in claiming that from now on the way is open for a general "liberation of labor." Even "progressive" concepts such as group work may turn into subtle, rigid means of exercising power (Deutschmann 1989b, 388f.; and PAQ 1987, 144). An additional consideration is: *"decisions on and planning of longer-term product, marketing, or indeed financial strategies will remain (...) the sole privilege of management."* (Mahnkopf 1989, 39; Hoerr 1989).

Here, in discussing possible impacts on workers, it is important to distinguish between assembly line production and job-shop production. In the past work was most rigidly organized in assembly line production; the operation cycles were traditionally short (often under a minute). The radical countermodel is replacement of the assembly line with stationary assembly by a working group of the type that has been used with great success in the Uddevalla Volvo factory.[14] In other cases the assembly line is retained, but the tasks and latitudes allotted to workers are greatly expanded, and the workers are assigned to groups which organize the distribution of work on their own. There is also much in this variant that indicates fundamental improvements compared with the traditional form of organization.

The situation in job-shop operations is more difficult. It in the past entailed a complex side-by-side of control and autonomy. It is not by chance that the 1980s CIM concepts aimed in particular at rendering events at the job-shop level more transparent for management, i.e. at improving the possibilities of supervision and control. In this environment any introduction of new organizational concepts can, if is not accompanied by social innovations, prove predominately negative – for the workers (who come under strong pressure to keep materials flowing at a brisk pace) and for the firm (because worker creativity potentials are not harnessed, because central supervision and control are invariably less flexible than more decentral organization). Yet it can also be observed that perceptible changes for the worse associated with the introduction of organizational innovations are temporary side-effects of a learning process the end of which is an adequate organizational model with a balanced relationship between supervision and autonomy, central and decentral control. What speaks in favor of this model is that organizational models like the self-controlled production island that were regarded as something esoteric in the mid-1980s (Herzog 1990) are today increasingly in use.

1.2.2   New Organizational Concepts in Product Development

At the end of the 19th century, the setting up of inhouse R&D laboratories was a central organizational innovation, and it constitutes an
important component in any explanation of the extraordinary development of the German chemical industry, which was in this respect a
pioneer. After the Second World War more and more (big) corporations began to concentrate their R&D laboratories and divorce them
spatially from production. What motivated this was the expectation to
realize economies of scale (by making technical and administrative
services available to all departments) and economies of scope (through
synergy effects that emerged through spontaneous or organized inter-
departmental research projects).

This hope came true only in part, and the more recent past has clearly
experienced the disadvantages of this form of organization. The underlying causes are that

–   the interactive learning processes between R&D and production
    are reduced, or even vanish, as a result of the spatial separation;

–   the R&D people have no contact to the market, i.e. to the users of
    the artifacts developed by them;

–   the substantive orientation of R&D develops not on the basis of
    problems stemming from production and inputs from marketing
    but as a result of introspective decision-making processes.

This decoupling of R&D has not only led to a situation in which a large
part of development efforts are detached from actual needs.[15] Even in
cases in which the development process is concluded with a successful
product, development itself for the most part takes too long and con-
sumes too many resources – a finding that stems from a comparison of
Japanese and Western firms.

Figure 17: Conventional and Simultaneous Engineering

Activity	Concept development	Design development	Design validation	Production development
Marketing Product Planning	▓			
Engineering		▓▓▓▓		
Testing			▓▓▓	
Manufacturing				▓▓▓

Conventional engineering

Activity		Concept development	Design development	Design validation	Production development
Marketing Product Planning		▓▓			
Engineering	Feasibility	▓			
	Production design		▓▓		
Testing	New technology	▓▓			
	Main programme			▓▓▓	
Manufacturing	Feasibility/ tolerancing	▓▓▓			
	Tool studies		▓▓		
	Tooling			▓▓▓	

Simultaneous engineering

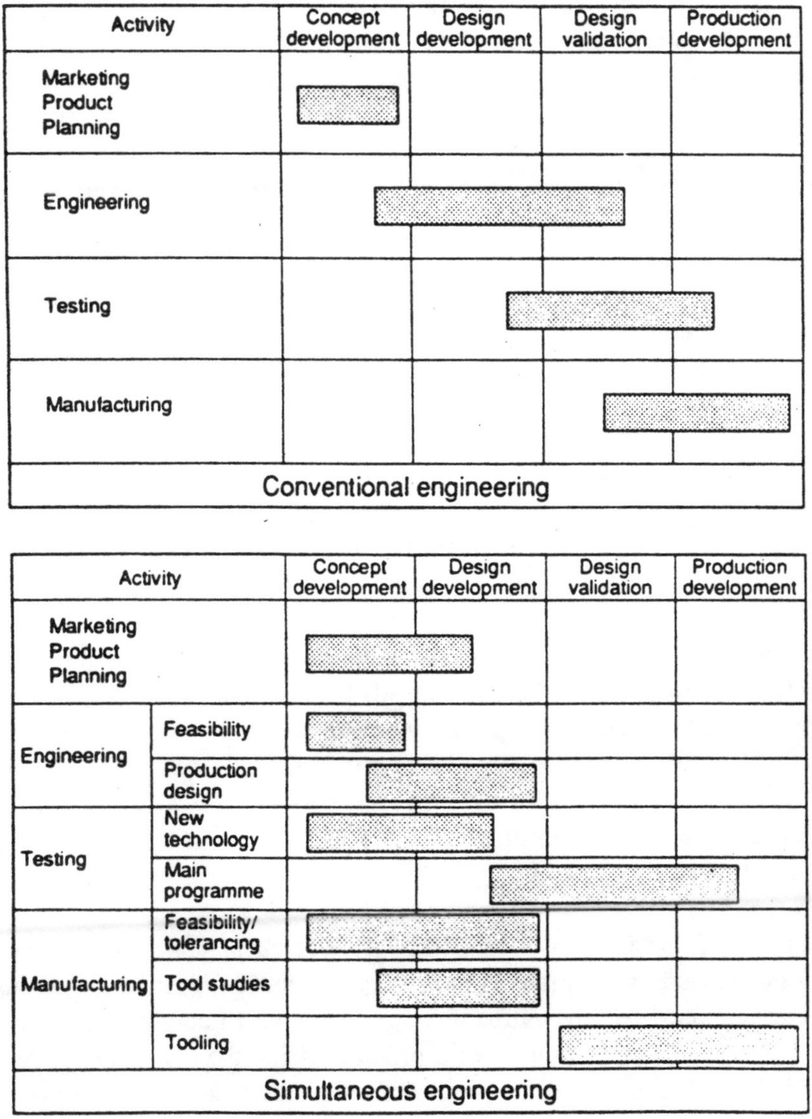

Source: Kochan (1991).

At the end of the 1980s, for instance, Japanese automobile manufacturers took on the average 70 % of the time and 60 % of the engineering
hours needed by their Western competitors to develop a product
(Womack, Jones, and Roos 1990, 118). The basis for this is the organizational model of simultaneous engineering (Kochan 1991, 4), which
includes two elements. First, an attempt is made as early as possible to
involve representatives of as many internal technical departments (as
well as marketing, procurement, and so on), suppliers, etc. with an eye
to overcoming the boundaries imposed by isolated areas by bringing
together various standpoints. Internally, this structure is strengthened
by reassigning R&D people over the age of 40 (when, in the Japanese
view, the zenith of creativity has been passed) to tasks in production
(Wakasugi 1992, 7). Second, product development does not proceed on
the cascade model, with different departments successively working on
a project; instead, different activities are approached in parallel (Figure
17).

The Japanese electronics industry provides another example. Its R&D
departments initiate only a relatively small proportion of R&D projects, impulses from customers taking on a disproportionately great
significance here. This differs strikingly from the practice of US corporations. In this respect there are worlds between the corporate philoso-
phies: while Japanese firms keep up close contacts with their customers, US firms operate entirely differently; in the words of an IBM managers: "... *we used to drive our business in a lot of areas by doing what
our laboratories thought it would be terrific to do.*" (Financial Times,
Dec. 2, 1988, 12)

Japanese firms also developed *design for manufacturability* as a further
organizational innovation. In the electronics industry, for instance, the
introduction of equipment to produce at low cost many product variants in small lots presupposes a product design that, instead of one-
sidedly optimizing the technical characteristics of a product, accom-
plishes this with the aid of elements designed to make possible production at low costs. One approach is to reduce the number of components involved, e.g. by using multifunctional subassemblies and integrating a variety of circuits in one efficient chip. But even product

improvements that at first glance look trivial, such as a reduction of half of the wire and screws needed for a television set, can have far-reaching consequences when corresponding innovations are available for the firm's entire line of products.

Simultaneous engineering and design for manufacturability have three effects:

–   they cut the use of resources, because they reduce frictional losses in R&D and achieve synergy benefits, and they make it possible to develop products that can be manufactured at less expense than before;

–   the increase in responsiveness, i.e. a firm can quickly respond to altered demand signals or new requirements (e.g. new legal frame-work conditions, e.g. on the environmental efficiency of products);

–   they increase the probability that successful products will be developed.

The demands faced by firms wishing to introduce simultaneous engineering are, to be sure, high, since it renders obsolete long-established organizational structures and behavioral patterns that may have been in practice for decades. Established internal power structures ("fief-doms") are no less put to the question than existing status hierarchies. Despite its obvious superiority, the introduction of new organizational concepts therefore often runs up against a variety of resistance, and not infrequently fails.

1.2.3   Policy Implications

While the findings of evolutionary economics and other disciplines regarding innovation behavior have obvious implications for policy interventions (i.e. as regards the political shape imparted to the technology-related business environment), the policy implications of new organizational concepts are less obvious, and indeed more complex. There are two issues at stake here: compatibility between fundamental microlevel changes going in the direction of more intensive participation and participatory social structures, but also sociocultural framework conditions; and the adequacy of conventional technology-policy instruments to promote innovations in the production process.

Microlevel change and social framework conditions. A controversial discussion has developed around the issue associated with the last point, viz. whether or to what extent new organizational concepts in product development and production are transferable. The original supposition that Japanese organizational concepts are culturally specific and depend on very specific conditions (e.g. lifelong employment), and are therefore generally not transferable, has been falsified by empirical data – Japanese firms have shown in the transplants in the US that they are able to realize in a different environment concepts similar to those familiar in Japan (Rehder 1988). In this context the fact was rediscovered that in the 1950s Japanese firms were themselves strongly influenced by US advisors. The transplant experiences do, however, also indicate that there exist substantial needs in terms of institutional change, e.g. in the pattern of labor union organization. "Union-free" transplants had far fewer problems than the ones in which established unions were active that had flourished under Fordist conditions. In these firms it proved relatively difficult to overcome longstanding confrontational behavioral patterns, but also for unions to develop new, internal patterns of legitimation (Scherrer and Greven 1993). New company-level organizational patterns thus presuppose changes in social patterns of regulation and organization. Whether this is accomplished inside or outside the sphere of state activity depends on the role played by the state in regulating the relations between capital and labor. In practical terms this can mean different things: in societies in which the state observes a hands-off attitude toward collective bargaining (i.e. has not even created, as in Germany, a legal framework covering the bilateral relations between the bargaining parties), it can be necessary to at least create legal regulations aimed at reducing, for both parties, the incentives to engage in highly confrontational behavior. In other societies in which the state (e.g. in the context of corporativist systems) has taken charge of regulating the relations between the parties to collective bargaining, it can prove necessary to strengthen the autonomy of the parties as a means of encouraging direct bargaining –

not only over wages but also on working conditions, job descriptions and the like.

New organizational concepts and technology policy. Technology-policy instruments designed to modernize industrial production often set their sights in the past on the technical component. This could be observed in particular in the 1980s, when programs aimed at diffusing the use of CIM components were introduced in various countries. The experiences with new organizational concepts did, to be sure, indicate that any such pattern of policy-level intervention was not only inappropriate but could even prove dangerous in that it tended to cement a given (abortive) model of restructuring industrial production. If the aim of technology policy is to stimulate the modernization of industrial production processes, it must today in particular pay sufficient attention to socio-organizational components. Initiatives with a shape similar to the program on the "humanization of working life" (launched in Germany in the 1970s), which were seen in the past more as humanistic-altruistic niche events, must today make up the core of production-process-oriented technology policy, because they contribute to mobilizing creative manpower potentials.

1.3   Networks and Competitiveness

Conventional economics deals with two transaction spheres: markets and hierarchies, i.e. market-mediated transactions between producers and buyers and transactions within firms. The recent past, however, has seen an increase in the number of transactions that cannot be assigned to the one or the other of these two categories. These include time-limited alliances between firms, just-in-time supplier networks, research cooperation, and the like. There is much to indicate that these forms of transaction cannot be plotted on a continuum somewhere between market and hierarchy, indeed that they constitute a third, independent transaction form: networks (see Table 13, which compares, in ideal-typical and, as regards networks, somewhat idealized, form, the three types of transaction sphere) (OECD/TEP 1992, 77f.). The phenomenon of networks not only questions conventional conceptions of

Table 13: Stylized Comparison of Forms of Economic Organization

Parameters	Forms		
	Markets	*Hierarchies*	*Networks*
Normative basis	Contract, property rights	Employment relationship	Complementary strengths
Means of communications	Prices	Routines	Relations
Methods of conflict resolution	Haggling; resort to courts for enforcement	Administrative fiat, supervision	Norm of reciprocity, reputational concerns
Degree of flexibility	High	Low	Medium to high
Amount of commitment among the parties	Low	Medium to high	Medium to high
Tone of climate	Precision and/or suspicion	Formal, bureaucratic	Open-end, mutual benefits
Relations between economic agents	Independence	Hierarchical	Interdependence
Source: OECD (1992), p. 78, adapted from Powell (1990).			

economic transactions, it is furthermore an element central to any understanding of technological learning processes and the diffusion of technological know-how. This is often even an important incentive, if not the explicit objective, of setting up networks.

It would, however, be mistaken to assume that an analysis of networks can be boiled down to yield a clear-cut grid demonstrating what an optimal network that leads to a maximum of competitiveness ought to look like (Sydow 1992; and Storper 1993). Differing views cannot be reduced merely to divergencies in methodological approach and theoretical framework; they also reflect real differences between different network types. The following subchapters are for that reason only partially complementary; they also present, in no small part, competing views. A concluding reflection seeks to categorize different network types and to identify the success conditions for networks.

1.3.1   Supplier Relations: the Superiority of the Japanese Model

The most widespread form of relations between firms are those between the supplier and his customer. In the industrialized Western
countries this relationship was in the past chiefly a transaction via the
market (arms-length relationship); it was regulated by contract and
could be terminated at any time. Still, it becomes evident in retrospective that beside purely marketlike transactions there always existed
another type which displayed characteristics of a network relationship
– a long-term, trust-based relationship marked by many informal contacts. Interfirm learning by interacting was able to develop in this type
of relationship: the buyer supported the supplier in solving given
problems; the supplier developed new products in close cooperation
with the buyer's engineers.

The realization that the development of a networked relationship is
more conducive to competitiveness than the practice of playing one
supplier off against another is an insight that derives above all from
Japan. As regards supplier relationships, the Japanese production system differs in two respects from the Western system (Nomura 1987;
Annavajhula 1989). First, the vertical integration of the manufacturers
of end products is far less pronounced than in the West.[16] These firms
generally restrict their activities to the scale-intensive assembly of
components and final assembly (Nomura 1991). Second, the structure
of the Japanese supplier system is pyramidal, not radial; only a minority of suppliers delivers to more than one customer. One factor defining this structure is that the majority of major Japanese corporations
belong to industrial groups (*keiretsu*) which – organized for the most
part around a bank and a trade firm – lead to the formation of multisec-
tor conglomerates. The formation of industrial networks within conglomerates is facilitated by the fact that market relations are replaced
by largely internal, for the most part informal, "social relations" which
make it possible to minimize transaction costs and risks. Close ties to a
major bank also diminish dependence of such firms on the external
capital market and reduce the pressure to earn short-term profits.

The Japanese supplier system differs from the Western system not only in terms of structure but also in terms of the organization of processes. Deliveries are as far as possible just-in-time, i.e. the customer is not forced to keep intermediate inventories. This presupposes close relationships and functions, e.g., only when a supplier takes charge of the quality control of the goods concerned – a function that, in the West, is typically performed by the buyer.

The close relationships between suppliers and customers are not restricted only to cooperation in production, they also extend to product development. What characterizes simultaneous engineering is that both the final manufacturer's departments and suppliers are involved in the development process.

1.3.2   Producer-User Interaction

A further type of interfirm interaction is the producer-user interaction described by Lundvall (1988). Lundvall criticizes the notion dominant in economics that the interaction between the manufacturer of a product and the buyers operates only via an anonymous market. He points out that in certain industries – and not only the ones in which complex, custom-made capital goods for known customers are involved – the interaction between producer and user is very close. This type of relationship is a typical element of interfirm interaction (Lundvall 1992b, 49). The close contact encourages technological learning processes and leads to the emergence of competitive industrial structures especially when the users are demanding and competition-minded:

> *"The fact that Denmark is strongly specialized in dairy machinery, Sweden in metal-working and wood-cutting technology, and Norway in fishery technology cannot be explained by the general factor endowments in those countries. Rather, we should look for the explanation in the close interaction between producers of such machinery and a competent and demanding domestic user sector."* (Lundvall 1988, 360)

This view particularly emphasizes the aspect of the cumulative character of technological know-how; it underlines the significance of learning by interacting. One feature of an efficient network is its pronounced technological externalities. These externalities develop between firms, either consciously (between suppliers and their customers or in an alliance) or unconsciously (via personnel fluctuation, informal exchange of information, and so on); they also develop between firms and research, technology, and training institutions. They are model examples of positive external effects which entail gains for all firms involved that are greater than the losses facing the individual firm. The disadvantage involved in the fact that no single firm is able to appropriate exclusively the benefits of its own innovations is more than compensated for by the enhanced competitiveness of the network; a network permits

> *"a collective rather than an individual form of rent appropriation and requires social and cultural preconditions which some nations possess more widely than others."* (OECD/TEP 1992, 84)

The existence of marked technological externalities makes possible rapid interactive, cumulative learning processes (Rosenberg 1982, 120ff.) in the course of which a network of firms and institutions is able to master technological process or product innovations far more rapidly than isolated firms in other locations, and thus to achieve market successes. The existence of continuous cumulative learning processes can lead to the situation that a country (more precisely: certain branches of industry in a country) can build up absolute competitive advantages (Dosi, Pavitt, and Soete 1990, 148ff.). Such absolute advantages do not rest on static comparative advantages; they are instead based on the ability of firms integrated in networks to sustain or expand technological leadership. It is possible to analyze international trade on this basis; such an analysis would no longer seek to identify static comparative advantages, it would look for technological gaps which determine the structure of the world trade in manufactured goods. Empirical studies have shown that such technological gaps or leads can be maintained for longer periods of time within the context of an efficient system of innovation (OECD/TEP 1992, 250). These explanatory patterns illustrate *"why, since the late 1970s, some OECD countries have run long-term, almost permanent trade surpluses and others almost equally permanent deficits."* (OECD/TEP 1992, 251)

1.3.3 Clusters as the Central Element of the International Competitiveness of Nations

A further approach to the analysis of interfirm interaction was developed by Porter (1990) with the intention of explaining the differences in the international competitiveness of nations; what links Porter here with evolutionary economics is especially his criticism of the simplistic basic assumptions of neoclassical economics. He summarizes his central propositions in the following words:

> *"National prosperity is created, not inherited. It does not grow out of a country's natural endowments, its labor pool, its interest rates, or its currency's value, as classical economics insists.*
>
> *A nation's competitiveness depends on the capacity of its industry to innovate and upgrade. Companies gain advantage against the world's best competitors because of pressure and challenge. They benefit from having strong domestic rivals, aggressive homebased suppliers, and demanding local customers.*
>
> *In a world of increasingly global competition, nations have become more, not less, important. As the basis of competition has shifted more and more to the creation and assimilation of knowledge, the role of the nation has grown. Competitive advantage is created and sustained through a highly localized process. Differences in national values, culture, economic structures, institutions, and histories all contribute to competitive success. There are striking differences in the patterns of competitiveness in every country; no nation can or will be competitive in every or even most industries. Ultimately, na-*

tions succeed in particular industries because their home environment is the most forward-looking, dynamic, and challenging." (Porter 1990, 73f.)

In his analysis Porter emphasizes the significance of creating environmental conditions that both stimulate and enforce the development of competitiveness. He illustrates this with the aid of a "diamond" containing four elements (Porter 1990, 77ff.):

1. Factor conditions: These include, e.g. the availability of qualified manpower or adequate infrastructure. *"Contrary to conventional wisdom, simply having a general work force that is high school or even college educated represents no competitive advantage in modern international competition. To support competitive advantage, a factor must be highly specialized to an industry's particular needs – a scientific institute specialized in optics, a pool of venture capital to fund software companies. These factors are more scarce, more difficult for foreign competitors to imitate – and they require sustained investment to create."* (Porter 1990, 78)

   Here, disadvantages in general factor endowments need not necessarily prove disadvantageous, and they can even stimulate the development of competitiveness. If cheap raw materials or labor are available in abundance, firms will often yield to the temptation to rely solely on these advantages, and even to put them to inefficient uses. Conversely, certain disadvantages (high real estate prices, scarce labor and raw materials) can force firms to behave innovatively. This of course presupposes that positive impulses are generated by the other factors.

2. Demand conditions: The more demanding the customers in an economy, the greater the pressure facing firms to constantly improve their competitiveness via innovative products, through high quality, and so on.

3. Existence or lack of related and supporting industries: Spatial proximity of upstream or downstream industries facilitates the exchange of information and promotes a continuous exchange of ideas and innovations. Porter refers, among other things, to experi-

ences with industrial districts in Italy, whereby, however, he strongly qualifies their specifics (see below). On the one hand, he points out that even upstream industries should in no case be sheltered from international competition; and he notes on the other hand that when certain upstream industries are lacking, recourse can be had to the supply available in the world market.

4. Business strategies and structures and rivalry: Porter notes that despite all differences and national peculiarities one characteristic shared by competitive economies is that there is sharp competition among national firms. Statically, national champions may enjoy advantages of scale; but the real world is dominated by dynamic conditions, and here it is direct competition that impels firms to work for increases in productivity and innovations; here, anonymous competition often turns into concrete rivalries and feuds, in particular when competitors are spatially concentrated. *"The more localized the rivalry, the more intense. And the more intense, the better."* (Porter 1990, 83) This is all the more true, as its effect is to cancel out static locational advantages and compel firms to develop dynamic advantages.

The last point indicates that the four factors do not exist in isolation, but can intensify one another reciprocally: firms that operate under strong competitive pressure will confront supporting institutions (e.g. R&D and training institutions) with more concrete and demanding claims. This reciprocal intensification is found particularly in spatially concentrated clusters with competing firms, suppliers, and supporting institutions.

1.3.4   Industrial Districts and "Collective Efficiency"

Porter differs from rest of the discussion on industrial districts in his clear emphasis on the competitive principle as opposed to cooperation. In contrast, the discussion on industrial districts, marked as it is by experiences from the "Third Italy", but also from Baden-Württemberg, Jutland, and Flanders (Schmitz and Musyck 1993), is concerned with a balanced consideration of these two principles, including a strong emphasis on cooperation. It also underlines sociocultural factors (Sengenberger and Pyke 1992; Pyke 1992).

Becattini defines districts as

> *"a socio-territorial entity which is characterised by the active presence of both a community of people and a population of firms in one naturally and historically bounded area. In the district, unlike in other environments, such as manufacturing towns, community and firms tend to merge."* (Becattini 1990, 38)

Industrial districts display the following features (Asheim 1992, 4f.; and Schmitz and Musyck 1993, 3):

– sectoral specialization;

– dominance of small and medium-sized plants;

– a marked division of labor among spatially concentrated firms, which forms the basis for a dense network of supplier relations;

– a pronounced product specialization on the part of plants and firms, which stimulates the accumulation of specific know-how;

– intensive competition that is played out primarily through innovations, and not so much by undercutting prices;

– a well-functioning information network which quickly disseminates information on markets, new production techniques and methods, new primary products, and so on; collective institutions play an important role here;

– high workforce competence levels, resulting in part from formal training, in part from transmission of knowledge from generation to generation;

– a sociocultural basis for trust relations between firms and qualified workers;

– an active role for regional and municipal public-sector actors, who strengthen the innovation capacity of the firms concerned.

The constitutive characteristic of industrial districts is the lack of clear-cut hierarchies between the firms concerned; there is no major corporation that actively structures the district. Aside from spatial concentration, industrial districts are characterized by a specific industrial milieu and an inseparable link between the economic and the social sphere; interfirm relations are woven into a dense social network that generates relations based on mutual trust. This is the basis for cooperative relations in which free riders are penalized not economically but socially.

What is behind the interest in districts is the experience that in this context even small and medium-sized firms can achieve, and maintain, international competitiveness. This appears all the more important as these firms have, in the past, created the major share of new jobs. Districts could therefore have the potential to resolve the dilemma between international competitiveness and large business units with, all in all, stagnant employment figures.

In industrial districts, small and medium-sized firms can compensate for their disadvantages of scale by networking and thus achieving economies of scale and scope (Dijk 1992, 4f.); Schmitz (Schmitz 1989) coined for this state of affairs the term *collective efficiency*. The competitiveness of districts rests in strong measure on a rapid diffusion of incremental innovations, many of which come about within the district. On the other hand, hardly any radical innovations emerge in districts because of the chiefly small sizes of the firms concerned and their limited ability to engage in systematic R&D (Asheim 1992, 21). Even the diffusion of such innovations generally requires technology institutes and other (often state) institutions that advise users on the procurement and uses of, e.g., microelectronically controlled machines. Potential for developing technological capability depends on the capability level of firms and the presence of supporting institutions.

1.3.5   Core Competence, Technology Fusion, and Strategic Alliances

The acceleration of the process of technological change and the altera-
tion of its characteristics confront firms with contradictory requirements. There is on the one hand the constraint (or the temptation) to
concentrate on one's own core competence (Prahalad and Hamel
1991); this often entails deverticalization and – in the case of conglomerates – the sale of various business units.

On the other hand, it is becoming increasingly difficult for firms to
move within one technological trajectory only. In a number of industries, in particular in science-based industries and specialized suppliers,
the firms are today faced with the challenge of processing and bringing
together technological know-how from entirely different sectors. Kodama (Kodama 1991, 10ff.) has coined for this the term technology
fusion. Examples would include the combination of optical, mechanical, and electronic elements in machine tools or CD players.

Firms whose product spectrum is modified by the phenomenon of
technology fusion are faced with two challenges: access to know-how
outside their own core competence and financing drastically rising
R&D investments. Many firms see strategic technology alliances as the
solution to these challenges (Mody 1991; and Gugler 1992). Alliances
have advantages vis-à-vis other organizational forms. Their sunk costs
are lower than those required for purely internal development; they are
easier to dissolve than fusions; they thus offer a greater degree of
flexibility.

The number of strategic alliances increased sharply in the 1980s. Of
the roughly 4,200 strategic alliances registered by the MERIT database
(Hagedoorn and Schakenraad 1992) for the years between 1981 and
1989, one third were launched in the first half of the decade and two
thirds in the second half. Almost three quarters of the alliances focus
on three fields: information technology/microelectronics, genetic technology, and new materials. About one quarter were concluded in the
USA, some 20 % between US and European firms, and some 15 %

between US and Japanese firms; fewer than 4 % of the alliances included firms from NICs and developing countries (Freeman and Hagedoorn 1992, 37ff.).

The number of national or regional alliances thus clearly outweighs the number of global alliances, even though the latter are often the ones that make the headlines. There are furthermore strong indications that the years 1986-88 saw the peak number of new alliances and that the tendency has been downward since then (OECD/TEP 1992, 73).

1.3.6   Globalization of R&D

Even if only a more or less small percentage of strategic alliances is organized globally, there is no doubt that technological activities have been globally oriented since business strategies went global and the process of technological change began to accelerate. A number of firms began to organize their inhouse R&D on a worldwide scale, reaching cooperation agreements with universities and research institutions in different countries. Very different patterns are concealed behind the phenomenon of the globalization of R&D activities:

–   The creation of R&D units in subsidiaries to modify products and to develop specific products for the local market (Pearce 1991). This is the "classical form" of the internationalization of R&D; relatively autonomous subsidiaries would scarcely be conceivable without it. A more recent trend is that such R&D units are developing specific specialization profiles within the context of a worldwide corporate division of labor in R&D and – in connection with this – that development tasks are being solved in joint worldwide efforts (Meyer 1991). The diffusion of globalized networked corporate research has received strong impulses from the rapidly sinking costs for telecommunication services (OECD/TEP 1992, 224).

–   The development of R&D units at locations to make use of scientific and engineering personnel that is scarce and/or very costly in the country of origin. This a recent, quantitatively limited phenomenon that can be observed in particular in new industries (electronics, software, genetic technology); here, there is often a gap between the output of established academic training institutions and industry's demand for personnel.[17]

- The location of R&D units in regions in which there are dynamic networks of innovative firms and/or research institutions. The bottom line here is to share in the external effects that emerge in networks, e.g. as a means of keeping abreast with new technical developments. A further concern here is to encourage learning by interacting, i.e. more efficient and rapid innovation activities via interaction with other firms. In the past, both aspects represented an important motive for US corporations operating in Europe, and in the 1980s they led to a number of Japanese and European investments in the US, particularly in the pharmaceuticals industry (with an eye to American genetic technology research) and the electronics industry (OECD/TEP 1992, 225).

On the whole, the 1980s were marked by a moderate rise in R&D activities of transnational corporations outside their home bases. The positive balance resulted from the expansion of international R&D by European transnationals, whereas in the same period overseas R&D activities of US corporations showed a downward trend (Freeman and Hagedoorn 1992, 22) and Japanese firms were very hesitant in internationalizing R&D (in the period from 1981-88, 99.1 % of Japanese patent applications in the US stemmed from Japan, only 0.7 % from US subsidiaries of Japanese firms) (Pavitt 1992, 121). Three factors can be referred to explain the behavior of European firms: first, the existence of major transnationals in small countries (Sweden, Netherlands, Switzerland) that run important activities abroad; second, the push toward internationalization in connection with the creation of the Common Market; and, third, the jump in technological investment in the US undertaken with an eye to participating in the development of new technological fields, which was progressing particularly rapidly there.

The finding that R&D is increasingly globalizing is based in great measure on experiences with science-based industries (electronics, pharmaceuticals, genetic technology), which move at the cutting edge of technological progress (Pavitt 1984, 353ff.). For them it is vital to develop a global network structure that includes leading international firms and technology institutions; only in this way can they ensure that they will remain at the top of international best practice (Gelsing 1992, 123). But even they operate most of their R&D at home. In other industries (including technologically demanding ones), this is even more pronounced; in the automobile industry, for instance, only car-body design (thanks to differences in national preferences) and production engineering have been internationalized to any significant degree, while other activities (basic research, development of engines, power transmission systems, and so on) are chiefly conducted at home (Freeman and Hagedoorn 1992, 33).

1.3.7   Prerequisites for and Disadvantages of Networks

There is no doubt that networks are a central element in the development of industrial competitiveness. They encourage cumulative learning effects, promote the diffusion of innovative processes, and foster reconciliation between flexibility and specialization. Identification of networks provides an element complementary to the factors of innovation localized at firm level. Yet there is great diversity of network types, which, in addition, exist side by side, without any one type being able to lay claim to clear-cut superiority. The following categories can serve as an aid in systematizing them:

Formal vs. informal. Certain networks have a contractual or in some other way legally sanctioned basis (e.g. strategic alliances), others are without any such basis owing to the mutual interests of the parties concerned.

Hierarchic vs. nonhierarchic. Certain networks are clearly structured hierarchically (e.g. Japanese supplier networks, networks of hollow corporations),[18] while others display egalitarian structures that do not necessarily develop a tendency toward hierarchical organization over the course of time (as has been observed in certain Italian industrial districts).

Vertical vs. horizontal. One aspect that needs to be distinguished from the issue of hierarchies (which is a question of a power structures) is the question of the techno-organizational division of labor within a network. In terms of division of labor, certain networks are organized vertically along the value-added chain (e.g. supplier/subcontractor networks), others are structured horizontally (networks of researchers).

Time-limited vs. long-term. Certain networks (e.g. alliances) are established with an eye to a concrete goal and thus for a limited period of time, others (e.g. districts) are long-term arrangements. The development of networks is a difficult and demanding undertaking which – as the experience with alliances shows – involves a high risk of failure. But even once a network is operational, it remains costly, and maintaining it and keeping up its efficiency is a complicated affair.

Conditions for Successful Interfirm Alliances

An OECD report works out six conditions under which firms decide in favor of establishing networks (OECD/TEP 1992, 79):

– they own complementary assets with a high degree of tacitness which are essential to the development of new products or processes;

– the exchange of such assets and the learning processes linked with it require close person-to-person relationships;

– unstable economic conditions, technical uncertainty, and rapid changes in demand imply a premium on speed;

– high R&D costs force firms to pool their resources with those of other firms;

– flexibility and the possibility of reversibility are particularly important;

–   the partners expect a reciprocal relationship which is based on trust and penalizes free riders.

These six points, however, are apparently tailored primarily to a specific type of network – namely, strategic alliances. To be sure, for strategic alliances this list is at the same time too broad and too narrow. It is too broad to the extent that it creates the impression that it is tailored to all possible forms of networks. It is too narrow to the extent that it omits important factors that decide on success or failure.

In fact, many alliances have not achieved the goals they set themselves;[19] and managing them has proven to be a difficult task. Various reasons for this can be identified (Taucher 1988, 90):

–   rapid changes in environment, technology, or competition;

–   problems in coming to organizational terms with the complex tissue of cooperation;

–   unclear decision-making processes;

–   career considerations of the managers involved.

According to another study, alliances are all the more successful the more modest their goals and the more restricted the number of actors involved are. The risk of failure is particularly high for alliances that extend to several corporate functions; it

> *"is evident that the organizational cultures differ to such an extent not only between the cooperation partners but – in part even more markedly – between cooperation functions (e.g. marketing and research and development) differ so much that likelihood of success of cross-functional alliances is low."*
> (Rotering 1993, 1)

In fact, the alliances that prove successful are especially the ones which ended up with the one partner taking over the other[20] – a very traditional form of organization, in other words.

Problems in Maintaining a Network

If even the formation of strategic alliances between strongly managed firms is a complex undertaking fraught with snares, the development of collective efficiency structures and industrial districts is bound to be far a more difficult venture.

For a functioning network, a challenge as important as it is difficult is to find the golden section between structures too dense and too loose (Grabher 1993). A dense network can easily solidify, become structurally conservative and inimical to innovation, thus blocking development; one example for the past would be Germany's Ruhr District. Here the dependence of suppliers on the core industries led the former into an underdevelopment of marketing and development activities, thus bringing about a functional blockade. This was intensified by cognitive blockades in that dense communication largely prevented the assimilation of external impulses, thus making it inconceivable to attempt anything but a coal-and-steel orientation. This situation was finally exacerbated by a political blockade due to the close collusion between patriarchal entrepreneurs, conservative labor unions, and conservative (albeit social democratic) politicians and administrators.

Similar problems caused by overdensity and thus excessive inward orientation of networks can be observed both in Italian districts and in the Nike network: the more pronounced the inward orientation of a network, the less energy the firms involved will expend in observing systematically the other segments of the environment. To this extent

> *"loose coupling constitutes a type of 'cultural insurance policy' that networks can rely on in times of turmoil. Loose coupling of functionally largely autonomous actors makes it possible to create an elastic buffer against unforeseen events, local adjustments to environmental changes, and decentral learning and forgetting, and thus provides redundancy that heightens the adaptability of a network and diminishes the risk of cumulative mistakes and 'incorrect' learning based on*

positive feedback loops." (WZB-Mitteilungen 58/1992, 4, with reference to Grabher 1993)

An overly loose coupling can, to be sure, also prove fatal: *"too little internal cohesion and dense coupling ... expose networks to a creeping erosion of the supporting tissue of social practices and institutions."* (WZB-Mitteilungen 58/1992, 4) Experiences from Baden Württemberg indicate that the attempt of large firms to harness existing network structures can have this effect.

Network structures can prove dysfunctional when they – as in the US electronics industry – stimulate hyperentrepreneurship (Florida and Kenney 1991). The problem there is that dense network structures facilitate the establishment of new firms – supplier relationships are easy to establish, access to capital is comparatively uncomplicated. This, however, leads to a situation in which spin-off firms emerge before the original firm has even approximately reached its minimum-efficient operating size and a sufficient level of techno-organizational maturity. This can sometimes mean that learning processes and processes entailing the development of competitiveness are again and again interrupted or invalidated.

The question whether long-term competitive structures emerge in the network form specific to industrial districts is still in dispute. The industrial districts discussion has seldom looked beyond the individual district; it in certain ways appears as an end in itself, as a structure that is positive and thus, a priori, worth maintaining. In what way and to what extent structures and dysfunctionalities of an overall society and economy interrelate in such a way as to intensify or destabilize individual districts has as yet not been investigated. Yet this is a question all the more significant as districts often do not constitute a closed local economy but are, on the contrary, even integrated in the world economy.

A cautious view of industrial districts is appropriate in that the firms in them are efficient as long as incrementalism prevails (in Freeman's diction: when a stable techno-economic paradigm is established and the industry concerned is not affected by upheavals in the technological system). It is then that the exchange of information between firms constitutes an extremely effective form for organizing incremental innovations (as regards products and processes). If, however, radical challenges emerge (e.g. technological leaps, new, far more competitive competitors) that should end up in a process of radical change, industrial districts run into problems, for this affects "... the industrial district where it is weakest against the competition, namely developing a consensus around how to compete against global corporations. That consensus will involve means of shaping collective strategies and sharing the burdens of restructuring." (Best 1990, 265) The experiences made thus far indicate that the self-organization potential of networks are no better suited to mastering a situation in which radical changes in the environment require far-reaching internal reorientations and rearrangements than the hierarchical organizational pattern within big corporations.

1.3.8 Networks and Technology Policy

As yet it is possible to recognize at best in outlines the political implications entailed by the growing significance of networks. The discussion has thus far moved above all around the question of what control requirements are generated by the existence of Japanese-style supplier networks, for which traditional contract-governed regulations are no longer adequate (Bochum and Meissner 1990). On the other hand, the debate has scarcely touched on the consequences for technology policy, i.e. the possibilities not of restricting and controlling the negative effects of networks but of harnessing or stimulating their positive effects.

That the state can play an important role in networks has become clear, particularly in the analysis of industrial districts (Schmitz and Musyck 1993). In the European examples investigated, it was local or regional governments that assumed the various functions required to heighten the efficiency of industrial networks. This is particularly clear in the Italian industrial districts, which in the past were generally characterized by the stable predominance of one political party (depending on region, the Christian Democrats or the former PCI) (Storper 1993, 439f.). The low level of party competition, i.e. a lack of political polarization, was here closely related to the cohesion of the social actors, and this in turn made it possible to work out, for instance, technology-policy measures aimed specifically at jointly identified bottlenecks.

The discussion has thus far largely neglected to address the question whether central government has a role to play here. In its economic policy no less than in other sectoral policies, it does, it is true, create framework conditions that are of central significance for the success or failure of networks; it also contributes – e.g. through its procurement policy – to the further development and consolidation of regional networks (this could be observed, for instance, in the US defense industry) (Storper 1993, 446); yet it is – thus the postulate of a number of authors (Schmitz and Navdi 1994, 37) – hardly in a position to purposively create such networks. Traditional policy patterns imply more the opposite: classical regional policy has aimed to create a balance between strong and less strong regions (Hansen, Higgins, and Savoie 1990), and it in this way discriminated against efficient industrial districts. The Italian districts appeared to represent an alternative to centralized state activities, a "Third Italy," while the state was at pains to promote, at considerable expense and with little success, the "Second Italy," the structurally weak South.

The question sketched here as to what policies at what levels of government can stimulate the development of networks will be taken up again in the following chapter. This will involve looking into the question of what forms of interaction between state and nonstate actors emerge in the process.

2   Technology Policy for Industrial Competitiveness – on the Discussion in the OECD Countries

2.1   Argumentational Context of Technology Policy

The discussion on industrial and technology policy is conducted at various levels and in different theoretical and empirical contexts. The economic discussion is basically a normative one; the issue here is whether or not the state should (or must) intervene in the free play of forces in the marketplace. The sociological discussion is on the one hand a theoretical one; following the demise of the "control euphoria" of the 1970s, the issue now centers on the state's governance capacity. On the other hand, the discussion is an empirical one on concrete experiences with different approaches to technology policy, frequently based on comparisons between different countries.

2.1.1   The Economic Discussion

The discussion on technology policy in recent years has developed into an important theater of debates between neoliberal economists and their critics. One of the points of the argumentation advanced by the neoliberals is that technology development and innovation cannot be perceived as a dynamic, interactive process in which both firms and the state have specific roles; they construe it instead as a dichotomy between state governance and market-guided technology choice. The following statement illustrates this view:

> *"Industrial policy presupposes the ability of administrations to forecast the future development of research and technical progress so as to be able to identify the key technologies and industries. Only then would researchers and firms be able, with the aid of subsidies or specific recommendations, to be lured into the 'right' direction."* (Vetterlein 1992, 213)

The core category of the neoliberal argumentation is the juxtaposition of market failure and government failure; proceeding from this, it is claimed that government failure is generally the more serious problem. To the neoliberal mind, there are no forms of interaction between state and firms beyond hierarchic governance by an isolated state and acceptance of particular interests, whereby the latter amounts in the end to rent-seeking.

Critics of the neoliberals argue on different levels (Grossman 1990):

- They point – within the framework defined by neoliberal thinking – to the fact that market processes will lead to a suboptimal level of R&D and innovation efforts. A firm that invests in R&D must anticipate that it will be unable to appropriate the entire result of its efforts. Even if it is able to pocket innovation rents for a limited period of time, the fact still remains that both product and process innovation will find imitators within a relatively short period of time. The impossibility of any complete appropriation, the argument goes, is a first reason why firms fail to make R&D investments. A complementary view points out that R&D investments are a typical case of positive external effects: it is not the innovator who extracts the main benefit from an innovation, it is competitors in the same industry and the users. Furthermore, the fact that firms take over one another's innovations leads to an accumulation of external effects. The individual firm, on the other hand, is tempted to try its luck as a free-rider. And high minimum sums for relevant R&D and the risks resulting from the unpredictability of scientific and technical development processes lead to a situation in which firms prefer low levels of R&D efforts. For these reasons the state must promote innovation efforts, if these are to reach the economically optimal level.

- They criticize the problematical, simplifying assumptions of the neoliberals for failing to do justice to the reality of innovation processes. The latter never correspond to the assumptions of equilibrium economics concerning perfect information and perfect competition; therefore: *"whatever market solution emerges is necessarily imperfect. It is* always *possible to do better."* (Smith 1991, 264)

- The critics of the neoliberals point to the historical-empirical experience that in practically all countries that began their industrialization process after England the state has played an important
role in stimulating and guiding this process.

A differentiated rejection of neoliberal criticism must proceed from the
different types of innovation described above. At the level of incremental technological change, the market mechanism is the adequate
governance instrument. The challenge facing firms is to find an organizational model that makes it possible to quickly perceive and respond
to market signals. Central elements of a new competition strategy are
flexibility, i.e. the ability to produce efficiently different products in
medium lot sizes, and speed, i.e. an acceleration of operations from the
product idea to the finished product.

At the level of radical innovations and changes in the technological
system, on the other hand, a feature of market-controlled search processes is that they do not run according to a given plan and thus generate
few positive externalities. Positive externalities occur only when a new
corridor has been found. The example of the current changes in the
point of intersection of broadcasting, telecommunications, and data
processing may be used to illustrate this. It is currently not possible to
claim that there is a defined development corridor in this field, even
though individual tendencies are beginning to emerge (Landler and
Grover 1993; Ziegler 1993): the digitalization of television is leading
both to a fusion between television and PC technology and to a mix of
programs and software (in every sense of the two terms) – from the
battlefield on the evening news the leap to the computer-game battlefield, from the cultural program on television to the virtual visit to the
museum thanks to CD-ROM. The fusion of telecommunications and
informatics to form the field of telematics, long since announced, is
becoming reality, and the boundaries between individual and mass
communication are blurring. Moreover, it is becoming evident that
progress in digital compression techniques and the introduction of per-
tinent standards (The Economist, May 29, 1993, 74) are going to mul-
tiply the transmission capacities of existing distribution networks.

The preceding was a description of some framework conditions, not, however, of the concrete shape of an information and communication system of the future. Whether the new broadcasting capacities will be fully utilized and how they will be used in the future are as yet entirely open questions. Nor is it possible to say what types of products will define the picture of industry in the future. The activity of both the computer industry and the consumer-electronics industry is presently characterized by weakly structured search processes. Highly diverse ideas for products and services are launched, sometimes even marketed; but many innovations fail due to the lack of a corridor – users are waiting to see which transmission system, operating system, or other standards will prevail, other firms are holding back with investments needed to develop complementary products and services, and so on.

Industry's costs for this process are high, sometimes even endangering its existence. Deregulation and affirmation of market forces prove dysfunctional; the dichotomy that neoliberal economists see between the efficient, judicious market and the omnipotent, albeit mindless and inefficient, state is therefore, both in this concrete situation and in a situation of radical change in general, not convincing. Governance can create the conditions under which a new development corridor becomes visible; this is a sine qua non for firms to be able to pursue promising strategies and invest in new technologies.

Past experience has made two things clear. First, in a phase of radical change those actors become politically active who have an interest in slackening the pace of technological change, i.e. who are interested in ensuring the continued existence of existing corridors; this, for instance, was the essence of Europe's HDTV policy (Meyer-Stamer 1994). Second, the tendency to engage in pork-barreling creates a situation in which defined corridors that prove to be dead-end streets are at times very difficult to close (Cohen and Noll 1991). The central challenge facing technology policy in the context of radical technological change is thus to find a governance model that makes it possible to arrive at decisions on technology development that create new corridors; and this calls for an open-ended decision-making network in which more than merely partial and conservative interests are represented.

Can Industry-Specific Technology Policy Be Abolished?

A further economic argument for practicing an industry-specific technology policy arises from the consequences that would result from any attempt to abolish it completely, mechanisms of political legitimation being as they are. True, the critique of industrial policy (information problem, danger of rent-seeking, etc.) voiced by neoliberal economists is not unwarranted. But the consequence of deciding against any industrial policy can lead to inefficient results (suboptimal as compared with continuous industrial policy activities). The initial consideration is that it is very unlikely that it is at all possible to abolish industrial policy once and for all. Industries are often spatially concentrated, and this means that difficult crises in one industry can spell crisis for an entire region. A crisis situation in this region will step up the pressure on politicians to initiate specific measures in response to the crisis; and pointing to the positive welfare-raising effects of "creative destruction" is irrelevant in a situation in which creation and destruction occur in separate locations. In a situation of this sort, the obvious option for politicians is to take industrial-policy measures aimed at cushioning the impacts of the process of destruction or structural adjustment, for example, subsidies for firms that agree to reduce layoffs. Measures of this sort have two advantages for the politicians involved. First, they have directly visible positive effects (fewer jobs are lost). Second, technically it is not very difficult to implement them, especially when subsidies are not linked to specific performance criteria (that require a large measure of technical competence on the part of those in charge of supervising them, i.e. the state would have to be able to verify, on the basis of quantitative indicators, any improvement in the efficiency of firms). Any preservation-oriented industrial policy that blocks the process of structural change instead of shaping it is thus the logical outcome of an environment in which industrial policy per se is taboo and is made use of only in acute crisis situations in the form of ad hoc activities. Put differently: the industrial policy of countries like Germany or England is dominated by structurally conservative activities not despite but on account of the regulatory (*ordnungspolitisch*) rigorism prevalent in the country.

Ordnungspolitik vs. industrial policy is thus, in empirical terms, a false opposition. The right opposition would be *Ordnungspolitik* plus *ad hoc* industrial policy vs. anticipative industry-related technology policy, strengthening of the quality of industrial locations, and intelligent management of the process of structural change in industry.

2.1.2 The Sociological Discussion: Who Governs Technical Change?

A central theme of the sociological study of innovation is the potential for intentional governance of technological development. This question is usually discussed at two levels: Is it possible to govern technology at all? And if so, what instruments should technology policy make use of, and at what levels?

The sociological discussion on innovation reveals conflicting views on whether it is possible to govern the process of technological change. The theoretical-conceptual discussion has moved back and forth from a position of governance pessimism to a position of governance optimism. The original governance pessimism resulted from the science-push view that technological change is driven by pioneering scientific innovations, which can only be harnessed economically after they have matured and potential commercial applications have become apparent. In this view, inventions cannot be planned, and basic scientific research cannot simply be governed. The science-push thesis was later superseded by the demand-pull thesis, according to which social, though often also business-related, needs trigger specifically targeted research efforts (Rammert 1992).

The more recent discussion has proceeded on the assumption that neither of these two theses – each of which assumes a clear-cut sequence from basic research to the finished product – adequately describes the process which links science, research, development and the market. There is rather a complex interaction between actors located at various points along the innovation chain. The discussion on the governance of technology centers on the question to what extent it is possible, in the context of this interaction, to influence this process in an active and purposive way. This discussion is strongly influenced by the more extensive controversy on the possibilities of political governance of social relations, including the economy (Martinsen 1992). This larger debate focuses on the evaluation of "sociotechnological" governance patterns of the type pursued in the 1960s and 1970s. There is not much doubt that the policies to shape social contexts pursued in this period were not particularly successful; this is one of the findings of the comprehensive research on the problems involved in implementing political programs. The reasons can be found in two factors: the growing complexity of modern industrial societies and reversal of the competence differential between state and social actors.

Growing social complexity creates a situation in which the consequences of individual policies, as well as the interaction among them, are difficult to grasp. Political initiatives get stuck in the "policy entanglement trap"; *"...instead of the premises of utter sovereignty and internal hierarchy germane to early modern thinking on the state, government policy is today tied into an increasingly ramified and dense nexus of transactions and inherently social dependencies and negotiation-based relationships"* (Scharpf 1991). Governance pessimists thus conclude that governance can at best be the result of self-organization within social subsystems, whereas attempts at governance at the level of society as a whole are doomed to failure (Luhmann 1989). To underpin their argument, the governance pessimists point both to negative experiences in the field of technology governance and to examples in which the state consciously refrains from any attempts at governance. One example is the Europe-wide EUREKA R&D promotion program, which is geared to stimulating cooperation between firms from different countries, but which pointedly avoids efforts of the governments involved to determine the content and direction of the cooperative research agenda (Willke 1988).

The reversal of the competence differential finds expression in the fact that the state is increasingly forced to rely on the technical competence of social actors to regulate given social activities. It is inconceivable, for instance, that the state itself could set technical standards in all areas of industry. The expense of developing the necessary technical competence within the bureaucracy would exceed the state's resources and would in any case be inefficient since the required know-how is already available in society. Moreover, since the requisite technical knowledge is widely dispersed in society, no single group holds an information monopoly that would allow it to manipulate standards-writing to its private advantage. This example supports the supposition that the state's potential role in social governance is much more limited than often assumed.

However, governance optimists can point to instances of successful goal-oriented technology policies, for example, in complex sectors such as telecommunications (Schneider and Werle 1991). They hold the view that the solution to the competence problem, as well as in part the solution to the complexity problem, is to transpose to society the process of deciding on rules with defined policy fields. Germany's DIN Commissions, which define technical standards, are an example of this. In this case the state assumes a function as organizer and supervisor, rather than sole executor, of the decision-making process. Though not monopolizing rule-making functions, that state plays several vital roles:

- it ensures that certain procedural rules are observed;

- it ensures, as the case may be, that the important actors are involved (in the DIN Commissions, for instance, a consumer council and an environmental coordination unit have been set up) (Voelzkow 1993, 116);

- it can threaten to issue regulations on its own, which, for the actors involved, would most probably be suboptimal so that there is an incentive for a constructive discussion process (Scharpf 1991, 629).

This kind of governance pattern, in which the state superintends a process of negotiated rule-setting among societal actors, may be described with the familiar concept of "policy networks." Policy networks gain in significance as decisions which clearly go beyond merely technical decision-making, and which were formerly the province of the state alone, are negotiated in networks which involve a number of actors. Policy networks – with state participation, though not necessarily under state leadership – are emerging in various areas in which political initiatives are negotiated. According to researchers who have examined such experiences in a systematic way, the concept of policy networks constitutes *"not only (...) a new analytical view of an unchanged reality. The concept of policy networks signals instead, for the understanding prevalent today, an actual change in the structures of political decision-making. Instead of being created by a central authority, be it executive or legislative, policy today often emerges in a process in which a great number of both public and private organizations are involved."* (Mayntz 1993, 40)

The danger of policy formulation in policy networks is that individual actors represent only parochial interests and that, moreover, the costs of negotiated polices will be shifted, or "externalized", to broader communities or to society as a whole. Two points argue against this objection, however:

–   Experience has shown that, in traditional political structures, it is very difficult to implement specific policies against articulated interests, even when they represent the broader public interest. This is particularly true of specific sectoral policies: industrial policy or technology policy will for the most part aim to stimulate or direct certain types of behavior on the part of social actors (especially firms). If these actors flatly refuse to cooperate, and the state's sanction potentials are limited (which can be typical of technology policy, for what sense would it make to penalize a firm for not availing itself of R&D subsidies?), any such policy is doomed to failure. It is therefore essential to include the relevant interests in the process of policy formulation It may be noted that formally recognizing that key social groups have a *de facto* influence over successful implementation does not jeopardize larger public interests.

- Moreover, the border between the representation of particular interests and objectively necessary information-gathering is a fluid one. In classical pluralist systems, relations between the state and social actors were hierarchical and radial, and direct interaction between societal actors was limited. It was the state's responsibility to gather the information required to formulate policy, to synthesize policy proposals, and to discuss them with individual interest groups. In network-like negotiation systems societal actors interact directly with one another.

The success or failure of negotiation systems depends on both the form and the character of the interaction between actors. Each actor must have a considerable degree of internal coherence, e.g. to be able to tackle internal conflicts (without calling upon external arbitrators such as, in corporatist systems, the government or the judiciary). The success of the interaction rests on various factors:

- the basis of trust between the actors concerned;

- the willingness to disclose relevant information;

- commitment to a fair exchange, reciprocity, or a just distribution of costs and benefits;

- orientation towards solving collective problems or achieving collective gains, i.e. an approach which aims at more than a minimum consensus. This point is crucial if governance decisions in the specific sense of the term are in fact made within a policy network.

The rules of interaction fundamentally require *"that each participant restrict his scopes of action by considering the possible divergent interests of other participants and the effects that one party's actions may have on them – not only in order to anticipate and avoid possible sanctions, but also because each actor is conceded his own legitimate claim to such respect of his interests."* (Mayntz 1993, 49)

Policy networks frequently emerge on their own. Sometimes, however, they are stimulated from outside; one example is the regional industrial policy or structural policy in Germany (Jürgens and Krumbein 1991). The organization, moderation, and prevention of any externalization of costs frequently require – even though this may at first seem paradoxical – state intervention. Yet the paradox is resolved when considering the fact that networks are often sectorally or spatially limited, i.e. there still is some "superordinate" authority; in the case of regional structural policy, for instance, this is the government of the state concerned. The state can ensure that external moderators are installed who are – perceptibly for the local actors – neutral and in a position to advance confidence-building between the local actors. It can also – like the German government in the case of DIN – influence the composition of networks, i.e. ensure in particular that those actors are included who might otherwise have to bear the externalized costs. Even when it does prove possible to substantially extend a network, it is quite likely that this will not only create, but at the same time restrict, scopes of action. *"The creation of policy networks narrows the range of ideas likely to receive a hearing as it establishes authoritative voices and modes of discourse."* (Weir 1992, 210)

It is thus important to recognize that hierarchical governance forms and pluralistic structures for interest representation will never be entirely replaced by "heterarchical" policy networks. Hierarchy and heterarchy simultaneously complement and obstruct each other: heterarchical organizational patterns make governance possible in many areas; but they are in need of hierarchical governance. Hierarchical authority, expressed in the state's role, will often take the form of procedural governance to ensure a sufficient degree of transparency in the composition of networks and the way decisions are reached within them; this prevents them from developing in the direction of secret societies. Furthermore, policy networks need a source of innovation equivalent to the entry of new firms to the market when industries are in a phase of radical change. This function is assumed in the political sphere, for instance, by social movements. It must be possible to expand a policy network to include such actors as they emerge in order to introduce new views and identify new problems. For instance, the German energy policy network clearly suffers from the fact that its composition has not significantly changed since the 1960s; thus, its capacity to learn and to adapt is severely limited.

The foregoing was meant to be a general outline of possible modes of governance and introduces the analytical distinction between hierarchic and heterarchic governance. When discussing the possibilities for governing technological development and the possible aims of technology policy, it is helpful to introduce a second distinction, namely that between different types of technological change. Many authors implicitly refer to radical technological change when they talk about possible governance patterns for technological development (when, for instance, they analyze the development of nuclear technology or telecommunication systems). However, the growing interest in industrial standardization processes stems from the realization that incremental change is also a critical aspect of technological development. The same is true of the discussion on legal instruments of governance, in particular the fuzzy legal construct of "state of the art" which the German legislators have included in technology-related legislation to ensure that regulations remain valid in a dynamic context – i.e. gearing legal language to the process of incremental innovation (Roßnagel 1993). Indeed, the discussion of technology governance gains clarity when a distinction is made between technology policy with reference to incremental technological change and technology policy for radical change or changes of 'technology system'. Incremental innovations *"occur more or less continuously in any industry or service activity although at differing rates in different industries, depending upon a combination of demand pressures and technological opportunities. ... Radical innovations are discontinuous events and in recent times are usually the result of a deliberate research and development activity in enterprises and/or in university and government laboratories. ... Changes of 'technology system' ... are far reaching changes in technology affecting one or several sectors of the economy, as well as giving rise to entirely new sectors."* (Freeman 1987, 61ff.)

In fact, the discussion gains in clarity when a distinction is made between technology policy with reference to incremental technological change and technology policy for radical change or upheavals in the technological system.

Technology Governance in the Face of Radical Change

One feature of radical technological change is that it challenges established development corridors (trajectories in Dosi's (1982) sense) and paves the way for the definition of new paths. The search for a new corridor can, in principle, proceed in two different ways. The first variant, recommended by neoliberals, is the ungoverned search process: the process of adjustment is left to market forces, i.e. each firm searches for a new organizational pattern of its own, a new strategy, a new line of core products. Some firms may join forces to seek and define a new technological corridor through joint efforts. There are two types of incentive for a firm seeking to define a new corridor through its own ideas and efforts. The first incentive is that a first-mover in the new corridor will enjoy major innovation rents. The second incentive results from the opportunity to define or modify a standard within a given framework; this establishes a competitive advantage *vis-à-vis* competitors.

Since, however, the participants in this type of search for a new corridor move in many different directions, the social costs of the search are high. Since it is, a priori, unlikely that the majority of firms will by chance explore in the direction that proves right in the end, it is highly probable that a large share of the search costs will have to be written off as losses. Apologists of the market are not impressed by this objection: "In a Western-style market economy system it is a simple fact of life that companies are faced with the need to find future markets on a trial-and-error basis. This is something that cannot be replaced by 'collective reasoning', no matter what kind of corporate group is involved." (Glos 1992, 109)

The other variant is a search process governed by all important actors. This was a core element of the Japanese success model, and MITI's famous formulation of "visions" was nothing other than a search process shared by MITI bureaucrats and representatives of the most important firms involved in defining development corridors. This should not be confused with one-sided governance decisions at the central level which the state then seeks to implement by providing targeted research funds or by establishing norms and standards (Hilpert 1993). As soon as a joint search direction, i.e. a corridor, has been found, a critical mass of investments in R&D and production capacities is certain to follow without delay, and this in turn gives rise to cumulative learning processes. To this extent, a policy focus on state technology subsidies, (which have for the most part been low in Japan), is misguided, since an incorrect direction of technology search encouraged by subsidies can generate even higher search losses than free-market competition. The advantage of definining technological corridors for firms lies in the possibility to avoid undesirable developments and thus wastering resources, not in any substitution of subsidies for internal funds.

The Japanese governance model was comparatively successful: in the early 1970s the Japanese identified microelectronics as a future key technology when Germany was still struggling to attract steel works and oil refineries (Koshiro 1986). Another example is the development of the gallium arsenide chip: although the US invested far more resources in its development, Japan was several years ahead of the US in the mid-1980s, for MITI-coordinated mechanisms were used to define a joint development corridor (Van de Ven 1993, 351f.). The argument that it was in Japan that important industries such as consumer electronics emerged without any industrial policy (or even against the tide of industrial policy) can also be turned around: the inability of the consumer electronics industry to organize a joint search process for radical innovations raises the costs for individual firms, retards development, and explains the absence of really new products that, in the early 1990s, would be able to help industry out of its crisis.

Technology Governance in the Face of Incremental Technological Change

In a phase of incremental technological change it is more difficult to justify active state governance of technological development, since as soon as a corridor has been defined, market-mediated, decentralized company-level governance is likely to prove to be the superior model. Here there is a need for active governance above all when negative externalities (e.g. environmental damage or safety problems) emerge. This is a classical field for state governance of technological issues, although it is also a field in which shifts in relative technical competence have increasingly removed decision-making from the public sector and turned it over to panels established by industry. In this case, the state supervises compliance with given procedural rules, i.e. engages in contextual governance.

While active governance is less relevant, a more passive form of governance may still be important. This is always the case when discretionary technology-related policies are implemented that are in themselves not necessarily controversial. The establishment of a technology institute at a given location for a given industry, for instance, is discretionary governance in the sense that it is also a decision against establishing an open number of technology institutes for all conceivable other industries. This example points to the main function of technology policy in the context of incremental technological change: the shaping of the business environment, i.e. the development of technology institutes, advisory services, specialized training institutions, and so on, which are designed to support firms in their technology-related search and learning processes. Here, the main task of technology policy is to shape the mesospace, rather than the detailed governance of individual lines of technical development.

Technology Governance between Hierarchy and Heterarchy

In the field of technical development, the state is frequently the only actor in a position to internalize externalities, take general interests into account, and introduce longer-term considerations. In so doing, however, it faces difficulties in that its technical competence is limited and the decisions it takes entail a high risk of failure. This "competence bottleneck" makes hierarchical governance difficult and forces the state to involve the social actors that possess the necessary know-how. But these actors will often have established interests of their own. In a situation of radical change, this can mean that their actual interest is to prevent, delay, or shape in a specifically distorted manner the definition of a new corridor that would depreciate part of their knowledge. Yet in a situation of incremental change firms will also offer resistance to any state-level regulatory interventions opposed to their immediate interests.

It can thus be assumed that a "heterarchical" model of technology governance is not a panacea and that any such model will entail sizable problems and constraints (Table 14). The success is most likely in situations with two specific "constellations" of conditions:

- Technological change is incremental, development corridors and joint views are well-defined. An example is a regional technology policy involving various local actors who reach agreement on measures designed to strengthen an industrial location, or the policy pattern in industrial districts. Another example is the greater part of standardization activities which do not require the definition of a new corridor, which involve a relatively low number of relevant actors (e.g. where the concern is not to define a standard that affects a number of different industries) (Kubicek 1993), and in which the standards concerned do not affect the core of the competitive advantage of the firms involved.

- An acute crisis in which the conservative interests geared to perpetuating a corridor are weak and at the same time no obvious corridor has as yet been clearly defined, so that the benefits of defining a corridor in time are evident to those concerned.

Table 14: Constellations of Technology Policy		
	Incremental technical change	*Radical technical change*
Success probable	shared problem definition and problem-solving orientation of actors involved, e.g. regional technology policy to strengthen locational advantages, standardization	acute crisis, conservative interests are weakened, no clearly defined corridor
Failure probable	political disarticulation, no shared problem definition between political actors	early phase of radical change, no acute crisis of established industries yet, conservative interests are strong

Governance is complicated in two other constellations:

- An early phase of radical change in which the reward for anticipatory policy would be substantial (i.e. no deep structural crisis is driving change), while the interests geared to the preservation of structures are still strong. Any such constellation is further complicated when the process of radical technological change is linked with the market entry of new firms – they will find it difficult to join existing networks between established firms and other actors, while these networks at the same time become dysfunctional due to the exclusion of important actors.

- A constellation of political confrontation in which – owing to past conflicts and the mistrust stemming from them or because of far-reaching ideological differences – it proves impossible to bring about a shared vision of the actors involved.

2.2   Instruments of Technology Policy

Governance of technological change and technology policy are by no means synonymous. In a state whose key actors are agreed that no active technology governance should be exercised, there can still be some kind of technology policy. To be sure, governance patterns and the choice of technology-policy instruments are in practice interrelated. If, for instance, a government rejects specific programs, but nevertheless wishes to stimulate the general climate for innovation, it will tend more to select generic instruments (e.g. depreciation benefits) than instruments that entail a discriminatory impact (e.g. direct subsidies). If, on the other hand, in a different context marked by a basic consensus on the necessity of technology governance, a decision on technology policy has been reached in a network with all relevant actors, this need not prejudice the choice of instruments: once a decision has been taken to promote selectively a given branch of industry or a line of technological development, the question still must be answered whether the best means to this end is direct funding or tax incentives, institutional promotion or stepped-up training activities.

Technology policy is an intricate field. There have been various attempts to create order and clarity here. Ergas (Ergas 1987), for instance, attempted to systematize the basic pattern of technology policy in the leading industrialized countries by contrasting mission-oriented policy with diffusion-oriented policy. While countries such as the US, Great Britain, or France pursue technology policy chiefly within the framework of large-scale programs (aerospace, nuclear technology, weapons technology), banking in so doing on commercially viable civilian spin-offs, countries such as Germany or Sweden are far more strongly geared to programs designed to stimulate a broad application of technological innovations in various branches of industry. The problem with this view is that it entails a high level of aggregation, as Germany has of course had just as many missions (e.g. the development of an aerospace industry) as France or Great Britain have had diffusion-oriented programs (Rush 1989).

Another attempt to create order starts out by assigning policy measures to stages of an innovation process (Meyer-Krahmer and Kuntze 1992, 103). This is supplemented by cataloguing as completely as possible the instruments of technology policy (Table 15).

Table 15: Instruments of Conventional Technology Policy	
In the narrow sense:	In the broader sense:

1. Institutional support
  - large government labs
  - Fraunhofer-Gesellschaft,
    Max- Planck-Gesellschaft
  - universities
  - etc.
	4. Public purchasing policy
	5. Corporatist measures:
	  - targeting, long-term visions,
	    technology assessment
	  - advisory body for technology
	  - awareness

2. Financial incentives
  - indirect support
  - indirect-specific support
  - R&D projects / consortia
  - risk capital
	6. Training
	7. Economic framework
	  - anti-trust policy
	  - legal framework
	  - influencing private demand

3. Other infrastructure plus technology transfer via
  - information and consultancy
  - demonstration centers
  - cooperation, networks, experts
  - technological research centers	

Source: Meyer-Krahmer and Kuntze (1992), p.103.	

Any such catalogue will, however, create no more than limited order, for though it specifies the important instruments, it does not systematize them. And this approach also tends – by introducing "corporativist measures" – to intermingle the processes of decision-making and implementation.

Proceeding from the instruments named in Table 15, state technology policy can be broken down into five fields (Figure 18):

– institutional promotion of research and technology institutes,

– direct promotion of inhouse R&D projects,

– indirect promotion of inhouse R&D,

– promotion of the transfer of technology from research and technology institutes to firms,

– promotion of research cooperation between research and technology institutes and firms.

Figure 18:

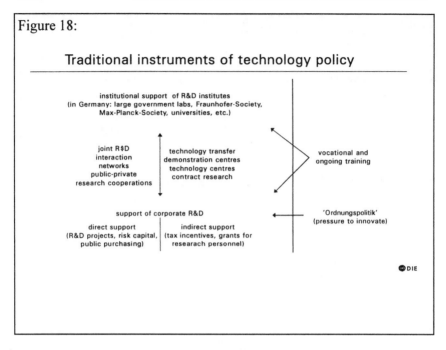

Traditional instruments of technology policy

institutional support of R&D institutes
(in Germany: large government labs, Fraunhofer-Society,
Max-Planck-Society, universities, etc.)

joint R$D
interaction
networks
public-private
research cooperations

technology transfer
demonstration centres
technology centres
contract research

vocational and
ongoing training

support of corporate R&D

direct support
(R&D projects, risk capital,
public purchasing)

indirect support
(tax incentives, grants for
researach personnel)

'Ordnungspolitik'
(pressure to innovate)

⊕DIE

Flanking for this is provided by a training policy that ensures that the required person-related know-how is available and by a regulatory economic framework geared to inducing firms to engage in innovation efforts in the first place.

2.2.1   Technology Institutes

One central feature of the development of science and technology after the Second World War was a direct outcome of experiences made during the war: the establishment of state laboratories designed to bridge the gap between basic research and applied research and development; technological breakthroughs had a major impact on the outcome of the war, and ventures such as the Manhattan Project to develop an atomic bomb demonstrated the potential of large-scale research in the public sphere. In the postwar era the development of state-level R&D infrastructure therefore – especially in the US – enjoyed a high level of legitimacy (Freeman 1992, 175; and Nelson and Wright 1992, 1951f.).

Even though today most innovation activities are conducted and financed by firms, technology institutions, primarily of a public nature, continue to play a key role. Most small and medium-sized firms are unable operate their own R&D departments; the minimum number of employees required for this purpose is 100 in high-tech industries and 1000 in low-tech industries (OECD/TEP 1992, 27). These firms are – aside from close cooperation among one another or with big corporations – forced to rely on cooperation with technology institutions and outside research facilities. The sine qua non for success is close cooperation between external researchers and employees of the firms in question.

But big corporations also are increasingly willing to cooperate with research institutes and universities. This cooperation for the most part comes about informally, through personal contacts, and leads successively to formal arrangements (OECD/TEP 1992, 71). In most OECD countries the cooperation between research and private industry is stimulated by the state. Following some initial hitches, it has generally proven possible to establish a functioning division of labor between both sides.

The discussion over technology institutes and the role they might play suffers from the tendency to categorize as such very different types of institutions. Technology institutions differ with regard to

–   their proximity to applied research;

–   the ability of state agencies governance them;

–   the type of their cooperation with firms (see Chapter 2.2.4).

A taxonomy was developed with reference to empirical experiences made in the US in order to be better able to assess the factors of closeness to applications and controllability;[1] it contains, as a function of the degree of intervention of the private and public sectors, nine matrix fields to which institutions can be assigned.

Government influence was measured in terms of the share of public funds involved in overall funding, while the influence of the market was judged on the basis of self-assessments made by the institutions. Table 17 makes it clear that classification and ownership are less clearly linked than commonly held ideas (science – state, market-oriented research without any state influence – industry) would lead one to expect. 184 of the total of 407 industry-owned institutions displayed a moderate to high level of government influence. Conversely, this implies: while government institutions are concentrated in the field of science, they make up less than half of the institutions polled in this sphere; and universities are not only active in the field of science.

A further finding indicates that it is not the simple classification along the lines of science/state – applied research/industry that is incorrect. It is also difficult to clearly define institutions in terms of basic research or applied research, since the institutions investigated contained a good number of hybrids that regard both fields as their main concern. One finding that was particularly striking is the pronounced application orientation among the institutions that saw the influence of the market as low; this self-assessment may, however, have been influenced by the fact that in the US an applications orientation has been seen as politically positive. Nevertheless, these findings reflect the evolution of institutions that have responded to changing framework conditions by redefining their profile. The application-minded development laboratory and the science-oriented research institution have increasingly revealed themselves to be more ideal types than institutions encountered in empirical reality.

Table 16: Number of US R&D Institutions by Types

Level of market influence	Level of government influence		
	low	*moderate*	*high*
low	Private niche science - (insufficient data)	Mixed-source science: 54	Public science: 133
moderate	private science and technology: 59	Mixed-source science and technology: 73	Public science and technology: 77
high	Private technology: 175	Mixed-source technology: 82	Public technology: 25
Source: Crow and Bozeman (1991), p. 168.			

Table 17: Ownership of US R&D Institutions by Types

Level of market influence	Level of governmental influence		
	low	*moderate*	*high*
low	- (insufficient data)	Government: 2 Industry: 6 University: 33 Other: 13	Government: 52 Industry:10 University: 63 Other: 8
moderate	Government: 0 Industry: 53 University: 3 Other: 3	Government: 0 Industry: 53 University: 13 Other: 7	Government: 37 Industry: 22 University: 14 Other: 4
high	Government: 0 Industry: 170 University: 4 Other: 1	Government: 1 Industry: 76 University: 4 Other: 1	Government: 5 Industry: 17 University: 3 Other: 0
Source: Crow and Bozeman (1991), p. 169.			

Table 18: Research Mission of US R&D Institutions by Types

Level of market influence	Level of governmental influcence		
	low	moderate	high
low	- (insufficient data)	62,5 77,4	63,5 60
moderate	20 90	32 85,3	26,9 79,2
high	10,5 98	7,5 00	9,1 100
First figure: basic research as major mission. Second figure: applied research as major mission (in per cent, several entries possible). Source: Crow and Bozeman (1991), p. 170f.			

2.2.2   Direct Promotion of Inhouse R&D

Direct promotion of R&D in one firm or a group of firms aims at stimulating certain technological developments. The reasons for this must be sought in overriding political goals (e.g. environmental protection, energy supply, defense) or in the marked externalities attributed to a given technology. In most OECD countries this is, quantitatively, the more important form of firm-related R&D promotion; only in the US, Australia, and Austria tax instruments – which are normally regarded as indirect support – make up more than half of government expenditures in this field (OECD 1994, 86).

The effectiveness of direct support is a controversial issue – not least because its effects are difficult to demonstrate to the extent that finding answers to the core questions poses methodological problems:

– Would R&D efforts have materialized in the absence of promotion?

– Are government promotion funds matched by adequate company efforts?

– Do the public benefits used to justify public support actually materialize?

Because of the methodological problems involved, evaluations of direct promotion are often based on case studies that frequently do not give rise to encouraging results; for Great Britain, for instance, Ergas estimated the costs of the Concorde project and the gas-cooled nuclear reactor at over 20 billion US-$, i.e. a volume that, at the end of the 1980s, amounted to two years of total government R&D expenditure (OECD 1994, 9). Examples of other failures are not difficult to find (Cohen and Noll 1991). Still, this type of R&D promotion goes on; the initiative launched in the spring of 1994 in the US to develop and manufacture flatscreens (Carey 1994), for instance, falls under this category.

2.2.3   Indirect Promotion of Inhouse R&D

The goal of indirect promotion is to establish an incentive structure that encourages inhouse R&D, but does so without supporting given technological fields at the expense of others. The most important instrument here is tax incentives; these may be bolstered, for instance, through subsidies for R&D personnel costs.

The use of tax incentives to encourage inhouse R&D is, mainly for one reason, an indirect instrument, i.e. one not restricted to individual programs or lines of technological development: implementation is in the hands of the tax authorities, and they are as a rule not willing (and are apt to lack the technical competence) to make decisions on the deductibility of specific inhouse measures. Tax instruments aimed at stimulating R&D are encumbered with three problems:

-    it is in advance difficult to estimate how costly they will turn out to be, i.e. the size of the losses of revenues entailed by them (Dahlman 1993, 27);

-    they benefit above all firms that operate profitably, a case that is often not given in newly founded firms for a longer period of time (OECD 1994, 85);

-    they discriminate between industries to the extent that actual R&D spending differs from industry to industry.

The last point becomes evident when the R&D intensity of different industries is looked into (Table 19, Table 20). The industries with low levels of R&D spending include the food and paper industries, which have in recent years undertaken sizable innovation efforts to comply with more stringent environmental regulations. These efforts are, however, often not shown separately in accounts, because they cannot be defined clearly in organizational terms but constitute a component of current process optimization efforts.

Table 19: Intensity of R&D Expenditure in the OECD Area. Weighting of 11 Countries (1) - R&D Expenditure/Output Ratio					
1970			**1980**		
High			**High**		
1.	Aerospace	25.6	1.	Aerospace	22.7
2.	Office machines, computers	13.4	2.	Office machines, computers	17.5
3.	Electronics & components	8.4	3.	Electronics & components	10.4
4.	Drugs	6.4	4.	Drugs	8.7
5.	Scientific instruments	4.5	5.	Scientific instruments	4.8
6.	Electrical machinery	4.5	6.	Electrical machinery	4.4
Medium			**Medium**		
7.	Chemicals	3	7.	Automobiles	2.7
8.	Automobiles	2.5	8.	Chemicals	2.3
9.	Other manufacturing industries	1.6	9.	Other manufacturing industries	1.8
10.	Petroleum refineries	1.2	10.	Non-electrical machines	1.6
11.	Non-electrical machines	1.1	11.	Rubber, plastics	1.2
12.	Rubber, plastics	1.1	12.	Non-ferrous metals	1
Low			**Low**		
13.	Non-ferrous metals	0.8	13.	Stone, clay, glass	0.9
14.	Stone, clay, glass	0.7	14.	Food, beverages, tobacco	0.8
15.	Shipbuilding	0.7	15.	Shipbuilding	0.6
16.	Ferrous metals	0.5	16.	Petroleum refineries	0.6
17.	Fabricated metal products	0.3	17.	Ferrous metals	0.6
18.	Wood, cork, furniture	0.2	18.	Fabricated metal products	0.4
19.	Food, beverages, tobacco	0.2	19.	Paper, printing	0.3
20.	Textiles, footwear, leather	0.2	20.	Wood, cork, furniture	0.3
21.	Paper, printing	0.1	21.	Textiles, footwear, leather	0.2
(1) Australia, Belgium, Canada, France, Italy, Japan, Netherlands, Sweden, United Kingdom and United States. Source: OECD/TEP (1992), p. 32.					

The central problem of indirect promotion is thus that it fails to fulfill precisely the function that was used to justify it: namely, not to favor one industry at the expense of others. It benefits the industries in which R&D spending may be high, but which also have no problems when it comes to showing it in accounts.

Table 20: Distribution of R&D Expenditure in Industries (%)					
	France	Germany	Japan	England	USA
	(1985)	(1985)	(1986)	(1986)	(1985)
Electrical equip-ment	25	26	18	31	22
Machinery and computers	8	11	21	11	14
Chemicals	17	21	16	18	1
Automobiles	10	15	14	7	9
Aerospace	19	7	(a)	17	23
Scientific instru-ments	1	2	3	2	7
Other industries (b)	20	18	28	15	15
(a) Less than 0.5%. (b) Including services. Source: National Science Foundation (1989), quoted from Freeman (1992), p. 179.					

2.2.4   Technology Transfer

Promotion of technology transfer is designed to encourage the transfer of two types of know-how from research and technology institutes to private industry: on the one hand, up-to-date know-how that has been developed in these institutions with an eye to applying it in industry at a later point of time; on the other hand, know-how that has been acquired within the context of specific programs (in the field of weaponry, say), i.e. active stimulation of spin-offs.

There are substantial differences between technology institutions that pass on their know-how to firms. In Germany, for instance, the Fraunhofer Institutes or the CIM Technology Transfer Centers play a role entirely different from that e.g. of the Steinbeis Foundation. Fraunhofer Institutes develop new types of technical hardware and processes and support firms in introducing them. The Steinbeis Foundation, on the

Table 21: Types and Main Activities of Technology Institutions		
	Process	*Product*
Routinized know-how	technology-extension (type Steinbeis-Stiftung), business consultancy [1]	business consultancy [2]
High-tech know-how	interactive research (type Fraunhofer-Institute, specialized in process technology) [3]	interactive research (type Fraunhofer-Institute, specialized in product technology) [4]

Table 22: Patterns of Industries and Technology Institutions		
Type of industry	*Main sectors*	*Relevant technology institutions (matrix-field from Table 21)*
Supplier-dominated	agriculture, housing, private services, traditional industries	[1]
Scale-intensive	bulk goods (steel, glass); assembly (durable consumer goods, cars)	[1]
Specialized suppliers	machinery, instruments	[4]
Science-based	electronics / electrical, chemicals	[3], [4]
Based on Pavitt's typology (1984).		

other hand, organizes know-how transfers from institutions specialized in advanced technology but not fancy high-tech to medium-sized firms that have no more than a limited budget for activities of this sort (Cooke and Morgan 1990, 23f.). These differently defined tasks can be classified in terms of how demanding the know-how they transfer is and whether the know-how is process- or product-related (Table 21).

A classification of types of technology institutes and industries going beyond this schema can be made with reference to Pavitt's typology (Table 22). It gives a general idea regarding what type of technology institute is relevant to what type of industry. This classification does, it is true, move at a high level of aggregation; there are, for instance, also apt to be firms in traditional industries (e.g. the food-processing industry) whose behavior is more like that of science-based firms (e.g. acquisition of biotechnological know-how). The point of Tables 21 and 22 is more to provide a warning against any undifferentiated view of the possible nexus between technology institutes and firms – the demands placed on the level and makeup of technology institutes depends heavily on the sectoral profile of the industry concerned.

Technology-Oriented Business Incubators

A specific type of technology institute will have to be considered here: technology-oriented business incubators, which – typically initiated by the state[2] and located close to a university or research institute – provide researchers with the possibility to translate their research results into products. The model is Silicon Valley, where several of the first firms in the microelectronics and computer industry were founded as spin-offs of Stanford University. The primary function of technology-oriented promotion centers is not necessarily technological, it is often financial and commercial-administrative. What significance, what potential, and how much success such institutions have had is a controversial issue. All in all, evaluations of experiences in Germany have come more to positive results, though one author noted that *"for the majority of entrepreneurs, the sojourn in the TGZ* (Technology Promotion Center – JMS) *neither was nor is of existential significance."* (Burkhardt 1994, 23) The British experience in this field, on the other hand, has evidently been negative. The problem here is that the promotion centers replicate the basic problem posed by inhouse R&D laboratories out of touch with production: the promotion centers are designed in such a way as to deter firms from initiating production activities in the center. What they stimulate is firms that engage in research, development, including prototype development, but without going into serial production (Quintas, Wield, and Massey 1992). And this means that the administrators of such centers are proceeding on two faulty assumptions, namely, the idea of a unilinear sequence of research, development, and application and the idea of a clearly defined firm trajectory, including a clearly definable time at which a firm has concluded its development phase and can relocate in an industrial park in order to start out with serial production. The point missed here is the necessity of interaction between research, development, and production.

The success or failure of technology-oriented promotion centers is evidently highly dependent on their specific environment, i.e. both on the general national environment (growth conditions for new firms; performance of potential demanders, i.e. usually national industry at first; general economic- and technology-policy framework conditions) and on the environment specific to a center (presence of efficient R&D institutions, specialized suppliers, and other specific services). If the framework conditions are on the whole favorable, an incubator can lower the threshold of independence; if they are unfavorable, an incubator will be able to achieve little.

2.2.5   R&D Networks

The dependence of technological progress on the results of scientific research has increased throughout the course of time. Some industries – science-based industries – are very closely interwoven with science; this is particularly true of the industries dealing with chemicals, biological technology and genetic engineering, electronics, and new materials.

Recent empirical research has led to a redefinition of the relationship between basic research and applied research and development. The traditional view postulated that

> *"like in a cascade, the results of basic research flow into the field of applied research, are there transformed into new technological products and processes from which in turn industrial (mass) production takes its cue."* (Hack 1988, 56)

The image implies the notion of a technology push, i.e. that scientific breakthroughs thus find their way into new products. Yet this notion is as far removed from reality as the demand-pull thesis according to which research responds to well-articulated needs of the downstream stages.

One feature of successful systems is an intensive feedback process between the three stages: the design of applied research is geared to the problems posed by development. Bottlenecks in development, and (paradoxically) breakthroughs in development as well, stimulate basic research; the latter case is motivated by interest in understanding the physical, chemical, or other laws on which a given, empirically identified phenomenon is based (Rosenberg 1982, 141ff.; and Nelson 1992b, 13) – surprisingly many phenomena (e.g. those with which chaos theory is concerned and those dealing with dynamic, turbulent events, e.g. aerodynamic phenomena or combustion events in engines) have yet to be explained satisfactorily (OECD/TEP 1992, 27).

The existence of feedback loops explains why firms engage in, and fund, basic research; there is a direct and an indirect incentive. The direct incentive consists of investigating bottlenecks that have turned up in production and are impeding progress there. The indirect incentive is that inhouse research constitutes the ticket of admission to networks of scientists, i.e. access to scientific communication and with it early cognizance of scientific results (inhouse R&D as a "window to research") (OECD/ TEP 1992, 71).

In fact there is much that indicates that cooperation between firms and research can function particularly well when the cooperative efforts on the firm's part are borne by scientists; their problems in communicating with academic scientists are far fewer than those encountered by managers. But this leads to a dilemma: research cooperation benefits in particular firms that are able to afford an R&D department of their own, i.e. large firms; small and medium-sized firms, on the other hand, are often faced with "cultural" and communication-related problems (OECD/TEP 1992, 72). The exceptions are firms that have spun off from universities and research institutes, i.e. new innovation-oriented firms; this phenomenon explains the seeming contradiction involved in *"the persuasive evidence that spillovers from university research con-*

tribute more to the innovative activity of small firms than to the innovatory activity of large corporations. " (Acs and Audretsch 1992, 15)

Public-Private Research Cooperation

Research cooperation constitutes a specific model of R&D networks. Even between firms they are a relatively new phenomenon: in Japan the legal framework for private research cooperation was created in 1961; in the US antitrust regulations were modified only in 1984 so in order to make possible private research cooperation (Ouchi and Bolton 1988, 27f.). But since the 1980s the discussion has centered not only on interfirm research cooperation, it has also highlighted public-private cooperation. Two factors stimulated interest in this phenomenon: the success of such cooperation in Japan, which led to a sustained improvement in the competitive position of Japanese firms, above all in information technology; and – in this connection – the perception widespread in the US and Europe that these economies were falling behind, and the assumption stemming from it that the gap could be closed with the same instruments that had paid off in Japan.

Experiences with public-private research cooperation indicate that it makes sense to distinguish between implicit and explicit goals. The explicit goal is generally to gain mastery over a given technology (Meyer-Stamer 1993). Two types must be viewed separately here:

1. Catch-up cooperation. For the firms concerned this means closing a technological gap vis-à-vis (mostly foreign) competitors. This type includes the Japanese computer and the VLSI microelectronics project. The European JESSI program on microchip development initially appeared to be designed in this way. Here the function of cooperation is to heighten the effectiveness of search processes, i.e. to disseminate as quickly as possible information on which approaches do *not* work.

2. Cooperation in the exploration of new fields. Cooperative ventures of this type tend to engage more in research than in development. The type includes the Japanese supercomputer and Fifth Generation projects. The aims of the two types are to avoid redundant efforts, to utilize resources efficiently, to diffuse knowledge and experience as quickly as possible.

Many projects in the US and the EU have added to this explicit aim the implicit (and possibly more important) goal of overcoming dysfunctional industrial structures. Cooperative ventures of this type have also set their sights on a catch-up process or on the development of a new technology. In the wake of cooperation it turned out that cooperation also led to measurable results (patents, new products), and that it above all helped to overcome structural deficits of the industry concerned – in the case of the US SEMATECH chip project, the dysfunctional relationships between suppliers and chip manufacturers; in the case of JESSI and other European projects, the isolation of national firms and research institutions.

When different projects are looked at more closely, several conditions for the success of public-private research cooperation become evident (Ouchi and Bolton 1988; Heaton 1988; and CBO 1990):

Clear-cut, unambiguous, transparent goals. The time horizon should not be overly protracted, nor should too many goals be pursued simultaneously. It is not by chance that catch-up-type cooperative ventures have proven particularly successful.

Complementary interests. If the actors involved pursue incompatible interests or if goals differ too greatly from one another, a long process of coordination and fine-tuning is required to arrive at a consensus on the subject of cooperation.

Limited number of actors. Research cooperation should also be able to adjust flexibly to new conditions (e.g. a scientific breakthrough or failure in an important subfield) or altered framework conditions. This proves difficult when the number of actors involved is too large.

Limited financial commitment on the part of the state. If firms are required to invest resources of their own in such ventures, it is less likely that the technology developed will turn out to be "baroque" and that work will focus on applicable technologies that can be transformed into marketable products.

Conditions attached to state support. State support – be it financial or commercial – should always be linked to certain success criteria. Early Japanese cooperative ventures excluded firms which had made little of a project from participating in ensuing projects.

Stimulation of competition. One feature of the successful Japanese cooperative ventures was that several firms shared in the results of a project – an arrangement that proved highly conducive to competition among them.

2.2.6   Technology Assessment

Technology assessment (TA) is an instrument at loggerheads with the typology of government technology policy outlined here. To be more precise, it is – unlike the types named above – not an instrument aimed at achieving given goals of technology policy. It must be seen the other way around: TA must be understood as an instrument located upstream from decisions on technology policy. It is an instrument that has been in use in a variety of countries for some time now. To be sure, TA is faced with far-reaching methodological and institutional problems. The following are the most important points of criticism of TA:

– *"The basic problem of technology assessment is the insurmountable inadequacy of prognoses: forecasts unsatisfactory due to the great complexity of the matter at hand and the constant changes in the framework conditions and difficult problems involved in assigning given 'consequences' to given changes in the uses to which technology is put."* (Langenheder 1986, 13f.; and Lutz 1986) TA – when it gets too far into technical details – is subject to the risk of falling behind the dynamics of technological development; nor does the latter progress in keeping with "iron laws of nature;" it is instead marked by the economic logics addressed above, by social factors, and not seldom by chance events.

– It is more than difficult to reach a consensus on the criteria to be used in assessing technology; different interests lead to different catalogues of criteria and assessments. Seriously misguided assessments occur in particular *"when the concern is to envision in sufficiently concrete and detailed terms, and to correctly assess, completely new situations about which there as yet exists no concrete experience. The development of city planning in the 1960s and 1970s ('model housing developments', satellite towns, urban renewal, etc.) may be used to illustrate this point. This is exactly the situation facing the assessment of new technologies."* (Langenheder 1986, 15)

– The situation in Germany was marked by a trend characterized by a functional shift of TA in the direction of gaining acceptance for technology. TA in this way becomes – contrary to the intention of its founders – an instrument of power (Langenheder 1986, 12f.; Reese 1986, 165).

But this is not to say that TA should be ruled out in principle; *"providing the political sphere and the public with more rational orientation aids and decision-making criteria than are currently available is not tantamount to rejection."* (Lutz 1986, 569)

It is, for instance, possible to develop scenarios that show *"what might happen if things go on the way they have been developing, if the present constellation of social forces remains unchanged, if no fundamental changes are planned or initiated."* (Langenheder 1986, 14) Yet there is no reason why TA should not go even further.

The path takes its way *"... through a systematic, differentiated, and comprehensive analysis of the social processes that determine the development and utilization of technology; it furthermore continues through an examination of the social structures in which these processes take place and the decision-related rationales and constellations of interests that are crucial here; it goes on, finally and above all, through empirical research (and theoretic definition) on the social and economic circumstances in which technology is used, the developments emerging from them being tied into technical innovations."* (Lutz 1986, 569)

This consideration is based on the insight that technologies do not emerge spontaneously, they are shaped in all phases of their development by social processes. As regards practical implementation, the suggestion has been made that the separation between engineer-level technology development and sociological assessment research be abandoned (Langenheder 1986, 18f.); in terms of governance theory, this implies an expansion of the nexus of actors in which technological developments are shaped. An early integration of TA in the process of developing a technology implies an open, broadly inclusive discussion of the problems in view of which a technology is set to be developed (Langenheder 1986, 16f.). TA and technology design should be combined in order to arrive at a broad-based company-level and social decision-making process by ensuring the participation of users and other persons concerned. *"There is a need for forums at the lower levels of the process in which public opinion is formed, and there it is important to formulate in a comprehensible language and to discuss the TA-related knowledge available, be it certain or uncertain."* (Reese 1986, 168)

There is, incidentally, a measure of irony in the fact that even limited TA is faced with similar problems in the private sphere. A broad-based empirical study found that *"some four fifths of managers' forecasts of growth for new products, markets or technologies fail to hit the target ... One of the biggest areas for error is technological forecasting, or identifying new products based on innovative technology that will produce growth markets. Most of these forecasts have been dead wrong ... because the people who made them were seduced by technological wonder. They ignored the market the technology is intended for and assumed that consumers would find the technology as enticing and irresistible as they did."*[3]

2.2.7   Conclusion

The success of technology policy depends both on what instruments
are used and how they are used. Reference to Pavitt's typology provides help in understanding why an instrument such as stimulation of
cooperation between technology institutes and firms, which has
worked out perfectly in some industries, has no more than limited
prospects in others. It is thus necessary to examine cautiously the issue
of which instruments can be used to achieve given technology-policy
goals; in an economy marked by supplier-dominated branches of industry, a strategy entailing the forced expansion of high-tech research
institutes is not apt to accomplish much. A successful technology policy will operate with a package of instruments whose make-up is contingent on the structure and development level of industry. Its effectiveness will furthermore depend on the pattern according to which
decisions on these instruments are taken; this point refers in turn to the
significance of the related patterns of political governance.

2.3   Levels of Action Open to Technology Policy

It is not only the diversity of instruments and the persons to whom they
are addressed that makes it complex to formulate and analyze technology policy. An additional factor is that technology policy is formulated
and implemented at different levels – aside from the central state,
which has traditionally been the focal point of analysis, actors at the
local, regional, or supranational level are playing an increasingly important role.

2.3.1   National Innovation Systems and Technology Policy

With regard to the analytical level constituted by the nation state, recent investigation into the national innovation systems sought to employ a broader pallet of tools to examine the structural bases of the
connection between technological development and industrial com-

petitiveness. It is an attempt to place the three levels made up by firms, networks, and the state in a context and – proceeding on the assumption: the whole is more than the sum of its parts – to look into the interactions that are responsible for the fact that certain countries are distinctly more successful (here: more innovative and productive, and thus more competitive) than others.

The term *national system of innovation* was first introduced by Freeman. He defines it as follows:

> *"The network of institutions in the public and private sectors whose activities and interactions initiate, import, modify and diffuse new technologies may be described as 'the national system of innovation' (...) The rate of technical change in any country and the effectiveness of companies in world competition in international trade in goods and services, does not depend simply on the scale of their Research and Development and other technical activities. It depends upon the way in which the available resources are managed and organised, both at the enterprise and at the national level. The national level of innovation may enable a country with rather limited resources, nevertheless, to make a very rapid progress through appropriate combinations of imported technology and local adaptation and development. On the other hand, weaknesses in the national system of innovation may lead to more abundant resources being squandered by the pursuit of inappropriate objectives or the use of ineffective methods."*
> (Freeman 1987, 1 and 3)

This view thus goes far beyond the approaches outlined in the chapter on networks. For Porter, the main actors are the firms; he concedes to the state at best a supporting role. In the industrial district discussion, the state and other social actors do play a role, but only at the local level. In the discussion on national systems of innovation, on the other hand, society as a whole – in its function as stimulator or inhibitor of innovation processes at the company level – constitutes the level of analysis.

A comparative project focusing on 15 countries made an attempt to define the constitutive features of national systems of innovation. Surprisingly, many similarities emerged, particularly between countries making up a group.[4] *"The US and Japan look much less different than advertised, once one brings Australia and Israel into the comparison set. And much of the US-Japan difference can be seen to reside in differences in their resource bases and defence policies;"* (Nelson 1992a, 354) and indeed, in many countries national security was a persistently significant influence on the shape taken on by an innovation system. Another striking factor was a pronounced institutional continuity in the developed industrial countries throughout the past 100 years; the US is here the most important exception; its research and technology infrastructure was largely restructured during and after the Second World War. The following central elements of successful national systems of innovation were identified:

–   a strong technological base in firms; this strength did not necessarily correlate with size and level of R&D spending or the support provided by the state, though there was a correlation with strong competitive pressure;

–   in many industries, a strong interaction among national firms along the value-added chain; exceptions included the pharmaceuticals industry (whose firms are largely autosufficient) and the aircraft industry (where worldwide supplier networks have been established);

–   an interaction between firms and universities, which was frequently far closer than was generally assumed – with reference both to research activities (in the context of a technological community) and targeted training with an eye to the needs of industry;

–   an educational and training system that provided qualified, learning-oriented manpower and above all supported advanced training and lifelong learning;

–   policy patterns conducive to innovation in fields other than technology or industrial policy, i.e., for instance, in fiscal, monetary, or trade policy – a pro-export bias stimulated innovation efforts in the firms concerned; technology and industrial policies, on the other hand, seemed to be of lesser significance, and they were for the most part not very coherent;

- an adequate, i.e. not exaggerated, focusing of innovation efforts and technology policy on high-tech industries; the connection between marked competence in these industries and dynamic development in general tends to be a loose one, and the empirical examples are not quite up to date; systematic efforts aimed at strengthening innovativeness in a broad ensemble of industries are evidently more important.

These findings cannot be compressed to make up a recipe book for an innovation system that is guaranteed to work; specific national peculiarities are too pronounced for that. And furthermore, the features common to a national system are often more likely to be found in existing economic, political, and sociocultural framework conditions, and it is less likely that they will be able to be assigned to state technology policy or research and technology institutes.

The term national system of innovation is misleading inasmuch as it suggests a single system that can be defined in terms of geographic boundaries. The notion that one single systemic context encompassing all innovation activities within the borders of a national economy will emerge is, however, false. In fact, this amounts to a somewhat unhappy attempt to reduce two phenomena to one concept. The first phenomenon is the observation that innovations are generated in systems that 1) are marked by a variety of feedbacks and 2) permit a distinction between system and environment; the prevalent structure is neither the solitary inventor nor the arbitrarily composed network. Innovations are stimulated by splitting up research and development tasks and exchanging information in a network of actors (which is definable, though variable, in its composition over the course of time), while at the same time a certain level of rivalry continues that can give rise to the impetus toward innovation activities. While the important stimuli for innovations include external pressure, the more important factor is apt to be internal rivalry.

The second phenomenon stems from divergent national framework conditions. The main reason why the national system of innovation in the US has many characteristics fundamentally different from those in Germany or Japan is that a quite different pattern of capitalist development emerged in the US than in Japan or Germany (Belson and Wright 1992). What constitutes nation states is their specific history, i.e. the path to development taken by their social and economic institutions. There are in addition sociocultural specifics, e.g. a more or less elevated social status for engineers. Whether a country was a latecomer, is pursuing an inward-looking development strategy, or has tried its luck with a socialist development model − each of these options will have shaped the incentives according to which innovative capacities have developed in firms, universities, and research institutes. There are specific national patterns of innovation activities that can be explained in terms of specific national framework conditions.

The second observation indicates that the level defined by the nation state will continue to constitute an important level in investigating the process of technological change. Because of the continuing existence of national specifics (Soskice speaks of *"different national systems of institutions"*) (Soskice 1994, 271) patterns of innovation and technology policy will continue to differ from country to country. But any attempt to use the nation state as an exclusive frame of reference to understand adequately innovation processes and scopes of action open to technology policy is bound to fail. It is − thus the argumentation that follows below − more helpful to look into the connections and interactions between the local, national, and supranational levels, between local clusters and global alliances.

2.3.2   National Technology Policy vs. Globalization?

One important objection to the appropriateness of national technology policy, and indeed to any view restricted to individual states, is that economic activities are becoming increasingly globalized. Each of the last four decades has been marked by a specific push toward globalization: the 1950s by the globalization of trade (or to be more specific: by the overcoming of the trade barriers which had, since the end of the First World War, caused the decline of world trade, which had until then been flourishing); the 1960s by the internationalization of business activities, including particularly developing countries; the 1970s by the internationalization of capital markets; and, finally, the 1980s by the globalization of numerous product markets and – closely linked with it – competition among firms and business strategies. The increase in nontariff trade barriers has modified and inhibited this process, but not prevented it; the growing wealth in the developed industrial societies and some NICs and the worldwide assimilation of consumption patterns have proven more powerful.

The globalization of business strategies and the acceleration of technological change has gone hand in hand with the globalization of technological activities. A number of firms started globalizing their inhouse R&D and sought agreements on research cooperation with universities and research institutions in various countries. Strategic alliances not only went beyond national boundaries, they have also been concluded between firms from different regions of the world.

In globalizing their R&D, firms are responding to the existence of regional innovation networks. In so doing, multinational corporations are seldom concerned with opening up low-wage locations in the style common to footloose industries.[5] Rather, their concern is to gain a foothold in especially promising networks and to keep abreast of technical innovations. This does not imply that regional innovation networks are being replaced by global research networks. The reason why, for instance, most big electronics corporations have their "listening posts" in Silicon Valley is that they there find an especially innovative setting (Teece 1992, 100). It is not merely that the technological limits of many ranges of product are defined here. Another important factor is the close networking and intensive interfirm interaction that makes it possible for relatively small firms to hold their own in innovatory competition with much bigger and wealthier competitors at home and abroad (Saxenian 1990). And the explanation for the R&D investments of multinational pharmaceutical corporations in England is the high quality of biochemical research in that country (Freeman and Hage-doorn 1992, 33).

The extent to which networks of scientists and engineers are internationalized is a controversial issue. Pavitt (Pavitt 1992, 121) claims that these networks exist chiefly at the national level. He argues that close personal contacts and regular exchange are the sine qua non for their successful operation; it is, he continues, due to the limitations imposed by great distances and language barriers that they are thus far for the most part localized nationally. Nelson and Wright, on the other hand, point to the increasing internationalization of such networks.

> *"Employees often move across national borders, within a firm or between firms. These are truly international networks, involving highly trained scientists and engineers, employed in universities and in industry, undertaking significant R&D efforts."* (Nelson and Wright 1992, 1959)

In Nelson's eyes, an additional factor is that – at least in questions of management – a process of cultural assimilation is observable; managers and management researchers have noted an increasing assimilation of the behavioral patterns of firms across national borders (Nelson 1992a, 368).

But the question here is whether this applies for industry in general or whether it is more true of "new" industries and industries with a high intensity of R&D. There is no question that, for instance, electronics is a global industry – with products homogeneous the world over, global sales strategies, and internationally diversified manufacturing locations. But this is not true of other areas of the electrical industry, e.g. the production of washing machines (Baden-Fuller and Stopford 1988). It must thus be assumed that, in terms of the worldwide mobility of highly qualified manpower and the global perceptual schema of management, experiences from electronics or genetic engineering are not simply transferable.

2.3.3 Regional Technology Policy

The globalization of industry does not constitute a contradiction to technological initiatives at the regional level, on the contrary: regional technology policy strengthens regional industry for global competition; and successful technology policy heightens a region's attractiveness for firms internationally on the lookout for strong, efficient, and attractive locations.

Regional technology policy operates in all five fields of technology policy, though it concentrates in particular on networking between firms and technology institutes. Its objective is to strengthen the local economy, which often has a clear-cut specialization profile; its method is to develop technology institutes and training institutions geared to the specific profile of local industry. This is the main advantage of regional initiatives: supported by functioning formal and informal communication channels, they are not forced to invest undue effort and expenses in identifying projects; the bottlenecks are evident to local actors, and if a solution is not obvious, it will be found more quickly in communication among them than it would be in a centralized system.

In other words, the core of technology policy is transfer of technology aimed at heightening the competitiveness of local firms. Cooke (Cooke 1992) distinguishes between three institutional types of regional technology transfer (Table 23):

- The "grassroots model" in which chance historical events have given rise to a technological network: *"A local university may recognize itself or be recognized as having a particular competence in a specialized field which is of value to a local industry. A particular municipality may decide that firms in its locality require technology transfer. A private company might recognize a market niche for selling its technology transfer expertise."* (Cooke 1992, 369) Funding is local, research initiatives are directly application-oriented, and there is a low level of coordination. Cooke cites as examples the Japanese experience with technology centers for small and medium-sized firms (*kohsetsushi*).

Table 23: Three Models of Regional Technology Transfer			
	Grassroots model	Network model	Dirigist model
Initiative	local	various levels	central
Funding	diffuse	guided	controlled
Research capability	applications	mixed	basic research
Coordination	low	potentially high	high
Specialization	weak	flexible	strong
Source: Cook (1992), p. 370.			

– The network model that, apart from local initiatives, also goes back to higher-level initiatives, but without overly regulating local activities, thereby discouraging local initiative. The nexus of actors includes both state agencies and firms and intermediary organizations. Cooke here refers to German experiences.

– The dirigiste model in which policies designed at the central state level lead to regional spillovers; state actors are dominant in this model. Local technology transfer here results as a side-effect of the activities of big state research centers. This model stands for experiences from France, where, however, only few regions (above all Rhône-Alpes) have succeeded in organizing any major spillover to local firms.

As opposed to other studies that sing the undifferentiated praises of local initiative (e.g. Pellegrin 1994), this typology has the merit of pointing out that even local technology policy is fraught with conditions: in a federal setting, as in Germany, the conditions are initially more favorable than in a centralist setting such as that in France. But this is not to imply that decades, if not centuries, of experience with federal decision-making structures are necessary to think about regional technology policy:

– Even centralist countries grant, at least certain regions, a certain measure of autonomy. An example of this is Wales, where an active regional industrial and technology policy was developed in the 1980s, and it has measurably contributed toward reindustrialization (Price, Morgan, and Cooke 1994). One of the important actors involved was the Welsh Agency, which developed from an agency in charge of distributing subsidies into an actor with strategic scopes of action.

- Decentralization is one of the most important instruments used by OECD countries in their efforts to reform the public sector (OECD 1993b, 12f.).

The last named point opens up additional political scopes of action for actors at the local and regional level – even in cases in which technology policy is not one of the fields explicitly set to be decentralized. Regional technology-policy initiatives frequently

- stimulate the interaction between firms and longstanding training and research institutions,

- stimulate regional training and research institutions to gear their profile of activities more strongly to the needs of the regional economy (the willingness to do so will be particularly great when the financial situation is critical on account of spending cuts at the central level and regional networking makes it possible to develop additional sources of revenue).

It can be mistaken to look only at formal competences, thereby neglecting existing problems and incentive structures. Successful regions, e.g. the Italian industrial districts, are marked by a dense network of relations between the state and social actors in which specific policies are formulated with an eye to specific needs or acute bottlenecks.

2.3.4   National Technology Policy between Globalization and Regionalization

It would be mistaken to draw from tendencies toward globalization the conclusion that from now on national-level technology-policy interventions no longer have any part to play. It is important here to distinguish between *mercantilism* and *structure-building*. Even in the past, mercantilist-oriented technology policy met with little success; protection and support of national champions – a widespread policy pattern in Europe in the 1970s – very rarely proved able to give rise to efficient, dynamic, and innovative firms. The experiences made with the EC's technology policy demonstrate that such policies will have even fewer prospects in the future. It was especially in the field of electronics that this policy displayed mercantilist traits, i.e. it sought to strengthen purely European firms against competition from Japan and the US; this approach met with little success (Meyer-Stamer 1994a, 1994b). The European electronics industry's competitive position further deteriorated in the 1980s; and the leading electronics firms have in recent years shown an increasing inclination to seek alliances with US and Japanese firms. The EC's attempt to restrict support to purely European firms have thus come to an end; EC-supported R&D activities are now benefiting the international electronics industry.

Laissez-faire may turn out to the better alternative to any mercantilist policy. The experiences of the 1980s, however, indicate that laissez-faire is, if at all, a second-best alternative, one that can make sense when social structures are encrusted to such an extent that innovative approaches are impossible. Yet laissez-faire is not a promising approach to improving industrial competitiveness; the competitive position of the two countries most consistent in their adherence to this slogan, i.e. which refrained from targeted technology-policy interventions (namely, the US and Great Britain), has not significantly improved. Quite on the contrary, the initial broad acceptance met with in the US by President Clinton's economic and – in particular – technology policy shows that frustration over the failure of laissez-faire is widespread.

As an approach, structure-building technology policy is today relatively (i.e. relative to the definition of technological corridors) uncontroversial. Its objective is to improve industrial competitiveness: competitive advantages neither simply exist, nor do they emerge spontaneously, nor are they created merely by dynamic entrepreneurs or firms. Competitive advantages emerge within the framework of a system of innovation marked by a specific national framework, and they emerge in a dynamic process of interaction between firms, business-related institutions, and the state, with the state appearing in the form of local or regional organizations and in the shape of a central executive or a national legislative. The general framework conditions are determined at the central level: labor legislation, (for the most part) education and training policy, research policy, environmental policy, and so on.

The regional or local level will then decide what to make out of these framework conditions – whether it will prove possible to motivate different actors (local politicians, administration, labor unions, churches, and perhaps others) to seek a consensus, to define new objectives (e.g. rehabilitation of polluted areas), to create new institutions (e.g. to diffuse technical innovations), to reform old institutions (e.g. vocational schools), and the like (Klönne, Borowczak, and Voelzkow 1991).

On the other hand, it will hardly be possible to define technological corridors at the regional level. It is even questionable whether the national level is suited to the purpose; two examples can be cited to illustrate the problems faced by national approaches:

– In the field of genetic engineering, the leading industrial countries are pursuing different patterns of governance. In the US approval procedures for outdoor experiments or production plants are liberal and flexible, because the need for control is, a priori, considered to be low. In Europe, on the other hand – and here especially in Germany – there is great skepticism over this technology, and the need for control is thus regarded as high. The outcome is that the development corridor is marked by a sizable degree of uncertainty – not necessarily in technical terms, but definitely in legal terms. While in Germany the high level of regulation has led to a high level of legal certainty, firms in the US are faced with an incalculable liability risk.[6] The outcome is that both locations offer environments that, due to their specific control patterns, display high degrees of uncertainty and thus impede investment. Supranational control might possibly show the way out of this dilemma.

– In telecommunications, R&D costs have reached levels that make it practically impossible for the development of new transmission systems to pay for themselves in one or a limited number of national markets (Vietor and Yoffie 1993). The advantages of supranational governance are thus obvious, and they have already materialized in the EU in the case of mobile communication: early agreement on a Union-wide standard created a degree of certainty for firms sufficient to stimulate early investment, thus leading to a clear-cut lead for European firms over their Japanese and US competitors (Handelsblatt, Feb. 22, 1994, 18; and Lüdemann 1993).

It is thus becoming more difficult for the central state to define its role in technology policy (Grande 1993): structure-oriented measures are increasingly governed by decentral actors who, thanks to the density of communications networks, have less difficulty in identifying the support requirements of firms; attempts to govern radical technological change are shifted to the supranational level; and even seemingly uncontroversial activities such as the maintenance of national research laboratories become more and more difficult to control, since these laboratories, first, are increasingly geared to applications (and are thus controlled by users, who are often private firms) and are, second, more intensively woven into worldwide networks. It has not yet become entirely clear how state-level actors – particularly in Europe, where the supranational level has made strong gains since the 1980s due to the expansion of EU research-related activities – will respond to this situation. One constructive approach would be to encourage decentral activities, to provide financial support and stimulate the horizontal exchange of experience between decentral actors.

2.4   Conclusions: Points of Departure for a New Technology Policy

The discussion on technology and industrial competitiveness is marked not least by the proliferation of things new – new technologies, new organizational concepts, the new competition (Best 1990), the new learning (Acs and Audretsch 1992). The discussion on technology policy has as yet not shown itself to be up to these tasks; it has been marked by traditional categories and policy patterns. The task at hand is to transform recent insights into the characteristics of technological change into a new technology policy.

Any new technology policy should bear the following points in mind:

- a broad definition of the concept of technology, a strong emphasis on the "soft" components of technology, and the central significance of interactive learning in in-company and intercompany networks;

- a disctinction between different types of innovations (Freeman's typology) and different types of industries with very specific characteristics of development and diffusion of technologies (Pavitt's typology);

- the new view of the interaction between basic research, applied research, and development;

- the new view of the simultaneity of globalization (of markets, firms, R&D activities) and decentralization (of the shaping of locational factors);

- utilization of network-like governance patterns in technology policy.

2.4.1   "Soft" Technology Components, Networks, and Technology Policy

Technological capability in industrial firms is essentially dependent – this is shown by experiences with computer-based hardware and new organizational patterns – on the intelligent management of "soft" factors, i.e. organization, formal qualification, and nonformalizable knowhow. The foundation of competitiveness is not that a firm is in possession of state-of-the-art machinery, it is that a firm organizes its production process in such a way as to be able to respond quickly and flexibly to changing market signals.

Technology policy must therefore not aim solely to stimulate the development and introduction of technical hardware. The dangers involved in any such orientation are illustrated by the experiences made with European technology policy for the electronics industry in the 1980s: its goal was to support firms in developing new products, but in so doing it missed the point that this was not the bottleneck concerned. The bottleneck was that the firms were unable to transform the results produced by their development departments quickly enough into marketable products (Meyer-Stamer 1994b). The problem was not one of technical hardware, it was one of organization. Similar problems emerged in programs aimed to diffuse CIM, like the one pursued in Germany.

A hardware-oriented technology policy does, however, have the advantage of often being able to produce easily measurable results, so that it is, at first glance, easy for policy-makers to prove their success – there are presentable prototypes, diffusion statistics on new manufacturing equipment, and the like. In contrast, a technology policy geared more strongly to "soft" components and designed to stimulate the development of networks is confronted with the problem that its effects are difficult to measure, and it involves problems in demonstrating success or adjusting policy instruments. One important precondition for any such policy is furthermore that the incentive structures in the agency in charge of formulating policy be modified in such a way as to induce the responsible actors to strive for results that are not easily quantifiable, and yet significant; the success indicator should not be the regular flow of funds, it should be the quantity of structural changes set in motion.

Formulation of a network-oriented policy will have good prospects only if the process of interfirm networking is not impeded by economic, legal, cultural, or other framework conditions. These include, for instance, restrictive antitrust legislation that rules out research cooperation between firms, or a business culture in which entrepreneurial individuality and clear-cut boundaries between firms are regarded as very positive. In a situation of this sort, instruments which are related purely to technology policy and run contrary to the framework conditions and the incentive structure generated by them will prove more or less ineffectual.

2.4.2   Innovation Types, Sector-Specific Innovation Patterns, and Technology Policy

Technology policy includes two areas that must be separated for the purpose of analysis: the active governance of technology development in situations of radical change or changes in technical systems, and the flanking and support provided for technological learning processes within technological development corridors.

In a context defined by radical innovations or changes in a technological system, the governance requirements stem from the necessity of reducing search costs; an additional factor may be – to the extent that the work of definition is performed in a national framework – the incentive to shorten the search process, thus providing national firms with an edge over their competitors in other countries. In the selection process between possible lines of technological development, it is at the same time important to ensure that no chance events or partial (company) interests win the day against other social interests that are at least of equal significance, though they may be more difficult to articulate.

As a rule market-controlled search processes are superior to state-governance in the context of incremental innovations. Technology policy here aims to improve the conditions for innovation processes so that firms can use innovations to secure or improve their market position. But since innovation patterns differ between industries (Pavitt's typology), there is no generally applicable policy pattern that can be used to support inhouse innovation processes. Instead, what is necessary here is – with reference to the instruments distinguished in Figure 18 and the classification outlined in Table 15 – a prioritization of the instruments to be used as a function of the innovation patterns prevalent in the target industry.

2.4.3   Interaction between Research and Development

Basic and applied research and technological development mutually influence one another. Even in science-based industries it is time to take leave of the notion of science or technology push. The notion that the results of scientific research need be merely interesting or relevant enough if they are to find applications is inappropriate. This gives rise to problems concerning market structure that have as yet not been perceived by neoliberal economists, for

> *"when the frontiers between science and technology are blurred and innovation is seen as an interactive process, it becomes increasingly artificial to set boundaries between 'precompetitive' and competitive R&D."* (OECD/TEP 1992, 235)

To the extent that firms exert direct influence on the orientation of basic research (and provide a financial contribution to it), it is no longer possible to argue that the (in view of the limited funds available necessarily selective) state promotion of basic research does not interfere with market processes. The task is therefore to make explicit, in research policy as well, the implications for technological development and its interference with market processes.

2.4.4   Globalization, Decentralization, and Technology Policy

Globalization and decentralization are not opposing terms. Their relation to one another may be one of tension, yet they are often complementary processes. Firms do not distribute their production plants at random, they look selectively for locations with attractive and demanding environmental and marketing conditions (Vet 1993). R&D centers are sited outside company headquarters in order to gain access to innovation networks, i.e. to profit from external effects that occur in a given place.

Globalization tendencies thus do not necessarily weaken the significance of policy in a national framework, even though this does make it more difficult to describe tasks at the central-state level. Technology policy can – in particular when it is formulated at the local and regional level in close contact with the persons concerned – contribute toward creating or improving attractive innovation networks. This enhances both the ability of local firms to hold their own in global competition and the attractiveness of a location for firms from outside.

2.4.5   New Governance Patterns in Technology Policy

The notion of a uniform technology policy governed centrally by the state is obsolete. The point of departure of more recent thinking on the governance of technological development and the support provided for innovation efforts is acceptance of the diversity of actors, intervention levels, levels of negotiation, and instruments. The classical instruments of technology policy – financial support of institutions engaged in research and technology transfer and inhouse R&D – are supplemented by instruments designed to promote soft factors – diffusion of information on new organizational concepts, network-building (Callon et al. 1992). Technology-related measures are formulated at different levels within networks of actors in which the state often plays a subordinate role.

Technology policy cannot be grasped adequately if it is seen as an activity restricted to given sectors, one that concerns only scientists in research institutes and universities, R&D people in firms, and their promoters in government administration. Technology policy is interwoven with the polity in two ways. On the one hand, governance patterns of technology policy are not independent of the evolution of governance patterns as such; in a society marked by a low level strategic capacity and confrontations between social actors, it will hardly be possible to establish a network of actors to formulate a long-term strategic technology policy. Moreover, macropolicy (general economic framework, legal system, etc.) and other sectoral policies have important implications for technology policy. On the other hand, the results of technology governance can entail far-reaching structure-modifying impacts on the polity; as soon as this become evident, actors normally not included in the nexus of actors concerned with technology policy will seek to gain influence on the formulation of technology policy.

3   Toward Competitiveness: Structural Change in Brazilian Industry and Politics

The year 1990 marked a turning-point in the framework of industrial development in Brazil. The Collor government, which had set out to initiate a process of industrial modernization, in June of 1990 adopted the core elements of medium- and long-term structural reforms which spelled the end of import substitution. The industrial policy worked out by Collor and his team was an attempt to initiate a transition from a sheltered domestic market to competitive structures. The label "neo-liberalism" that was used in the Brazilian discussion to designate this policy is not entirely appropriate: although liberalization and deregulation were important instruments, the liberal concepts were countered by neostructuralist ideas that found expression in the active policy components, in particular industrial and technology policy.

The central instruments of the new policy, which emphatically altered the incentive structure for businesses, were reduction of import barriers, deregulation, and privatization. The *similares* examination was abolished, as were the local-content regulations for some industries or the obligation to apply for a government license prior to any investment in a given branch of industry.[1] The decision-makers were nonetheless aware that any shock-like liberalization would necessarily entail fatal effects; the Argentinean experience of the late 1970s had not been forgotten. The new industrial policy therefore set its sights on a gradual transition. The numerous market reservations, i.e. absolute import bans, were lifted, while tariffs and other import duties were at the same time raised. Tariffs were cut to zero in some areas in which national suppliers were accused of abusing their market power. The effective tariffs were, however, raised in most areas, for instance by canceling outright the innumerable tariff preferences.[2] A gradual plan was presented for the period extending to 1994; it provided for a step-by-step reduction of tariffs to an average rate of 14.2 % in order to successively expose national industry to foreign competition (Longo 1993, 53; and Machado and Carvalho 1993). In addition, export and other subsidies were canceled. The only exemptions were for key technological sectors such as microelectronics; but even the market reservation for informatics products was allowed to expire when the informatics law was due to revision in October 1992. There were also plans to found an export finance bank and improve infrastructure, in particular port facilities; and plans were worked out to introduce antitrust legislation and control mechanisms against import-dumping so as to ensure an orderly course for market processes.

Collor's successor Itamar Franco largely continued with the policy of market-opening; this in part even entailed moving tariff reductions ahead in order to step up the competitive pressure in the domestic market (Machado and Carvalho 1993). Although the firms affected did offer resistance, they were unable to push through a return to the old rules. One reason for this is the structure of Brazil's corporatist industrial associations that, nolens volens, united both proponents and opponents of liberalization. This constellation made it difficult for the associations to mark out a clear-cut position. An additional factor was that leading industry representatives had previously spoken out in favor of a policy of liberalization and modernization and were thus unable to credibly oppose any such policy. A further aspect is that the state was here not concerned with actively implementing new, "positive" measures. In its own terrain – customs administration – the government modified some key framework conditions passively, by way of decree, i.e. without any creative impetus, but above all without any parliamentary participation,. On the other hand, only partial progress is evident for positive measures, e.g. antitrust law and strict measures against market-abuse practices that continue in oligopolistic sectors of industry. The continuing existence of traditional corporatist structures in subsectors is apparently also preventing market mechanisms from becoming operative; Soto (1993, 33f.) describes this with reference to the pulp industry, where the traditional price-setting mechanisms continue: prices are set on the basis of negotiations between the pulp industry and the paper industry, though they inevitably remain at levels distinctly below those in the world market – the paper industry has always been closely associated with the government agencies that supervise the sector and thus wields more political weight. Thanks to its privileged access to the machinery of government, it is able credibly to

threaten the pulp industry with sanctions (e.g. administrative impediments for exports).

Despite such practices the new framework conditions forced through
an adjustment process at the company level. They furthermore contributed to modifying the forms of interaction between state and social
actors in formulating industrial policy. These two areas and some initial steps toward a revised regional policy will be looked into in what
follows.

3.1   Change at the Microlevel: Company-Level Efforts at In-creasing Competitiveness

Industrial competitiveness comes about at the company level. The ideal
case is that all stages of the value chain are organized effectively and
efficiently: research and product development, the link between product development and production, procurement and materials management, quality assurance, production itself, sales, and after-sales service.

Firms that have emerged in closed economies are for the most part
afflicted with shortcomings in each of these functional areas. There is
hardly any research and product development, because the normal
practice is to imitate standardized products. Procurement and materials
management are often just as chaotic as production, because there is no
efficiency constraint. There is no quality assurance, because even low-
quality products are marketable. Likewise, there is no need to invest
any special efforts in sales. There is little pressure to develop an after-
sales service if there are no competitors to whom frustrated customer
could switch.

Moreover, Brazilian firms were often able to engage in cost-plus pric-
ing. To this extent, they had no incentive to introduce systematic cost-
control mechanisms (in the sense of cost optimization or minimization;
this point should not be confused with financial management, in which
many Brazilian firms have reached high standards):

"... even the most advanced Brazilian firms have problems with cost management. They are competitive in the international market in terms of product quality, but are not competitive in terms of price because their competitiveness in the external market was facilitated by the profit margin they enjoyed on the domestic market. As the domestic market is being opened to imports, prices are being re-aligned in accordance with the external market, with serious consequences for such companies. Such firms are obliged to 'walk backwards' to regain control of their cost dimensions and to re-think the meaning and scope of their Quality Programmes." (Fleury 1993, 19)

Even though the array of industrial-policy programs were implemented belatedly, only in part, or not at all, the gradual opening of the markets compelled Brazilian firms to take leave of their traditional behavioral patterns. Since 1990 they have been faced with the challenge of drastically rationalizing their operating functions. The following section will look into the question of what measures they are taking and what problems are involved. The analysis will concentrate on production and materials management and control, i.e. core areas of industrial production.

No doubt, this focal point on production restructuring is not unproblematical. The course of import substitution saw the emergence of a complex industrial base that cannot survive the liberalization process unscathed. There are firms which, due to their product spectrum and/or their stage of development in the field of product technology, have no chance to hold their own in the foreseeable future against international competition. Examples would be the machine-building industry and the electronics industry. These firms cannot even be saved by radical rationalization of their production process. But if this focal point has nevertheless been selected here, the reason is that these firms constitute a minority. The majority of firms is not a priori without chances, and they can rationalize and reposition themselves in the market in such a way as to ensure their survival and develop competitiveness in the medium term (IE/Unicamp et al. 1993).

3.1.1   Measures to Increase Company-Level Competitiveness

Cost Reduction through Layoffs

Many firms respond to the stiffened competitive situation by slimming down their structures, and what this first means in practices is cuts in manpower. The mass layoffs that have taken place since 1990 are to this extent not merely a reflex of the recession, instead they also mirror the efforts of firms to cut costs. One approach was critical observation of in-company production sequences with an eye to identifying redundant manpower; a second approach was in many cases to abandon entirely given areas of production that were judged to be underutilized and without promising future prospects.[3] The layoffs are sometimes also a result of the efforts undertaken by firms to cut back on their excessive diversification and concentrate on selected key areas.

Outsourcing

A second important measure linked with the point just addressed is outsourcing, i.e. the removal of activities formerly performed internally (Gitahy, Leite, and Rabelo 1993, 65ff.). This is done above all with non-production-oriented services – e.g. cleaning services, canteens, or security. Outsourcing of production-oriented services – for instance in the field of software – is far less common, since it is far more difficult here to find qualified subcontractors.

The case is similar with attempt to reduce vertical integration. Successful cases are known from the electronics industry, where there are a number of factories that are specialized in component-assembly; in quite a few cases this is the result of the systematic supplier development policy practiced by IBM. In other areas, e.g. in mechanical manufacturing, there is often a lack of qualified subcontractors; and the situation with regard to foundries is particularly complicated; many firms state that the latters' product quality is unsatisfactory. There are thus severe limitations on any efforts to reduce vertical integration.

Introduction of New Production Technology

What constituted the main approach to improving competitiveness in the industrialized countries in the 1980s has taken a backseat in Brazil: the introduction of new production technologies. It is important here to distinguish between industries with a moderate diffusion level and industries with a very low diffusion level. A moderate level has been observed in some process industries, particularly petrochemicals (Ferraz et al. 1992, 16ff.). Here, production is virtually impossible without modern digital process control; the firms, however, are pursuing a defensive rationalization strategy, i.e. they are introducing new technology whenever this cannot be avoided, but without harnessing it offensively to maximize productivity and quality or to diversify/upgrade their products, thus improving their market position (Carvalho 1992).

The level of diffusion is as a whole low in industries with discontinuous processes (Carvalho 1993, 22ff.; Meyer-Stamer et al. 1991). Firms such as the aircraft manufacturer Embraer that pursue a comprehensive CIM strategy (Fleury 1988, 20f.) are rare exceptions. The prevailing picture is that of a cautious, patchy introduction of new technologies, i.e. occasional CNC machines or CAD systems; other technologies such as flexible manufacturing cells or centers, robots or driverless transportation systems are very rare indeed. One striking aspect to be observed in the electronics industry is the absence of SMD technology.[4]

Surveys conducted among firms in industrialized countries indicate that the motive inspiring modernization is just as much quality requirements and volatile demand situations as it is considerations of cost in the narrower sense (Förster and Syska 1985; Shah 1989, 17; and Tajima 1990). In the past these factors posed few problems to industrial firms in Brazil; they generally had no difficulty in marketing domestically overpriced and low-quality products.

There were three additional reasons for the low level of diffusion of new manufacturing technologies (Schmitz and Carvalho 1989, 24; Lima 1989, 16):

- the crisis-ridden economic framework conditions led to a generally low level of productive investment;

- it was often unprofitable to step up the process of automation since labor costs were low;

- the costs for automation technologies were (not least due to the market reservation in the informatics sector) high.

For the latter reason domestically manufactured products such as programmable controllers and NC controls were, in the 1980s, between 1.8 and 2.3 times as expensive as they were in the world market; the price for Brazilian-produced NC machine tools were two to three times the customary international price (SEI 1988, 103; Fleury 1988, 39; and Tauile 1988, 16). This stemmed from a negative circle: the users refrained from buying machines because they were too expensive, and the national suppliers demanded high prices because they were unable to realize economies of scale due to their low production volumes. Another factor was that most producers of informatics products designed to automate production were new to the informatics sector and were therefore faced with learning costs higher than those of firms experienced in manufacturing other informatics products. Moreover, the number of suppliers had very little to do with the size of the market; the 5,274 programmable controls manufactured in 1988, for instance, came from 12 different factories (SEI 1989, 62).

Introduction of New Organizational Concepts

Progress has been made in introducing new organizational concepts. These are concentrated in two areas, and in each area their introduction is linked with a qualitative goal and a quantitative goal. The one area is improvement of product quality aimed at penetrating more demanding market segments and reducing the high costs stemming from rejects and reworking; the other area is acceleration of material flows and reduction of inventories with an eye to improving responsiveness to changes in the market and cutting the costs stemming from large inventories of primary and semifinished products.

Quality Assurance

Quality assurance strategies proceed from the Japanese philosophy of zero defects, quality at source, and total quality control. The objective is to identify defects and irregularities as early as possible and to eliminate their causes. Components of an introduction or a reform of quality assurance include:

-   The introduction of statistical process control. In a given rhythm, workpieces are measured and their average deviations from target dimensions are determined; too large deviations trigger an immediate search for the sources of error.

-   Programs designed to heighten quality awareness among employees, frequently stimulated by the Japanese *kaizen* concept.

-   The introduction of quality circles. This instrument was introduced in the early 1980s, and it frequently failed because it was not linked with further-reaching organizational changes or there was a lack of adequate compensation for the workers involved (Fleury and Humphrey 1993, 50). In many cases firms have learned from these errors in recent years and made a new start, this time successfully.

-   Shift of responsibility for quality assurance to the workers. This is – when it is linked with a drastic reduction of quality inspectors – the most advanced structural reform made in the field of quality assurance, and it has been documented only in a few cases.

Just-in-Time

The objective of introducing new logistical organizational concepts is to reduce processing times, inventories, and work in progress. Company-level efforts are prevalent here. The main approaches are

- conversion of inhouse material flows to the pull principle based on the model of the Japanese *kanban* system;

- reduction of lot sizes;

- modification of factory layout from a structure geared to work routines to a product-oriented structure; this goes as far as the introduction of cellular manufacturing. One of the reasons why the latter are particularly in demand is that they make it possible to limit costs; cellular manufacturing can be introduced with already available conventional machines, and they can also diminish the need to introduce computer-controlled production-planning systems.

- Introduction of preventive maintenance with an eye to ensuring that machines will run without interruption.

The diffusion of new organizational concepts has progressed differently in different sectors; in the metal-working, chemical, and petrochemical industries they are more widespread than in the shoe, furniture, glass, and cement industries (Gitahy, Leite, and Rabelo 1993, 18). But the degree of diffusion differs greatly even within industries (Meyer-Stamer et al. 1991). As yet new organizational concepts (above all just-in-time delivery) are not very widespread at the interfirm level (Posthuma 1992, 17ff.).

3.1.2   Experiences with New Organizational Concepts

Traditional Organizational Concepts and Labor Relations

Brazilian firms tend to be family enterprises;[5] what prevails here is a paternalistic, centralized style of management. The firms have also been marked by relationships of distance and mutual mistrust between management, while-collar employees, and workers. In many cases this has led to a situation in which workers at first perceive organizational innovations as a new instrument of control and repression and are therefore reluctant to apply these innovations in the way expected. Posthuma, for instance, reports a case in which initially excellent quality results were recorded following the introduction of statistical process control (Posthuma 1992, 11). This, to be sure, was not the outcome of high production quality; the reason was that the workers included in the calculations only parts that displayed low deviations. In this case it was difficult for management to convince the workers that the measurement and reporting of defective parts would have no negative effects for them and merely served to modify the production process.

The organizational outcome of the traditional type of labor relations was a system of extensive division of labor – on the shopfloor between workers, but also between departments such as production, quality assurance, and maintenance. Work was organized on the principle of command and obedience. *"What management wants the workers to do is obey instructions, and not to improve the production process."* (Humphrey 1989, 32; Carvalho 1993, 55ff.). The concessions that this concept can entail are illustrated by the following example:

> *"Expensive and state-of-the-art CNC lathes were introduced in a factory belonging to a metall-engineering firm making precision products and special materials. The workers were not permitted to alter the programs they received from the programming department, but they nevertheless did (without management's knowledge) so as to prevent any production stoppages. They at the same time demanded formal training in programming. When this was turned down, the workers one day decided not to correct the errors they detected in the programs (which of course was in line with the rules). The result was paralysis of production in the following production stages, because the parts machined were not up to standard, although all had been done according to the rules."* (Fleury and Salerno 1989, 18)

A further characteristic of traditional labor relations is their high conflict intensity. For lack of mechanisms for worker representation and orderly conflict settlement, industrial action was in the past a central instrument used to underline elementary demands (e.g. transportation, factory canteens).

In the past high rates of fluctuation were a striking feature of industrial employment in Brazil; a figure of 53.1 % of all persons employed in industry is reported for 1988 (Carvalho 1993, 70). The reasons for this lie both with the firms and with the employees themselves. The firms responded to fluctuations in sales and capacity utilization by laying off workers (and rehiring them when sales picked up). They also used firing as an instrument of discipline. Moreover, there were in the 1980s many firms that pursued an explicit strategy of dismissing workers who had reached a given stage of seniority, and later rehiring them – without seniority and at lower wages (Doleschal 1987, 180ff.). The workers' ties to their firms were loose – not least due to such management strategies, and thus workers were prepared to switch jobs to improve their wages even marginally. On the other hand, job stability has always been one of the most important demands raised by the labor unions.

New Organizational Concepts: Changes at the Shop-Floor Level

Since new organizational concepts are marked by delegation and decentralization of responsibility, participation and strengthening of individual initiative, and horizontal instead of vertical communication, their comprehensive introduction means little less than a revolution in the internal structures of firms. But this has thus far failed to materialize; the prevailing pattern in firms that have made progress in introducing new organizational concepts is marked by a number of limitations.[6]

Top-down Introduction of New Organizational Concepts

In the industrialized countries the introduction of new organizational concepts often takes the form of an interactive process between management and workforce. The main concern is not only to identify and deal with resistance at an early point of time. The most important concern is that workers have know-how on operations at the shopfloor level that can be utilized systematically for reorganization measures. The situation in Brazil is different: the introduction of new organizational concepts is decided on by management, usually at the top echelons. The process of introduction very rarely experiences attempts to harness systematically the experience-based knowledge of the workers; at best, the workers are informed in time of the impending changes.

Reorganization as a Learning Process

The introduction of new organizational concepts is for the most part marked by an incremental approach. Firms seldom have a masterplan covering a complete restructuring of a production process, they tend more to start out by introducing a given instrument (e.g. quality circles) or shooting for a concrete goal (e.g. certification as per ISO 9000). In doing so, they attempt to tailor the standard solutions offered in the literature and by consultants to their own realities, initially introducing only given new elements. These efforts often lead to a learning process the outcome of which makes systemic restructuring inevitable. Firms learn from their errors; the example of quality circles was mentioned above.

Partial Delegation of Tasks and Responsibility

Firms that achieve an extremely flat hierarchy, comprehensive polyvalent work profiles, and group work in connection with the introduction of new organizational concepts are rare exceptions. The usual case is

- partial delegation of tasks and responsibility, so that workers take on new tasks, but bear only limited responsibility (e.g. in the field of preventive maintenance, only for lubricating machines);

- reduction of levels of hierarchy, but without in any way infringing on management prerogatives;

- restriction of polyvalent job profiles to a strictly limited number of workers (seldom more than a quarter of the workforce);

- reduction of the division of labor, sometimes even including the introduction of rotation among work stations within a manufacturing cell, but without any genuine group work.

Introduction of Conflict-Resolution Mechanisms

The introduction of new organizational concepts is often linked with the introduction of conflict-resolution mechanisms, e.g. regular consultations between managers and workforce representatives.

But one thing that cannot be overlooked is management's persistent resistance to the presence of labor unions in factories and to the establishment of works councils (Faletto 1991, 12). Firms instead seek to introduce material and non-material incentives to inoculate their workforces against the "temptation" of organizing in unions.

Incentives for Workforces

Employment stability. The introduction of new organizational concepts renders any high fluctuation rates dysfunctional for the firm concerned. A stable workforce offers advantages in amortizing training investments and in organizing in-company learning processes. Quite apart from this, new organizational concepts only work when there is a minimum of trust between management and workers. It is for this reason that in many firms their introduction is accompanied by voluntary management commitments to dispense with any arbitrary hire-and-fire policy and not to lay off workers because of seasonal sales fluctuations. Employment stability is furthermore used as an incentive to counter potential workforce resistance to the introduction of new organizational concepts; for management in this way acknowledges the experience that in-company reorganization processes must be regarded as an exchange – with the workers exchanging stepped-up efforts and their know-how for certain benefits from the firm.

Intensified investments in training and advanced training. The benefits also include intensified investments in the training and advanced training of workers. Fleury and Humphey postulate: *"Firms are investing heavily in education, training, and motivation"* (Fleury and Humphrey 1993, 10); and in polls the firms themselves assign high priority to their investments in training and advanced training (CNI 1993a, 22). The data available do, however, not confirm that this is in fact being broadly implemented. A survey conducted at the end of 1992 found low levels of company spending for training and advanced training; two thirds of the firms surveyed spent under 100 US-$ per worker and year (PBQP 1992, 13). There is thus a gulf between rhetoric and company declarations of intent on the one hand and reality on the other.

Material incentives. Firms are reticent in introducing material incentives; this is linked with specific legal framework conditions (see below). Material incentives are basically limited to the introduction of voluntary social benefits with an eye to strengthening worker ties to firms.

Impediments and Problems Facing the Introduction of New Organizational Concepts (Internally)

The introduction of new organizational concepts in firms is an undertaking that is neither simple nor painless. On the contrary, it involves many problems and much resistance that often cast doubt on the success of modernization measures.

Recession

At the beginning of the 1990s, the economic framework for the introduction of organizational innovations was not exactly favorable. If employment stability is an important precondition or even a strong incentive, while at the same time the sales market collapses, mass layoffs can often not be avoided. But this for the most part entails the end of any explicit or implicit understanding on which the introduction of new organizational concepts is based. A further consideration is that in many firms qualification measures, a second incentive, are also rescinded in difficult economic situations because of the high costs to which they give rise when they are pursued seriously.

Another reason why these economic framework conditions have a negative impact is that they deter firms from making new investments. Yet experience shows that new organizational concepts are easier to introduce in new "greenfields" factories than in existing plants (Lima 1989, 15). Here, there are neither workers nor managers to put up resistance; and the new workforce can be recruited from the outset with an eye to the demands linked with new organizational concepts (above all as far as qualifications are concerned).

Moreover, firms in a recession-plagued environment tend to undertake markedly "defensive" modernization efforts: they prefer measures that offer promise of immediately measurable benefits (Ferraz et al. 1992, 9). This is more than understandable; but it is an approach in sharp contrast to the one practiced in East Asia. In Japan, but in other countries as well, firms are establishing a culture involving a constant search for incremental improvements – *"often with better, longer-lasting results that are realized over the longer term."* (Welliver 1992, 233)

Resistance among Medium-Level Management

The introduction of new organizational concepts does not only lead to layoffs of workers. Reductions of levels of hierarchies and shifts of responsibility to lower levels also render many white-collar jobs redundant, which means dismissals here too (Gitahy, Leite, and Rabelo 1993, 15). Others who retain their jobs see their status threatened by the new changes. For obvious reasons, both groups put up resistance to these changes. Fleury and Humphrey even identified this as the main obstacle encountered in the process of introducing new organizational concepts (Fleury and Humphrey 1993, 31; Ferraz et al. 1992, 29).

Resistance on the Part of Workers

On the other hand, workers seldom raise any fundamental objections to the introduction of organizational innovations; Fleury and Humphrey note: *"The apparent lack of labour resistance was somewhat surprising."* (Fleury and Humphrey 1993, 36) Workers offer resistance mainly either when they fail to see benefits or when the innovations are pushed through behind their backs. The introduction of new organizational concepts frequently entails an intensification of work processes, higher demands on labor, and layoffs (when the innovations lead to a jump in efficiency not accompanied by a corresponding expansion of production). If measures of the type mentioned above are not introduced as flanking, workers will put up resistance. The same thing happens when management introduces new organizational concepts without providing any information beforehand and workers, for instance, find a new layout when they return from vacation (Kaplinsky 1993b, 23).

Qualification Bottlenecks

In introducing new organizational concepts firms often encounter qualification bottlenecks in their workforce. Even though workers are in possession of considerable experience-based knowledge and practical skills, they often have major gaps in terms of general qualification (Posthuma 1992, 9; Carvalho 1993, 66f.), and functional illiteracy is just as incompatible with new organizational concepts as deficient mathematical skills (e.g. for statistical process control or deciphering simple XY diagrams). The situation becomes particularly complex when workers have long since developed techniques to conceal their functional illiteracy.

There are reasons to suspect that qualification bottlenecks will generate far greater problems in the foreseeable future than they have until now. The introduction of new organizational concepts has thus far been restricted to a minority of firms in the formal sector; all and all, these firms offer acceptable working conditions and wages and are therefore attractive to workers, particularly to better qualified workers. An additional factor is that mass layoffs since 1990 – which have also affected well-qualified workers – have led to a situation in which firms have no trouble recruiting manpower. Yet this situation can change to the extent that, first, economic activity picks up again and the more competitive firms begin recruiting again and, second, the surge of modernization also reaches less efficient firms (down to the informal sector). This will mean that sooner or later firms will end up in a pronounced qualification trap, for the potential pool of qualified workers – particularly as far as literacy and basic mathematical skills are concerned – is restricted, especially since the quality of general education sharply deteriorated in the 1980s, with the consequence that fewer well-qualified young workers are entering the labor market.

Inadequate Career Perspectives

Some firms have sought to come to terms with the qualification problem by setting a high threshold for job applicants (e.g. high school diploma). Their experience with this strategy has been negative. The firms have been unable to meet the expectations of relatively highly qualified employees in terms of remuneration and career perspectives and have therefore been faced with high fluctuation rates (Fleury and Humphrey 1993, 45).

Labor Legislation

Sometimes traditional legal regulations impede the introduction of new organizational concepts. For example, lathe operators put up resistance against the job description *polyvalent specialist*, since for them this would entail losing the privilege of being able to retire after 25 years of employment (instead of 30) (Author's company survey, May 1993). One other factor that complicates the introduction of new organizational concepts is that performance-related bonuses, once they have been paid a number of times, tend to be regarded as the property of the worker concerned.

Skepticism and Arrogance

It is not at all rare for firms, including foreign ones, to overrate their own competitiveness. Awareness of the necessity to improve efficiency and quality is often undeveloped. Individual managers intent on introducing new organizational concepts will therefore often be faced with strong resistance.

Surplus Suggestions for Improvement

Owing to the great store of experience-based knowledge available and the absence of formalized bottom-up channels of communication, the establishment of such channels often gives rise to a flood of suggestions for improvement that go beyond management's capacity for change. If, however, only a small part of these proposals are implemented, the typical result is frustration and cynicism on the part of workers (Fleury and Humphrey 1993, 34).

Costs

Even though the introduction of new organizational concepts is far less expensive than a CIM-oriented modernization strategy, it does involve costs – the engineering work required to redesign the flow of production and the training costs are no less a factor than the costs generated by production slowdowns during the process of conversion (Mody, Suri, and Sanders 1992, 1808). The costs tend to be particularly high when the introduction has not been properly prepared for and fails to lead to adequate benefits, or attempts to slim down operations, in particular to reduce buffers, lead to a collapse of the production process.

Inadequate Exchange of Experience among Firms

It is a documented fact that in the industrialized countries the exchange of experience among firms constitutes an important element of the introduction of innovations in industrial production. This can, for instance, be systematically organized through industrial associations (Fleury and Humphrey 1993, 27).

In Brazil, on the other hand, exchange of information among firms is generally not customary (Fleury 1993, 21). There are associations working in this direction, but their membership is limited.

Problems and Obstacles Facing the Introduction of External Just-in-Time

An important reason for the low rate of introduction of organizational innovations at the interfirm level is that the end users – particularly in the auto industry, the typical user of such concepts – were long hesitant to take resolute steps in this direction;[7] the main reason for this was that, in the low-competition and at the same time stagnant environment of the 1980s, they had little inducement to undertake efforts aimed a clear-cut improvement of efficiency. The fact that suppliers take the initiative vis-à-vis their customers does not accord well with the generally hierarchical relationship between the two; it would simply have been inconceivable for medium-sized national firms (which is what the leading automotive suppliers are) to push through an offensive modernization strategy against one of the automobile multis. To this extent, the low level of diffusion, the major problems, and the lack of change diagnosed by Posthuma (Posthuma 1992) are not surprising. Only when markets were opened up did the picture begin to change – as a result of growing competitive pressure and stepped-up rationalization efforts. Firms encounter a number of different problems here.

Arms-Length Relationship

Suppliers relationships in Brazil – as in many other countries, above all the US – were characterized in the past by an arms-length relationship: suppliers and their customers did not cooperate closely on the basis of a medium-term agreements, relying instead on market-guided transactions.

The conflict-oriented basic tendency in supplier relationships intensified in the course of the economic crisis of the 1980s. Four phenomena were observed:

- In explaining their excessive costs, customers pointed to the inefficiency of their suppliers, frequently failing to search for inefficiencies and rationalization potentials in their own plants.

- Customers sought to unload crisis-adjustment burdens and seasonal fluctuations on their suppliers.

- Customers sought to "outsmart" their suppliers. For instance, a frequent practice was to hold up orders until a price adjustment was immanent so as to cash in on prices that were then particularly low in real terms; or to introduce unilaterally protracted terms of payment in order to profit from inflation.

- On the other hand, suppliers have also sought to modify these relations to their advantage. In the past this sometimes led to situations in which they were more willing to cease production than to operate at a loss. The outcome of both such practices and a lack of reliability was, for instance, that in 1990 one automaker had some 40 % of his production, nearly complete, waiting for a specific part at the end of the assembly line (Author's survey of firms, April 1991).

The relationships between suppliers and their customers are thus characterized by mistrust and mutual dislike, which has burrowed its way into the memory of both sides. Stabilization of the economic framework would thus lead to a change of behavior patterns only hesitantly and on the basis of gradual processes of confidence-building and *rapprochement*. Transition to a Japanese-style supplier network is thus bound to encounter considerable problems in the beginning.

Culture of Inflation

Brazil's culture of inflation did not merely complicate everyday dealings between business partners, due to inflation many firms also had fundamental doubts about the sense of just-in-time networks. Inflation invariably led to flight into tangible assets; and investments in stocks were therefore seen by many as a good means of protection against inflation. This view was, on the one hand, not unjustified, particularly when a firm was highly liquid and thus able to finance investments in stock from its cash flow. But on the other hand, this strategy had a marked speculative component to the extent that it was motivated by the notion that the rate of return or the anticipated loss in value was lower in financial investments.

Quality of Supplies

A just-in-time supplier network presupposes that the customer will be able to use deliveries immediately upon receipt, i.e. that there will be no need to inspect incoming goods, since the customer can rely on consistently high quality. But, owing to the past performance of most Brazilian firms, the end producers see little reason to do so.

System of Taxation

Transactions between firms are burdened with high, and in part cumulative, taxes (federal and state). This entails a sharp distortion in make-

or-buy decisions: a supplier must offer a price advantage on the order of 30 – 40 % if the sum total of sales price and taxes are not to exceed internal production costs.

Infrastructure and Practical Problems

The state of material infrastructure is in some cases an obstacle to the establishment of just-in-time supplier relationships. In the area of São Paulo, the road network is overburdened, and outside the state of São Paulo it is of insufficient quality, and it is therefore impossible to predict exactly how long deliveries by truck will take. Rail transportation is not an alternative, since both rail network and rolling stock are in poor condition. The poor quality of the telephone network also poses problems to its use for electronic data transmission.

Another consideration is practical problems. One firm reported on inadequate packaging techniques – 70 – 80 % of packaging materials could not be reused. Furthermore, the just-in-time planners were confronted with a surprising obstacle to timed deliveries: because the truck drivers who delivered parts were entitled to use the subsidized firm canteen, deliveries were invariably concentrated around meal-times.

Networks

In Brazil there is no gentle transition from oligopolies or trusts to networks – the conditions required to establish networks do not exist. An OECD publication (OECD/TEP 1992, 79) specifies six such conditions:

– Firms have complementary assets, in particular company-specific, tacit knowledge. Whether this is the case for Brazilian firms is questionable. But even if it were: in Brazilian firms there is a strong preference for internalization and vertical integration, and this is, at least for the time being, an obstacle to cooperation.

- An exchange of such assets, and the learning processes associated with it, would require close, personal contacts. This, however, would presuppose that a firm already knows that it is in the midst of learning processes; it is a long way from the existence of learning processes to awareness and promotion of them on the part of firms/managers, and in Brazil very few firms have embarked on this path.

- Economic dynamics, technological change, and quick changes in demand patterns reward any implementation of product ideas. But time-to-market has not been a serious problem in Brazil, since even obsolete products found their buyers. This situation is gradually changing in the wake of the liberalization process.

- R&D costs are so high that they can only be borne by several firms in concert. This problem has hardly occurred in Brazil, because firms have engaged in little R&D.

- Networks represent an adequate organizational form when the structures required are flexible and reversible, and associated with few sunk costs.

- Potential partners expect reciprocity, i.e. there must be willingness to develop confidence and possibilities to penalize opportunistic behavior. It is precisely these factors that seem to be alien to Brazilian industry – due to the specific history of the development of intercompany relations, but also because of macroeconomic framework conditions that have stimulated free-riders.

3.1.3   Conclusions

In the Brazilian discussion the question of how to asses the introduction of organizational innovations is highly controversial. While many authors detect no more than marginal or superficial changes (Gitahy, Leite, and Rabelo 1993; Carvalho 1993), others identify a far-reaching process of change (Fleury and Humphrey 1993; Ferraz et al. 1992).

These contrasting interpretations are shaped by the specific frame of reference they use. Compared with Japan's state of development, the level of modernization in Brazil is doubtless fully insufficient; Brazil also looks bad when compared with Europe, particularly with regard to certain social achievements at the company level (confidence-based relations and management-workforce relations based on mutual respect, orderly settlement of conflicts). Brazil's industry is no doubt far from being able to close this gap – which is why some assessments are skeptical.

On the other hand, a process of profound change is quite evident – especially in leading firms. True, they too are still far from any organization of production along the lines of Uddevalla. But compared with the *status quo ante* the changes are far-reaching, and they mark the transition from no trust to some trust (which will ultimately develop into relations based on high trust). These firms are thus in the process of restructuring company organization and the character of the relations between management and workforce. This means initiating a process of "late modernization" of in-company social relations. In phases of rapid industrialization, i.e. from the 1950s to the 1970s, industry engaged in a certain measure of technical modernization. But relations between management and workers remained at the same level, one resembling that predominant in 19th century Europe, when rigorous regulations were set up to discipline workers and cement patterns of internal domination (Wirtz 1982). Today this is changing under the pressure of circumstances. It cannot be ignored that awareness of the need to enhance efficiency and improve quality has grown perceptibly since the policy of liberalization began. Today the scene is no longer dominated by a small number of big corporations as various firms are engaged in systematic efforts in this direction; and management is learning that new organizational patterns and redefined relations with workers constitute conditions central to any improvement of competitiveness.

Three general conclusions may be drawn here:

- New organizational concepts can be successfully employed in Brazil – despite initially incompatible conditions, i.e. conflictual labor relations, paternalistic entrepreneurial cultures, and lack of experience with participation at all levels;

– such concepts are no longer employed only by top performers; they are successively gaining currency in other firms as well (CNI 1993);

– even when employed only partially, they entail substantial efficiency gains that find expression, for instance, in distinctly reduced quality costs and lowered stocks of semifinished products; these effects are measurable (Table 24) (Meyer-Stamer et al. 1991, 94ff.).

One thing must, however, be noted with regard to the issue of competitiveness. Even though the modernization efforts currently underway are encouraging, it has as yet not become clear to what extent Brazil's industry will be able to improve its relative competitiveness (i.e. in relation to its direct competitors in the world market). The initial level, poor in many branches of industry, is just as much a reason for skepticism as the fact that in recent years the investment rate has declined sharply; and the current figures (in real terms, in the last quarter of 1992, roughly 14.5 %, the better part of it for building investments)[8] contrast sharply with both the general discussion and experiences made here and there. But they are in line with the experience of BNDES and its affiliated organizations, which are faced with serious problems with outflows of funds:[9] The greatest demand in relative terms was for small-scale loans (below 1 million $) needed to finance organizational innovations and procurement of some new machines. There is no doubt that Brazilian firms are well advised to give priority to organizational innovations (introduction of quality assurance, layout modifications, reduction of stock, reductions of processing times). But the technological level of production processes in industry is on the whole so low that increased investment in modern plant is inevitable; and thus a persistently low inclination to invest in new machinery would cast doubt on the success of modernization efforts as a whole. Any sustained improvement of competitiveness presupposes stabilization of the economic framework and a return to a path of growth, since only this would stimulate the required investments in plant and machinery.

Table 24: Relative Efficiency of Brazilian Capital Goods Producers, 1990 and 1993

	Brazilian capital goods producers		World Class Manufacturing Standard
Performance indicators	*1990*	*1993*	
Rework Percentage of parts needing to be reworked	30	12-20	2
Production quality problems - rejects per million (WIP only)	23-28,000	11-15,000	200
Warranty/repair costs as a percent of total gross sales	2,7	0,2	0,1
Through-put time average - from day of receipt of order to day of delivery	35	20	2-4
Production lot size Pieces per lot	1000	100- 250	20-50
Annual inventory turns (raw and WIP only)	8	8-14	60-70
Average set-up time (good part to good part in minutes)	80	30-40	10
Value-added time as a percent of total production lead time	10	30	50
Defects in machinery idle time in % of total time of use	40	21	15-20
R&D investment % of turnover	< 1	1-2	3-5
Proposals for improvements % of employees who make at least one proposal per year	0,1	1-2	50-70
Training % of working hours per employee and year	< 1	< 1	5-7
Levels of hierarchy from CEO to shop floor	10-12	4-8	7
Source: Gazeta Mercantil, quoted from FESBRASIL 1/1993, p. 7.			

3.2   Old vs. New Governance Elements in Industrial and Technology Policy

To stimulate structural adjustment in industry, the Collor government pursued a carrot-and-stick policy: the stick was monetary policy on top of foreign trade policy, the carrot consisted of various programs involving tax breaks and other financial incentives.

Even for the later Sarney government restrictive monetary policy was a central datum for firms, in that this policy lead to a recession in Brazil, which had two consequences. First, the profits, which had hardly declined during the so-called crisis years of the 1980s, went into a tailspin. It was this that created an awareness among firms that radical change in economic policy was immanent and that entrepreneurial responses to it had to be sought.

Second, it led to a situation in which many private firms stepped up their export efforts; even in earlier years many industrial firms had seen in exports a way out of the growth trap posed by a stagnating domestic market. Exports were not encouraged by the development of the exchange rate, and export subsidies were cut. The firms were thus forced to use efficient production as a means of becoming competitive. Monetary policy had a second effect in this connection: since it drove interest rates up to high real levels, many firms sought to increase productivity more through organizational than technical innovations.

3.2.1   Failed Attempts of a Traditional Industrial and Technology Policy

Between August 1990 and February 1991, three major programs were launched to support structural change in industry.

Programa da Capacitação Tecnológia (PCT). This program was designed to strengthen technological capacity in industry. The point of departure was that competitiveness rests on mobilization of dynamic comparative advantages and, in particular, technological capacity. PCT set its sights on two levels at which the technological capacity of Brazil's industry was to be improved. The first level included general measures:

– strengthening of the human capital base,

– awareness-building and strengthening the motivation to introduce new technologies,

– development and dissemination of the management know-how required to absorb technological innovations, in particular for R&D and production planning,

– Improvement of technical infrastructure, i.e. research centers, laboratories, etc. with an eye to industry's needs,

– consolidation of information networks for the dissemination of knowledge on new technologies and their economic prospects.

PCT's second level of intervention was aimed at directly supporting firms:

– financing of R&D projects and/or programs,

– financing of the procurement of technological equipment,

– support of joint ventures with Brazilian firms,

– financial stimulation of the transfer of technology from large firms to small and medium-sized firms.

Programa Brasileiro de Qualidade e Productividade (PBQP). Following the long phase of insulation, the level of quality in the Brazilian market was inadequate. The aim was thus to develop sectoral strategies and measures to improve quality. The approaches included

– strengthening of awareness in matters of quality and productivity among both consumers and producers,

– development and dissemination of management innovations,

– improvement of the human capital base.

The program was aimed above all at disseminating information and building awareness. Financial instruments played a very small role.

Programa de Competitividade Industrial (PCI). PCI's goal was to restructure industrial subsectors. The intention was to promote industrial segments that seemed to offer particular potentials; these were on the one hand segments in mature industries that were already competitive and had comparative advantages and on the other hand new industries which appeared promising in this respect. PCI included the following measures:

– firms that invested in new machinery and equipment qualified for tax relief and accelerated depreciation possibilities;

– the informatics law was to be modified;

– INPI was to continue to control technology imports, but was now required to reach its decisions within 45 days; it was allowed to raise objections only if the technologies to be imported were completely obsolete;

– the local-content rules governing access to state credits and government procurement were cut from 85 % to a maximum of 70 %;

– 3.8 billion US-$ was earmarked to bolster the formation of human capital.

Only one of these three programs was rapidly implemented, namely, PBQP, which did not operate with financial incentives and could therefore be implemented without congressional approval. PCT, on the other hand, was adopted only in May of 1993, and PCI disappeared from the scene.

It was not only the political framework – confrontation between government and parliament, impeachment procedures against Collor, problems with the consolidation of the Franco government – that impeded implementation and reduced the programs' effectiveness; a factor of equal significance was the makeup of Brazil's industrial policy. The most important instruments were tax incentives and subsidies aimed at stimulating modernization investments. These instruments were, however, unable to accomplish much as long as few firms were investing on account of the poor economic situation. Since short-term economic stabilization failed to materialize, the attempts to support and control the structural adjustment process in firms with the aid of conventional industrial-policy programs were bound to fail.

The situation was not just that the government was not in a position to stabilize the macroframework. It also periodically changed the fundamental rules, and in addition sought to implement active, creative policies. All in all, this gave rise to a picture of confusion, erraticism, and inconsistency which led firms to perceive the state above all as a disruptive factor. Firms started to develop measures aimed at increasing their flexibility as a means of being able to respond quickly to new erratic turns of policy.

The lesson to be learned here is: conventional mesopolicies have limited prospects of success if there is a lack of any supportive institutional tissue and if these policies are counteracted by macropolicy:

- Industrial policy was traditionally negotiated at the sectoral level between state agencies and firms. Firms accepted the target corridor, which was sometimes set by government, sometimes bargained for, because the state offered them benefits – no competing imports, low-price imports of primary products and machinery, low levels of competitive intensity in the domestic market, favorable financial terms. All these benefits were done away with once markets were opened up; what remained was an offer of tax breaks, which made little business sense in view of the poor profit situation and, furthermore, were less attractive than the traditional instruments.

- In the face of poor macroeconomic management, the firms lack confidence in any form of government intervention, even though it may be intended as support. This increases their irritation with programs designed by authoritarian technocrats far removed from practical realities and not formulated in a close dialogue with the actors concerned.

3.2.2   New Governance Patterns in Industrial and Technology
         Policy

The situation with unconventional programs that – like PBQP – have
introduced new elements into industrial policy is somewhat different.
PBQP differed from other and earlier programs in that it set its sights
on awareness-building, the dissemination of information, and management consulting. An additional new element was the fact that the
implementation of these instruments was in large measure left up to
nonstate organizations. It is, however, difficult to assess this program's
exact contribution in that company-level efforts aimed at improving
quality often emerged plainly and simply from the necessity to survive
in markets growing ever more competitive. Surveys of firms indicate
that PBQP is at least not a central element of their quality offensive.
They are on the whole nor very familiar with it, and the smaller the
firm, the less likely it is to be familiar with the program: 30.6 % of
large firms indicate that they are familiar with it, while the figure for
medium-sized firms is 25 % and that for small firms is only 10 %.[10]
The data need not be interpreted as a failure of the program; they stand
more for the anticipated limited successes with a new approach that
presupposes intensive learning processes on the part of the state no less
than the firms concerned.

One institutional innovation that met with more success in the short
term was the *câmaras setorais*, i.e. bargaining panels for individual
industries. Such panels existed in the Sarney era as a forum for negotiating over prices. The Sarney government at first sought to set up
Executive Groups for Sectoral Policy (GEPS); but this attempt at coordinating industrial policy with representatives of private industry
failed due to marked mutual mistrust (Salgado 1993, 306). The
câmaras setorais were set up in the spring of 1991 as a means of preventing an explosion of inflation in the phase in which price and wage
controls were relaxed. A total of 31 panels were established. Particularly remarkable results were achieved in the automobile industry panel
(Salgado 1993), which succeeded in initiating a process of structural
change in this industry, leading to a vitalization of overall economic
activity. The chamber was composed of representatives of government,

the automobile and automotive industries, car dealers, and the labor unions. They reached an agreement on reducing the prices of automobiles and thus dynamizing the market via lowered taxes, rationalization, and lowered profit margins. The labor unions at the same time agreed to waive any strikes for a given period of time; for this they received assurances of employment stability.

It is difficult to decide whether a functioning policy network was already established here: the distribution of costs and benefits was unequal, since it was doubtful (and difficult to verify) whether manufacturers and dealers would really reduce their profit margins. Nevertheless, the bargaining process established here was seen in the Brazilian discussion as a major advance, if only to the extent that the labor unions were accorded a constructive role. The relative success of this chamber is doubtless linked to the fact that the auto industry is in every way strongly concentrated, thus rendering the number of actors involved more or less visible at a glance. Furthermore, the transparency of the measures proposed (apart from the issues of profit margins) was great, i.e. implementation was easy to verify. In other chambers that dealt with dispersed branches of industry, it was far more complicated to reach tangible results.[11]

3.3   Regional and Local Policy

Important political changes are underway at the state and municipal levels. The case of the northeastern state of Ceará, which attracted the notice of the international press, is not unique. This state managed on its own to revitalize public finances, increase the effectiveness of state services, and rehabilitate its school and health-care systems.[12] There are similar tendencies in Piauí and Paraíba, likewise states in the northeast.[13] In Salvador, the capital of Bahia, the largest state in the northeast, the prefect launched a program aimed at improving the quality and productivity of public services. These are all examples that are regarded in Brazil as indications that reforms are also possible at the local and regional levels. This insight is apt to step up the legitimation pressure on old-style governors and prefects. In the past, breaking out

of the traditional clientelist constellation was for politicians an undertaking fraught with risks and holding out promise of uncertain benefits.
The risk involved was that of not being elected in the first place; or, for
lack of a clientele that ensured both legitimation and the implementation of policies, of not coming up with viable majorities; or, due to a
lack of benefits for clientele, of not being reelected. To the extent that
politicians show that it is possible to break through the traditional
logic, the risk/benefit rationale can shift quickly.

Regarding industry-related policies, thus far the chief state-level policy
geared to making locations more attractive to industry has been races
for subsidies (Lasmar 1994). Once scopes have been discovered for
shaping local and regional economic framework conditions, new approaches open up for a technology policy that can be used to enhance
the competitiveness of local industry and improve locational quality
(Lavinas 1994, 22). The point of departure is the existence of industrial
clusters, which exist in many areas of Brazil: the manufacturers of
ladies' shoes are concentrated in the Vale dos Sinos in Rio Grande do
Sol, the producers of men's and children's shoes in Franca and Birigüi
in the interior of the state of São Paulo; the leading manufacturers of
tiles are located in the south, poultry processors in the west of Santa
Catarina. The auto industry, and a large share of the capital goods industry, are concentrated around of São Paulo. The better part of the
electronics industry is in Manuas (though this is for political reasons),
and the petrochemical industry is concentrated in Cubatão near São
Paulo, Camaçari near Bahia, and Triunfo near Porto Alegre (this, too,
for political as well as technical reasons).

The cluster most thoroughly investigated is the one in the Vale dos
Sinos (Schmitz 1993). It consists of roughly 1,800 firms with over
150,000 employees. Two thirds of the firms are independent shoe
manufacturers or subcontractors, the others supply primary products,
machines, and special services. Apart from a number of large "Fordist"
firms, most others are small and medium-sized companies. This is a
place for which Alfred Marshall's dictum, "the information is in the
air," is applicable; this does not mean *"that all information is shared,
but clearly in such a cluster secrets are hard to keep."* (Schmitz 1993, 7)

Six specialized industrial associations and three training and technology diffusion centers provide forums for the dissemination of information. It is striking that the local or state-level governments evidently were not involved in the development of competitiveness in this cluster, which accounts for roughly 30 % of Brazil's shoe production, but 80 % of its shoe exports.

But it is not such that Brazil, in the past, never experienced approaches involving local technology policy. Aside from attempts in São Paulo to organize the transfer of technology from the local university to industry, there were several initiatives aimed at establishing technology parks in which new entrepreneurs who had developed ideas for innovative products in their university research might be settled (Medeiros 1990; and Villaschi 1992b). Systematic evaluations of these experiences are not yet available. The prevailing view emphasizes two points: first, some of the technology parks work well, i.e. the number of firms in them is on the increase, and the survival rate is high; second, however, these are isolated experiences that are restricted to a specific location and whose spillover effects are slight, even within a larger area.

There is very little documentation available on local or regional technology-policy initiatives aimed at improving the competitiveness of existing firms; Haddad (1994, 32f.) mentions programs in Ceará that were planned to disseminate modern management techniques in industry, but without going into details. In Santa Catarina the state government commissioned the state industrial association to formulate an industrial policy; but the corresponding activities were basically restricted to commissioning a study on possible industrial-policy, and the results were apparently not appreciated by those who commissioned the study.[14]

3.4 Conclusions on the Brazilian Case: Prospects for a New Technology Policy

Brazil confirms experiences made in other Latin American countries: in the phase of import substitution

- an industry emerged that is only partially competitive, in part because it undertook too few (and often distorted) R&D efforts owing to the incentive structures generated by the country's inward orientation;

- what emerged was not a national system of innovation but a landscape of weakly networked research and technology institutions;

- a blockade constellation emerged in the political system that has minimized the state's governance capacity.

Two things have become evident in the phase of transition to a new development model. First: the adaptability of firms – this is shown by an analysis of the process of change at the microlevel – is greater than might have been supposed in view of the deterioration of their performance in the 1980s and the relatively unfavorable sociopolitical framework under which they operated. A contributing factor was that the process of opening up to world market competition did not occur in the form of a shock, it proceeded gradually. This provided firms with the time needed to organize internal learning processes. These learning processes refer in particular to the reorganization of production and quality assurance. It must here be noted in turn that the introduction of new organizational concepts is less complicated than might have been expected in view of the country' protracted history of conflictual labor relations. This supports the thesis that central elements of the "Japanese production model" can be employed in socio-economic-political environments that differ fundamentally from the framework in Japan.

Second, in the phase of import substitution political structures developed that minimized the capacity to engage in learning processes and actively shape the process of adjustment to new global framework conditions. Apart from foreign-trade policy, in which the executive branch has autonomy of action and was therefore able to hold its course, economic policy has thus far been erratic; there is a close reciprocal causal relationship between unstable macroeconomic development and ad hoc interventions on the part of the state, and this is the reason why the credibility of long-term mesopolicies has been low. This is all the more true when the latter operate with financial instruments, since, for instance, the target group of industrial- and technology-policy programs knows that it cannot rely on financial commitments on account of the special features of the budgeting process in Brazil. With this in mind, the proposal to implement on a broad basis the above-outlined "New Technology Policy" would seem to disregard Brazilian realities. The concern in the immediate future will thus be

– that the most important actors succeed in elaborating a joint vision;

– that actors at levels other than central government discover and explore the scopes open to (technology) policy and that this be encouraged and possibly stimulated by central government;

– that selective experiments be conducted at different levels with new instruments.

3.4.1   "Hard" and "Soft" Factors of Technology

One feature of the company-level adjustment process is that the firms – owing to the uncertain economic situation and problems in financing investments – place greater weight on "soft" factors than on "hard" factors, i.e. are more interested in reorganization than in the introduction of new, computer-based hardware. The company-level reorganization process is impeded above all by two factors: the conventional approach to labor relations, which often obstructs company-level negotiations and accords, and the general economic-policy framework and specific fiscal framework conditions, which often subject interfirm relations to severe trials. Technology-policy initiatives should accordingly also aim to further disseminate information on new organizational concepts (as is already the case with PBQP); but, and above all, what is required is political initiatives outside the sphere of technology policy in the narrower sense (see Section 3.4.5).

3.4.2   New Industries vs. New Technologies in Old Industries

Informatics policy, the most important policy as far as new technologies are concerned, was in the past linked with a shift of priorities toward the development of new industries, and not the diffusion of new technologies in existing industries. In fact, the latter was even impeded to the extent that informatics policy stimulated the emergence of a distorted supplier structure in the field of computer hardware and software: firms tended mainly to push into areas in which the entry barriers were low. This entailed a weak development of sectors with high entry barriers, which are often of strategic significance for other branches of industry; these include, e.g., the development of applications-specific microchips, automation of production, software, and systems integration. This development is not encouraged by the currently predominant informatics policy, marked as it is by an odd combination of laissez-faire and indiscriminate protection for existing firms. A vicious circle has become dominant: the uncertain economic situation and the investment weakness resulting from it has restricted the demand for strategically important products and services, and thus there is little incentive to enter this market; this in turn limits the number of suppliers, and prices and quality are not particularly attractive for potential users. To the extent that the Brazilian state regains its governance capacity in industrial and technology policy, it could become necessary in this field to stimulate the development of a corresponding supplier structure by means of public-sector interventions.

All in all, the main objective as regards new technologies will in the future be to promote their use in existing branches of industry, e.g. to step up the efficiency and quality of production in process industries or to diversify the product spectrum in areas such as food processing. This results from the circumstance that competitiveness cannot be sustained merely or even chiefly through organizational innovations;

this requires the use of new technical hardware, which is as yet not very widely diffused. Policy interventions, often at the local or regional levels, can focus on concentrating competences and render more effective the process of identifying technology components that are already available elsewhere and need to be adapted to specific needs.

3.4.3   Science and Technology

The unsuccessful search for a national system of innovation has shown that a large gap between the system of science and the productive sector has thus far been predominant; attempts to initiate joint development projects have led to success only in very few areas. This reflects the dominant incentive structure, which has failed to induce scientists and firms to approach one another.

It would be mistaken to assume that the liberalization process will alter this incentive structure either fundamentally or in a short period of time. Firms' need for support in the restructuring process creates above all demand for technical and management consulting that leads to rapidly realizable results, but not to a need for long-term joint research projects with universities or technology institutes. The institutions in the science system are in part attempting to adapt to this demand by, for instance, offering consulting services for the introduction of quality programs. It is here that needs are pressing, and there is also an incentive in that such institutions can in this way achieve additional revenues that can often offer relief in difficult financial situations. The model of joint research and development projects between firms and research institutes familiar from the industrialized countries will gain appreciable footing in Brazil at best over the medium term, and will do so in industries that come closer to the internationally dominant technological limits and, in solving process-related or product-development problems, avail themselves of methods similar to those used in science.

3.4.4   Globalization and National Technology Policy

Brazilian policy reflects expectations that the country will be able to benefit from the globalization of industrial activities. This expectation is justified in one respect, i.e. as regards the potentials of industrial exports; here – in view of the missed chances noted above – there are scopes that can be harnessed to the extent that firms improve their competitiveness.

There is less justification for other types of expectations, i.e. the contribution to the process of industrial modernization provided by foreign firms that are or will be operating in Brazil. Experiences made thus far have shown that the foreign firms already present in the country are not playing much of a pioneering role in efforts aimed at improving competitiveness. The reason for this is basically that they adjusted to the local environment during the phase of ISI and are therefore not necessarily a priori more competitive than efficient local firms. Furthermore, they – unlike the latter – do not necessarily accord high priority to adjustment in Brazil in the context of a global business strategy and are thus not automatically provided with massive support by their corporate headquarters. Expectations with regard to new foreign investment are optimistic, it must be asked, however, how justified this optimism is. At the end of a protracted phase marked by low levels of foreign investment, economic stabilization will presumably lead to fresh inflows of foreign capital, which, to be sure, can quickly subside again – not least because Brazil offers few specific locational advantages and direct investment thus depends above all on the absorption capacity of the national market or the Mercosul market.

3.4.5   Perspectives of Political Governance in Brazil

In the second half of the 1980s, the following description of politics in Brazil could hardly be disputed: *"Brazilian politics follows a pattern of personalistic relations, colossal clientelism, strong regionalism, little or no party discipline, and extremely nebulous ideologies. The underlying assumption is that politics consists of what is taking place among the gentlemen in the legislative and executive branches; the rest of the population is effectively excluded. In this political world, the logic of representation operates only intermittently – basically, when there is no way of avoiding it. In its absence, the concept of accountability disappears ..."* (O'Donnell 1988, 296). In the meantime O'Donnell's description is in need of qualification: it still applies for congress and the relations between government and congress at the federal level (and certainly in most of the states). But is less and less true of the relations between the political-administrative system and organized social groups; the traditional corporatist system is being complemented and in part supplanted by other forms for the representation of interests and coordination of policies.

Learning processes are here becoming visible at all levels. Actors in the executive have begun to learn that their power is not so great as they once assumed. The main reason is that the resources that once constituted the state's power base (which has at times been limited), namely, money and a vision, i.e. a concept for a development model, are today only partially existent: there are competing visions and social projects, and these, for lack of adequate financial resources, are moving in a vacuum.

Social actors have begun to learn that they can rely neither on the money nor on the strategic competence of the state. The corporatist organizations are no longer directing their demands to the state, instead they are undertaking efforts to develop direct relationships. The CUT labor unions, which represent roughly one third of those formally employed, have for some time now shown an increasing tendency toward a pragmatic, dialogue-oriented line; this is particularly true of the key unions like the *metalúrgicos* in the southern industrial suburbs of São Paulo. On the business side it is striking that the export-oriented firms are not becoming more politically active as a means of working toward economic stabilization. The main reason is that any departure from the corporatist system will in any case entail high costs, while the benefits remain uncertain. New types of associations and institutions are emerging – if only cautiously – outside the existing corporatist system, e.g. PNBE (*Pensamento Nacional de Bases Empresariais*), a federation of modern small and medium-sized firms, and IEDI (*Institute Econômico de Desenvolvimento Industrial*), which was organized by some 40 leading private firms and has thus far served above all as a think tank (Lamounier 1991, 14; and Mathieu 1990, 161).[15]

The solution-oriented negotiations conducted in the *câmara setorial* for the automobile industry, and possibly in other chambers as well, do not merely form a clear-cut contrast to the permanent confrontation between government and congress. An optimistic interpretation states: what is emerging here is the establishment of a new political model in which the structures of authoritarian corporativism are being overcome and replaced by structures that resemble policy networks. This is a demanding undertaking that is far removed from any traditionalist corporatist system in which entrepreneurs and labor unions direct their demands not to one another but to the state. That negotiations in a policy network lead to concrete results is, in the Brazilian context, a surprising and – in view of the possibility that a new societal governance pattern may be gaining ground – encouraging finding.

It is evident that a new governance pattern is called for, since the fact cannot be overlooked that a centralist, hierarchical governance model in this society, which has in the meantime attained a high level of functional differentiation, has reached it limits. The Collor government's two stabilization plans, both of which were highly control-intensive, did not fail only as a result of lack of competence on the part of the technocrats; an additional cause was the fact that no fine control of the different variables was possible. Today the traditional form of hierarchical governance is failing in Brazil both on account of the state's limited competence and because of the strong veto potential wielded by social groups (Santos 1993). Another factor is that state actors have lost credibility due to erratic policy changes in the past. One more thing that has become evident is the limits imposed by the traditional form in which interests were organized, especially in the business camp, where large and small, weak and effective, solely inward-looking and export-oriented firms were compelled to unite in one and the same *sindicato*. It proved increasingly complex in this framework to define joint interests at all, to say nothing of articulating them vis-à-vis the state. The complexity of industry and governance requirements is better dealt with through a differentiation of the pattern according to which interests are organized in this area, especially since there are as yet no indications that the pendulum is swinging in the opposite direction, which would be an inflation of small and very small groups representing common interests.

A new governance model in Brazil must include three levels:

– reestablishment of a minimum of governance capacity at the central government level;

– a redefinition of the division of tasks between central government, states, and municipalities;

– modification and supplementation of corporatist structures and reconstitution of the relations between state and social actors.

Governance capacity at the federal level. The central government's governance capacity is today low because of the limited competence of the executive, the low level of creative will on the part of the legislative, the blockade constellation between the powers of state, and the complex articulation between state and social actors. There is nothing to indicate that this situation can altered over the short term; the government that came to power in 1995 will basically be confronted with the same governance problems as its predecessor. In view of this finding it should not be assumed that central government will be able to take on a leading creative role in shaping a new, no longer inward-looking development model.

In fact, it could be seen as a substantial success if the federal government should manage to stabilize the economic framework and rationalize the budgeting process. During the past 15 years, Brazil's economic framework has been marked by a great measure of unpredictability. A rather stable framework would be a significant condition for firms to develop strategic options (and this means in Brazil: to be able to plan for a period of more than a few months); these strategic options would include stepped up investment in R&D. Reorganization of the federal budget and reform of the budgeting process would also be significant steps with regard to the scientific-technological infrastructure, since stable financial allocations to state universities and federal research institutions would be elementary conditions for any improvement or reconstitution of the effectiveness of these institutions. Moreover, the federal government could also take steps toward rehabilitating the MSTQ system and gearing it more to the needs of firms.

Further-reaching reform projects that have direct effects on efforts toward increasing competitiveness at the macrolevel appear even more complicated. These would include the pending reform of the system of taxation, which, in its current form, is dysfunctional in that it sharply discriminates between economic sectors, combines a selectively high tax burden with tax revenues that are all in all low, and, moreover, is too complex. A reform should include, among other things, a reduction of the high levels of federal and state taxes imposed on transactions between firms, since this stimulates vertical integration in firms and discourages interfirm transactions (and thus the emergence of speciali-zation-oriented networks of firms). There is also the need to reform of existing corporatist structures; this is the sine qua non for the introduc-tion of direct wage negotiations between industrial associations and labor unions as well as of a legislation on rights of codetermination at the workplace.

Without the adjustments at the macrolevel described above, initiatives at the mesolevel would largely evaporate, i.e. be counteracted by the incentive structures generated by conventional patterns of regulation. Quite apart from this, they would in all probability overburden the administrative and political competences of the executive. One of the initial concerns for the future will be to strengthen the administrative competence of the executive before it in turn can start out strengthen-ing, across a broad front, technological capability in other areas. This is also an important precondition for raising the state's relative autonomy vis-à-vis social actors.

Industrial- and technology-policy programs typical of the early phase of the Collor government that sought to stimulate innovative behavior with the aid of various incentives will also fail in the future if they are not worked out in close dialogue with the target group. *Câmaras setoriais* can provide an adequate forum for such a dialogue, particularly with regard to industries that are distributed throughout the country and are faced with similar problems. There are, however, few such industries; it is no coincidence that the automobile industry chamber was by far the most successful one. The majority of industries are concentrated regionally in a number of locations, and individual clusters in different parts of the country are faced with different problem complexes (such as, e.g., the shoe industry, where several clusters have serious problems with competitiveness, while the problem facing the firms in the Vale dos Sinos is mainly the entry into new export markets). Initiatives at the federal level are not very promising here; technology policy should preferably be formulated at the regional level in such cases.

A new division of tasks between central government, states, and municipalities. Regional technology policy of course presupposes a clear-cut definition of responsibilities among the federal, state, and municipal levels. Otherwise the formulation of local or regional policy would be in danger of being depreciated or counteracted by measures stemming from central government (Schultze 1990); this would reduce the incentives for local or regional policy actors to formulate concise policies. Thus far the division of tasks among central government, states, and municipalities has been defined only vaguely. In principle the Union is responsible for all national tasks and services, though there are also often parallel structures at the state and local levels. The provision of the 1988 constitution stating that a fixed share of federal tax revenues is to be passed on to the states and municipalities is not incorrect in principle; the problem has been primarily that there is no clear-cut definition of how these funds are to be employed. One conceivable solution would be – particularly in view of the fact that intelligently run state and local authorities are at times literally awash with money – the consistent introduction of the principle of subsidiarity: many tasks for which federal institutions have until now been responsible could be taken on by the states and municipalities (and in this way be controlled and monitored far more effectively) (Piquet Carneiro 1993, 153ff.). This, for example, would be one approach to a rehabilitation of the country's educational system; its poor state and the lack of properly qualified manpower resulting from this situation are, over the medium term, doubtless the greatest obstacle to any far-reaching improvement of industrial competitiveness.

There are also points of departure for local or regional initiatives in technology policy, in particular in a reorientation of existing technology institutes and universities, which, owing to the financial crisis facing the state, have considerable interest in earning additional revenue through consulting and research commissions. The concern here is less long-term, expensive development projects for firms than directly effective contributions to company restructuring projects, above all in the field of quality assurance. Stepped-up cooperation between research and industry can lead to rapid improvement of processes where it proves possible to identify complementary strengths between such institutions and existing industrial clusters that were not perceived in the past due to the incentive structures in place then.

Furthermore, a decentralization of functions would contribute toward relieving the federal government of some of its duties, in this way easing the financial crisis with which it is faced; and this in turn would constitute a central precondition for any effective containment of inflation, and hence also for a solution of the economic crisis.

Reconstitution of the relations between state and social actors. Local and regional policy dialogues can at the same time serve as a vehicle for a reconstitution of the relations between state and social actors and among the latter. To be sure, they presuppose a measure of articulation skills on the part of politicians of different parties and social actors, the existence of which is questionable. Such dialogues would have a twofold aim: on the one hand, the solution of given problems; and on the other hand, practice with techniques of conflict solution. Here the federal or the state governments could be faced with a new task: formulation of programs and provision of incentives designed to stimulate local or regional policy dialogues and contribute to closing existing competence gaps (e.g. by employing external moderators).

This, however, is an option that will prove realistic only from case to case. Any return to an effective political governance in general and an effective technology policy in particular presupposes learning processes within and among the relevant groups of actors, and such learning processes will require time. Technology research has noted that some time passes between an invention, its first application, and its widespread use, and that this involves numerous learning steps and incremental innovations. This finding can be formulated by way of analogy for political processes as well: in Brazil radical innovation has taken place in the form of a general reorientation in terms of development policy. The concern now is to initiate political-institutional learning processes and incremental innovations that involve testing new forms of policy formulation and new policy instruments.

4   General Conclusions for Developing Countries:
       Points of Departure for a New Technology Policy

A far-reaching process of change is underway in the practice of technology policy in DCs which is illustrated by the example of Brazil. Technology policy in DCs was in the past characterized by a large measure
of voluntarism. Policies were shaped by the will of the political actors,
not the technological actors, and largely ignored the incentive structure
and rationality of action relevant to the latter. Technology policy was
viewed in isolation from other policies which often had far more influence on technological behavior: a turbulent economic macropolicy that
led to a situation in which firms thought in the short term, perceived
the state as the cause of turbulence, and failed to respond to incentives
offered by technology policy; a restrictive monetary policy that led
firms not to invest, not even in technology; a public budget policy that
(especially in phases of structural adjustment) made employment in the
public sector financially unattractive.

One aspect will have to be focused on in reformulating technology
policy: what incentives, what motivations, and what goals do firms,
technology institutes, and training institutions have? Here it would be
naive simply to assume that a change in the macroframework –
opening up to the world market, increasing competitive pressure – will
itself induce firms to develop a marked technological dynamic and an
efficient environment consisting of support institutions. Firms often
also have the option of developing evasive behavior patterns or pursuing a defensive technology strategy. Adopting a strategy that entails
the purposive development of technology-based competitive advantages presupposes conscious management decisions, and these are easier
to arrive at when they coincide with corresponding activities undertaken by other cooperating firms and support institutions. Cooperation
between firms and technology institutions will flourish only if the appropriate incentives preponderate on both sides and if joint aims are
formualted. The political actors therefore will have to be more concerned than they were in the past to ensure that technology-policy initiatives are compatible with other sectoral policies, especially finan-

cial and economic policy. This is a *sine qua non* for success that is valid for each of the five areas looked into in the following section.

4.1   "Hard" and "Soft" Components of Technology

In many DCs technology policy was in the past one-sidedly hardware-oriented. A good number of industrialization and technology-transfer projects failed due to a lack of consideration of the "soft" factors of organization and know-how as a consequence of the incompatibility between the hard and soft components. Technology policy must therefore be targeted to developing and strengthening all three components, i.e. hardware, know-how, and organization.

As the analysis of company adjustment processes in Brazil showed, this is true in particular with regard to the reorganization of firms with an eye to boosting their competitiveness. Other case studies corroborate the finding that there are many potential applications for new production concepts – and here especially their organizational components – in advanced developing countries (Meyer-Stamer 1994c). A study on cost structures in the international electronics industry shows that firms in NICs are the most efficient producers (Table 25). It is not only the visible wage costs, it is above all hidden wage costs, that constitute the difference, particularly when reject rates (typically high when traditional organizational concepts are in use) are part of the calculation. After all, a fully assembled printed circuit board rejected at the end of the assembly line for quality defects contains substantial wage costs. It is here that both lower wage costs and, above all, better organization and the reduced reject levels achieved with its aid pay off. An additional point becomes evident: firms from DCs with a long history of inward-looking development (Mexico, China) are faced with grave organizational shortcomings that cannot be balanced out even by the lowest wages.

Experiences from Brazil also show that it would be rash to take cognizance of paternalist company structures and an authoritarian and polarized social structure, and then jump to the conclusion that new organ-

Table 25: Stylized Cost Structure in the Electronics Industry				
Costs per circuit board in US-$				
Cost category	DC*	NIC**	NIC	IC***
	manual	manual	automat.	automat.
Material	50	50	50	50
Direct labor costs	3.51	6.42	2.62	15.83
Direct machine costs	2.23	1.87	10.05	12.76
Non-productive direct labor costs	1.86	3.19	0.86	5.66
Non-productive direct costs of material	1.96	1.31	4.04	6.92
Indirect labor costs	8.83	11.12	5.72	11.73
Premises	0.88	0.88	0.6	1
Administration	1.08	0.97	0.6	0.76
Inventory and floating capital	6.2	1.95	1.46	2.04
Value of rejects	24.1	12.65	4.63	9.09
Sum total	100.65	90.36	80.58	115.79
* = Mexico, People's Republic of China; ** = Korea, Singapore; *** = USA. Source: Mody et al. 1991.				

izational concepts are not realizable at the company level. Introducing them will prove more complicated than in advanced industrial countries that have participatory patterns in other spheres of society as well; and they will often only be able to be introduced partially (e.g. in the form of a top-down strategy). But this is one way to achieve measurable progress in productivity, flexibility, and quality. Here, too, it also becomes clear that there is a cross-link between technological changes (or their blockage) and framework conditions outside the domain of technology policy (in this case labor legislation).

At the interfirm level, technological dynamics result from close, often informal, interaction between firms. Here there are two reasons why DCs are burdened with disadvantages. First, it is part of the nature of late industrialization processes that a structure of efficient, specialized suppliers develops only gradually, and thus for a long time individual firms have a great incentive to strive for a vertical integration as extensive as possible; Brazil's experiences are in this respect typical. One thing that can prove fatal is – as in Brazil – to discourage reductions in vertical integration by taxing interfirm transactions.

Second, regional policy has often aimed at a uniform distribution of industrial firms throughout the national territory. This has, among other things, led to a situation in which no really efficient industrial agglomerations have emerged anywhere – existing industrial regions were weakened through government-stimulated relocations, no new agglomerations emerged. This type of regional policy is dysfunctional, but the political costs of doing away with it are high; appropriations of funds to weak regions to ensure their political support are not a feature typical of Brazil alone.

On the other hand, agglomerations have been observed in other DCs that in many respects follow the pattern of industrial districts. Yet often the element of spatial agglomeration prevails over the element of social agglomeration – firms are close to one another, but they mistrust one another, cooperative relations between them are underdeveloped, and there is hardly any flow of information. There is not much the state can do to rectify this situation.

In its attempts to strengthen networked industrial relations, policy is in any case faced with grave problems. It is precisely in the phase of re-orientation following the end of a long period of one-sided inward orientation that the risk is high that new "new entrepreneurs" will display a behavioral disposition that leads to marked skepticism toward collective activities of any sort – in particular when the state is involved. Even development of elementary institutions, e.g. in vocational training, runs up against resistance. Network-oriented policy will prove promising only if the important actors are convinced of the advantages of industrial networks. This implies intensive efforts on the part of state actors and "vanguard" associations. Large companies reducing vertical integration and trading companies might also play an important part in this respect. But even then it is questionable what instruments hold promise of success; it was already pointed out that the discussion centered on the industrialized countries offers hardly any points of departure. Yet on the other hand it often occurs that economic or legal frameworks impede the emergence of networks; appropriate reforms are necessary and possible here.

4.2 Radical Change, Incremental Change, and Sector-Specific Technology Policy

In many DCs industrial firms are today faced with a twofold challenge. In addition to the need to adjust triggered by the opening up of markets, the traditional advantage-related factors of the "old" and "new" international division of labor are losing their significance because of the process of radical change currently underway. In the "old" international division of labor, natural, static locational advantages were the shaping influence: natural-spatial conditions favorable to the production of meat or plants, deposits of minerals and other raw materials. In the "new" international division of labor, it has been low labor costs that have provided the incentive to relocate given production phases (simple assembly activities) in certain branches of industry (electronics, clothing).

As far as natural locational advantages are concerned, their significance is being sharply eroded by technological trends – above all substitution processes involving bio-engineered products and new materials, but also a more efficient use of resources with the aid of microelectronically controlled machines or technologically advanced power plants (Junne et al. 1989; Jha 1990; UNCTAD 1991b; Kounides 1989). This is why there will be no way back to the times in which DCs – more exactly: the upper and upper-middle classes in DCs – were able to build their wealth on the export of unprocessed raw materials. These countries (examples would be Argentina, Chile, or Malaysia) today have two alternatives: they can either come to terms with economic stagnation or even decline, or they can build up dynamic comparative advantages. In concrete terms: Instead of exporting raw materials that they have in some way produced or brought to the surface of the earth, they

- optimize agrarian production processes or mining techniques with the aid of new technologies;

- they make use of low-priced raw-material inputs to take the step into processing, here too by using state-of-the-art technology, but above all new organizational concepts;

- they improve their marketing activities abroad, not least by employing new technology, e.g. state-of-the-art telecommunications and database technologies.

The comparative advantages stemming from low wages are losing their significance as a competitive advantage to the extent that many industries are altering their competitive structures by introducing new production concepts. New organizational patterns are for the most part superior to Taylorist organization, although they do require qualified manpower. This is even true for "simple" industries like the clothing industry (Kaplinsky 1991).

The keyword that will in the near future determine industrial development is *shaping of competitive advantages* (Porter 1990; OECD/TEP 1992). In many DCs this first applies to industries that emerged in the phase of import substitution and are today forced to boost their competitiveness, and new industries that can take advantage of given static comparative advantages, though their longer-term competitive advantage will emerge through the creation of dynamic competitive advantages. The latter result in particular from creative use of technology, i.e. development of improved or new products and the efficient production and marketing of such products. This refers both to "mature" and "new" technologies (although it is important to point out that these should not be seen as alternatives – many industries will be concerned to employ both mature technologies and new technologies).

In fact, the discussion on the impacts of new technologies on industrialization in developing countries was for a long time somewhat shortsighted. One important strand of the discussion developed from the thesis that the surge of automation made possible by microelectronics would render superfluous the wage advantages offered thus far by sites in which activities had been relocated, and that this in turn would lead to a massive re-relocation. Failed automation projects in industrialized countries and the successful introduction of new organizational patterns in advanced developing countries have invalidated this thesis (Jungnickel 1988).

Another strand of this discussion proceeded on the assumption that new technologies would lead to the emergence of new industries. It was argued that this could open up a window of opportunity for advanced developing countries, because this would make it easier for them to enter these areas rather than other industries that are, in their life-cycle, presently somewhere between emergence and maturity, and thus pose high barriers to entry.

"What this means for lagging countries is that during periods of paradigm transitions there are two sorts of favourable conditions for catching up. First of all, there is time for learning while everybody else is doing so. Secondly, given a reasonable level of productive capacity and locational advantages and a sufficient endowment of qualified human resources in the new technologies, a temporary window of opportunity is open, with low thresholds of entry where it matters most." (Perez and Soete 1988, 477)

The weakness of this thesis is its underestimation of the continuities that exist despite radical technological change (Pavitt 1986); this became evident in Brazil's informatics industry in terms of weaknesses in the field of fine mechanics. Weak technological competence in the face of mature technologies cannot be compensated for by intensive capacity-building with new technologies; the latter is more apt merely to reveal weaknesses in dealing with mature technologies. The leapfrogging thesis according to which firms in DCs can overleap certain development phases is to this extent short-sighted (Wad 1982). The real issue is that firms in DCs can abbreviate learning processes by making use of the experiences of other firms (to the extent that these are available in textbooks or manuals or the minds of business consultants), and that they – particularly in organizational terms – need not go through every step of evolution that firms in more advanced countries have already covered.

The second weakness lies in the linkage of a high level of aggregation with empirical phenomena and a simplified view of industrial life-cycles. Radical technological change not only gives rise to new industries, it also leads to a restructuring of long-established industries; the watch industry is a good example of how radical technological change can fundamentally change a product long since available and the techniques used to produce it, thereby leading to far-reaching changes in the supplier structure. Windows of opportunity do not emerge only in entirely new industries, they tend also to appear in branches of industry that are regarded as old. In advanced developing countries technology policy can aim to stimulate and support entrepreneurship in new industries. It is, however, false to understand high-tech technology policy merely in the sense of "building up a computer industry." Windows of opportunity for leaps in quality and efficiency and for new products also open up when new organizational patterns are used in the clothing industry, when microelectronics is used in toys, or biotechnology is used in food-processing. These are industries in which suppliers from several DCs already have production know-how and – what is often just as important – marketing know-how and channels. The possibility of proceeding from this point is a central condition for the utilization of new technologies to build up competitive advantages. This is why firms in DCs will often have better prospects of success in this field than in entirely new industries.

In terms of technology policy, this means that clear priorities must be set for the dissemination of knowledge on new technologies and organizational patterns in existing industries. It will hardly prove possible to develop competitive advantages when firms are thrown back on their own resources. The creation of advanced factors and specialized factors does not merely presuppose a dense pattern of interaction between firms (and that is: with suppliers and customers, and with competitors), it also presupposes that entrepreneurial learning processes are supported by a variety of technology institutions. They can be developed by the firms themselves, though they often imply state activities; the state can create support institutions (e.g. vocational training, consulting services for SMEs) which – assuming the appropriate internal organizational incentives as given – can stimulate and support the emergence of technological networks.

Radical innovation in existing industries does not necessarily mean radical innovation in existing firms. The success of radical innovations is often linked with the emergence of new firms, because existing firms are reluctant to leave an existing technological trajectory. Encouragement of the introduction of radical innovations in existing industries therefore presupposes an environment that is favorable to the founding of new firms. The important elements include a functioning competition watchdog agency that ensures that established firms are unable to sustain market entry barriers at too high levels; and a functioning financial system that does not unnecessarily impede the mobilization of capital to found new firms.

4.3   Science and Technology

In DCs technology policy often rests on the thesis that a functioning system of science constitutes a sine qua non for social development and, in particular, for successful industrialization processes. This thesis is in need of qualification: it is also and precisely in DCs that the results of scientific research are not automatically harnessed for industrial purposes. In making their investment decisions, industrial firms are guided by economic incentives, not by scientifically generated potentials. There is a need for systematic efforts on the part of both researchers and the state to provide scientific findings with a character amenable to practical uses. The implies the creation of incentive structures in scientific institutions that encourage researchers to seek contact with firms.

Even when this succeeds, the contribution that an emerging national system of science will be able to make toward late industrialization will as a rule be small. Industrial firms that chiefly use – especially in terms of hardware – mature technologies (i.e. the great majority of industrial firms in DCs) are generally not faced with problems that can be solved only with the aid of scientific research. They are instead confronted by problems that can best be solved by engineers, technicians, and qualified workers; here and there external consultants (from markedly applications-oriented technology institutes or consulting firms) will be called in.

One of the main functions of the system of science will therefore be to train engineers and technicians, who should also have solid basic training in the sciences. The quantitative requirements in these areas are far greater than the demands placed on the training of pure scientists. Countries pursuing a project of late industrialization are therefore well advised to focus on the development of technical colleges and universities.

In addition, it also makes sense to concentrate systematic basic and applied research in industrially relevant fields to a limited number of sectors in which a country is capable of building up competitive advantages. Even here the function of research will be less to achieve major breakthroughs than to provide, through solid results, the scientists involved with a "ticket" to enter international research networks with an eye to making possible a transfer of research results made by the international scientific community.

4.4 Globalization and Decentralization

The globalization wave of business activities that characterized the 1980s occurred above all within the world of the industrialized countries. One indicator for this is that the share of DCs in overall foreign direct investment – an important indicator for globalization – was roughly 26 % in the first half of the 1980s and only 15 % in the second half (UNCTAD 1994, 12). The reason for this is above all that the ICs are highly attractive as markets (due to their purchasing power), but also as production sites (due to their well-developed business environments and efficient supplier structures). The chances for DCs to make up for these factors through, e.g., low wages are small; in fact, direct investments in DCs are concentrated in a few especially dynamic countries with an efficient physical, technological, and industrial infrastructure.

This underlines the finding noted above that DCs pursuing an industrialization strategy have no alternative to actively developing locational and competitive advantages. Such efforts are countered by globalization tendencies when a DC fails to develop a specific competitive advantage, when, for instance – as in the case of Brazil – an attempt is made to build up a microcomputer industry that produces neither better (more innovative, higher-quality, more attractively styled) products nor has a superior production process. The situation is different when a country succeeds in developing a competitive advantage in a field which, for instance because of the availability of especially favorable inputs, already offers a point of departure. If it proves possible for such a country to dynamize this advantage by developing a specialized supplier structure, technology institutes, and training institutions (which will typically be concentrated regionally), it will not, at least in the short run, be in danger of losing its position. And this means that the attractiveness of a location will grow for foreign firms.

Development of dynamic advantages can also prove possible in industries that see themselves confronted with stiff competition in other countries. This presupposes a combination of temporary infant-industry protection, the appropriate shaping of the business environment, and the introduction of performance criteria on which protection and support are made contingent; late industrialization will succeed only if the new industries learn faster then the established firms in ICs. Under these conditions it can be beneficial to be a latecomer, because it is possible to avoid typical errors by learning from other firms, in this way abbreviating learning processes.

4.5 Old vs. New Governance Patterns

At least three reasons suggest that it is time to abandon the notion that it makes sense to pursue an industry-oriented technology policy *sui generis* in advanced DCs:

- The relationship between state and firms is no longer clearly hierarchical even in advanced developing countries. Even in countries like South Korea, where the state played a key role in managing the industrialization process, the edge in competence held by state actors has been used up after a long period of capacity-building at the firm level (Messner 1992). In formerly inward-looking countries, the state lost both legitimacy and competence in the course of the crisis of import substitution. In both types of countries there are firms in various sectors that better understand the techno-organizational logic pursued by their industry than state actors. They know their competitors, and they observe the worldwide trends in their field. They thus are no longer in need of state guidance or supervision in defining their business strategy and, e.g., reaching decisions on acquiring technology abroad.

- The notion that technology policy in developing countries as opposed to industrialized countries is generally characterized by a catch-up situation is incorrect to the extent that this situation is often encountered in industrialized countries as well. A real or supposed lag vis-à-vis other industrialized countries typically is the reason why such countries formulate a specific technology policy. At the same time, in many DCs, after several decades of industrialization, the predominant question is no longer how to protect infant industries. The dominant industries have built up a certain measure of technological competence, though they may, after a long phase of protection from competitive pressure, be forced to undertake major efforts to increase their competitiveness on short notice.

- In both industrialized and advanced developing countries, the concern is to implement different types of technology-policy instruments for different types of industries. The difference between technology-policy measures for a supplier-dominated industry and a science-based industry in one and the same country is probably greater than that between technology-policy measures for one of these industries in a IC and an advanced DC.

One qualification is nevertheless necessary, in that the basic orientation of technology policy will differ between three groups of DCs:

–   In the first-generation East Asian NICs, the dominant patterns of technology policy are ones that correspond to those encountered in industrialized countries. Since the end of the 1970s, these countries have undertaken major efforts to develop a comprehensive, differentiated, and specialized network of technology institutions that work closely together with firms. The firms themselves have clearly stepped up their R&D spending. In these countries technology policy aims both to shape the process of radical technological change and to influence the further development of the techno-institutional landscape.

–   In poor countries the industrial structure is for the most part rudimentary. The dominant firms are small businesses, frequently in the informal sector, which exhibit technological learning processes that may be flanked by supporting institutions – e.g. technology extension. But the goal here is not so much to increase competitiveness in the sense of closing the gap to the best practice, but to impart elementary qualifications in dealing economically with means of production and inputs, in reducing quality fluctuations, or in the fields of bookkeeping and marketing. There also exist isolated larger firms, often state-owned and built up with development cooperation funds, that are frequently concerned with no more than securing operations or achieving a halfway satisfactory utilization of their capacities. These firms need – aside from an incentive structure that stimulates efficiency gains – above all qualified workers, technicians, engineers, and managers; but in poor countries the number of such persons is as a rule low, and it thus proves difficult to create a situation of personnel stability – qualified employees are enticed away by other firms, the state, or development cooperation projects.

- The large group of semi-industrialized middle-income-countries make up the middle ground between these two groups. Three patterns of technology policy can be observed here. The first is a continuation of traditional policy with a clear focus on militarily significant prestige projects. There is not much connection between such projects – say, in aeronautics and space or nuclear technology – and civilian industrial development; they for the most part provide no contribution to the development of industrial competitiveness, and instead absorb resources that could be harnessed for this purpose. The second pattern entails getting along largely without any technology policy; it can be observed in several countries that are consistently pursuing the neoliberal prescription and have reduced state activities to a minimum. Technology policy is here limited to selective interventions in areas in which the pressure stemming from acute problems is matched by political clout on the part of the industries concerned. The third pattern is a technology policy that supports, in existing industries, modernization processes and efforts aimed at improving competitiveness.

Implementation of the last-named pattern poses great demands to the competence of the state. A constellation such as that which existed in the past in the East Asian NICs (where a competent bureaucracy endowed with a large measure of autonomy was able to attack the problem of structure-building selectively and strategically; see Cumings 1984) is the exception. The rule is (following several waves of layoffs in which many competent employees have drifted off to the private sector, which offers higher salaries) a moderately competent, often demotivated administration that sees itself confronted by remnants of redistribution-oriented social groups. The transformation of this constellation into one marked by a situation of state autonomy and close interaction between state and social actors geared to problem-solving is a complicated and protracted process (Evans 1992, 179).

The central condition required to dynamize development in such an environment is the ability to formulate a development-oriented consensus between state and important social actors, i.e. an understanding that, first, development per se (and not maximization of development aid or the private welfare of the upper class) is one goal aspired for and, second, that it is necessary to aim for a specific corridor for developing a specialization profile. A basic consensus of this sort is the *sine qua non* for the social project of actively developing competitive advantages. The first task of central government is to secure stable, predictable framework conditions that encourage private initiative. Going on from there, state and social actors have to share the burdens for continuous investments in education and training, science and technology (that can often be built up on the basis of an existing infrastructure, even if it is sometimes in need of rehabilitation); this is the precondition for dynamizing the national base of comparative advantages, above all in areas in which potentially competitive industries already exist that are in need of a supporting environment. The state can also use selective, performance-related protection and targeted support to stimulate the development of given branches of industry. This, however, will prove successful only when the state gains a measure of autonomy vis-à-vis particular interests sufficient to enforce performance criteria. It is in this way possible both to develop an efficient national industry – a *conditio sine qua non* for any well-founded international competitiveness – and to attract foreign investors strong in terms of value added and technology.

This process can – particularly in large developing countries – not proceed on a nationwide basis. Instead, the discussion on regional policy has taken leave of the notion that it is desirable to aim for a uniform distribution of industries (Hansen, Higgins, and Savoie 1990). The industrial district discussion and other approaches to defining innovation and competitiveness point to the great significance that must be accorded to spatial concentration and the accumulation of external effects and learning processes that such concentration makes possible; even in São Paulo the economies of agglomeration achieved in this way outweigh the disadvantages stemming from extreme spatial concentration (Storper 1991). This opens up a new political access to the development of competitiveness: even if it should prove impossible at the central government level to reach a tenable consensus, this may prove possible within a local or regional framework. This does of course presuppose at the local or regional level a sufficient measure of competence and governance autonomy; local or regional technology-policy initiatives will develop particularly when it is clear that central government will remain abstinent in this area. It will remain the task of future investigations to illuminate the points of departure, scopes of action, and restrictions faced by a local or regional technology policy in developing countries.

These considerations result in an institutional profile of technology policy that differs fundamentally from the traditional profile. In the past technology policy was in many countries an activity that was the responsibility of an isolated unit – for instance a technology ministry that operated in competition with the planning ministry and the industry ministry. Moreover, a constellation of the type that existed in Brazil, where there were a number of largely independent sectoral agencies, was not untypical. The resulting governance pattern was hierarchical, centralized, and uncoordinated. A governance pattern of this type can in no case do justice to the new demands placed on the development of industrial competitiveness. For this reason there is a need for a new institutional pattern and a new governance pattern. If the important political actors share the view that technological competence is the key to successful economic development, technology policy will cease to be a niche event and begin to move into the center of economic and structural policy. Institutionally, this can imply questioning the existence of technology ministries or similar institutions. At the same time, technology will take on a new character at the central government level: the concern will no longer be to formulate detailed initiatives for individual (sub)sectors but to modify the framework conditions that block dynamic technological development. The detailed initiatives should – in a way analogous to the experiences made in the industrialized countries – be formulated at the regional or local level. The matter at hand is not to found state or provincial technology ministries or municipal technology offices but to create the conditions that make it possible for government-level actors and representatives of industrially relevant groups to formulate jointly initiatives aimed at improving locational conditions for technology.

A network-like governance pattern of this type presupposes among all those concerned a high degree of readiness to learn and to change. Only those societies will be able to close the gap to the developed industrial nations which succeed in creating in the political sphere institutional conditions and governance patterns that favor and stimulate learning and change. It is thus that "soft" factors such as organization and learning capacity become central determinants of the success of industry-oriented development models both at the company level and at the overall level of society.

Notes

Introduction

1   OECD/TEP (1992, 242). This definition is taken from the "Report of the US Presidential Commission on Industrial Competitiveness," which was elaborated in 1985.

2   For 1990 the UNIDO figures for Brazil indicate a net industrial output of 118.7 billion US-$. The DCs next in line are Korea (91.7), China (88.4), Mexico (57.4), and Taiwan (55.4); see UNIDO (1992c), A-18ff.

3   Although different definitions have in the meantime been introduced in English. The Collins English Dictionary (Glasgow 1991, 1583) distinguishes three variants: *"1. the application of practical or mechanical sciences to industry or commerce. 2. the methods, theory, and practices governing such application: a highly developed technology. 3. the total knowledge and skills available to any human society for industry, art, science, etc. ".*

4   See Barnett (1991, 1). Sharif (1988) proposed a similar systematization; he breaks down the component of know-how into two elements (knowledge and skills).

5   Blum (1990) exemplifies this with reference to Andean agriculture.

Part I, Chapter 1

1   "The 'TRIPS' Agreement and the Developing Countries," UNCTAD-Bulletin, No. 23, Nov.-Dec. 1993, 9.

2   See "Gesetz zu dem Rahmenabkommen der Vereinten Nationen vom 9. Mai 1992 über Klimaänderungen. Vom 13. September 1993," Bundesgesetzblatt for 1993, Part II, 1783ff.

3   See Katz (1987, 43). An anti-innovation topos also seems to rub off on the scholars concerned with the problem, for Katz postulates elsewhere: *"Little seems to have happened, for years now, in the basic automotive or steel production technologies employed by humankind"* (ibid., 44). When this comment was written, radical technological changes were perceptible both in the auto industry (à propos the superior productivity of Toyotism) and in the steel industry (à propos modification of competitive conditions due to the emergence of mini-mills).

Chapter 2

1   In 1990 the country ranked - behind Italy and ahead of Canada and Spain - eighth among the largest industrial countries; see UNIDO, Industry and Development. Global Report 1992/93, statistical appendix.

2   Industry did find a system of vocational training in 1942 (SENAI), but its quantitative output was insufficient.

3   Moreira (1993, 38). Peñalver et al. (1983, xii) speak of the *"accumulation of policy mechanisms, whose overall impact at the subsectoral level is not generally well known to the policy makers, and is often not consistent with a growth pattern that takes full advantage of the country's comparative advantage."*

4   See Section 2.4, below.

5   There was, in addition, a domestic savings gap between 1974 and 1976; see Batista (1992), 28.

6   Frischtak and Atiyas (1990, 6) offer a somewhat more balanced assessment.

7   The correlation coeffcient for this period is -0.378.

8   Moreover, the producers of paper were able to force cellulose producers to sell at prices far below the world-market level.

9   In crisis years rescue actions constituted a proportion of up to 40 % of the payments disbursed by BNDES; see Frischtak and Atiyas (1990, 71).

10 See "Government moves to modernise industry," Brazil Report, RB-88-06; and Frischtak and Atiyas (1990, 54ff.).

11 See "Zonas de incerteza," Veja, August 3, 1988; "As ZPE são um desastre" (interview with Wilson Suzigan), Isto é, August 10, 1988; "Stiff opposition to free-trade zones," Brazil Report, RB-88-08; and "Brasilien erläßt Regeln für neue Exportzonen," Nachrichten für den Außenhandel, August 25, 1988.

12 There were in addition taxes and levies amounting to 5 %; see Frischtak and Atiyas (1990, 15).

13 Advisory boards staffed with scientists were set up in CNPq; they reviewed and commented on applications, although the leadership continued to be in charge of decision-making; see Nussenzveig (1992, 139).

14 *"Net sales is calculated as total sales minus duties, taxes, imported inputs and components, commissions, transport, insurance, and other deductions"* (Dahlman and Frischtak 1993, 448, note 34).

15 332.3 and 1,184.9 US-$ resp.; see Kim (1993, 361).

16 Calculated on the basis of ANPEI data, cited after "A concorrência força a andar," Exame, April 28, 1993, 36.

17   Calculated on the basis of data on Brazil's industrial structure (Figure 7) and the R&D intensity of industrial sectors (Table 19).

18   See Banco Central do Brasil: Boletim, Separata (August 1993, 64-93); and UNIDO, Industry and Development Annual Report 1992/93, Statistical Annex.

19   Automotive: 24.3 % of the medium- to large-sized firms; electronics: 34.9 %; Chemicals and petrochemicals: 16.1 %; average of all industries: 9.5 %; see Dahlman and Frischtak (1993, 427).

20   Some examples are: Metal Leve, Cofap, and Fundição Tupy in the car parts industry, Villares and Gerdau in the steel industry, and Mariani and Ultra in the petrochemical industry. Scott-Kemmis (1988) notes that there are also some such firms in the pulp and paper industry.

21   It is thus, for instance, not unusual that upon request of a firm (and on the firm's premises) specific training courses are offered for limited periods of time, e.g. for two or three years. In 1992 800,00 of the 1.8 million students enrolled in schools attended courses organized in firms; see SENAI (1994, 23).

22   See "O Brasil tira zero," interview with Claudio de Moura Castro, Veja, May 5, 1993.

23   Castro (1989, 287) notes that the average university teacher in the 1980s published 0.3 papers a year. There were 7.69 students per teacher.

24   Table 5 includes all universities which ranked among the first ten (graduação), respectively among the first five (pós-graduação) in Brazil. 35 different courses were evaluated. Less than 10 universities offered the graduação course Engenharia de Produção; several other pós-graduação courses were offered by only less than five universities. The source of this ranking is, strange enough, the Brazilian edition of Playboy, No. 3/1994. Though the source in itself may be dubious, the survey, on which the ranking rests, is reliable.

25   See "Melhores e maiores da informática", Exame Informática, 12 July 1989.

26   See "Os donos da reserva", Isto é/Senhor, 10 May 1989; and "Um astral de uniaõ invade os negócios", Exame, 28 October 1987.

27   See "Is the Computer Business Maturing?", Business Week, 6 March 1989.

28   See, for example, "Pesquisa revela a insatisfaçaõ dos usuários", Folha de Saõ Paulo, 6 July 1988.

29   See "Integrar é tendência", Folha de Saõ Paulo, 26 October 1988.

30   See "The Software and Services Market in Brazil" (no author, no location, no date given, 1). This report has been prepared on behalf of the association of Brazilian software importing companies for a presentation in the US.

31   See the surveys carried out by the Stiftung Warentest, Test, 1988, No. 10, 1989, No. 10.

32 Tigre (1988) quotes a study which puts the price of IBM PCs in Mexico 267 % than in the USA.

33 On Brasil see Proença and Caulliraux (1989, 111), and for the international situation "Is the computer business maturing?", Business Week, 6 March 1989.

34 See "Instabilidade no mercado", Info, No. 77, June 1989.

35 See Brazil Informatics Newsletter, No. 1, November 1988, 5.

36 See "Como as empresas saíram de 1989", Exame Informática, 10 January 1990.

37 See "Taiwan holds its lead", Far Eastern Economic Review, 31 August 1989.

38 See Frischtak (1989), Sequeira (1990), World Bank (1991), Meyer-Stamer et al. (1991) and the results of a survey of Brazilian industry presented in "Diagnóstico do atraso", Veja, 27 February 1991.

Chapter 3

1 Data from the private economic information service Macrodados.

2 See R.W. dos Reis Velloso (1993, 127). The highest pensions are those of former congressmen, and they average 50.3 times the minimum wage (NB: the minimum wage - usually somewhere between 65 and 100 US-$ - is in Brazil a unit of account and not the lower boundary for wages or the existence minimum; the latter is considerably higher). Retirees of the judiciary receive 27.1 times the minimum wage, retired military personnel 22.2 times the minimum wage (source: FIPE, quoted after Diário Catarinense, March 19, 1994).

3 Data from the private economic information service Macrodados.

4 Calculated from Macrodados data.

5 See World Bank (1991, 111). Earners of incomes who have a checking account are automatically protected against inflation in that whatever positive balance they have is invested in the Fundão (Fundo das Aplicações Fianceiras, FAF). The Fundão is indexed and yields positive interests. When bank accounts are overdrawn (e.g. by payment of bills by check), the corresponding funds are deducted from the Fundão; see Nóbrega (1993, 96).

6 Between 1986 and 1990 the biggest party, PMDB, lost half of its senators and representatives, some of whom left congress to take on other posts, while the greater part switched to other parties; see Power (1991, 87f.).

7 There were a total of 72,000 such emandas to the 1993 budget; see Folha de São Paulo, March 12, 1994, 2.

8 Lamounier (1993, 130) sees this as the plebiscitary element of the political system.

9 Estimates are that at the federal level a change of government entails refilling tens of thousands of posts; see Evans (1989, 577).

10 See French (1991) on the controversial views on the emergence of corporativism, in particular the inclusion of the workers in it.

11 The corporativist associations were not represented in the most important economic panels, e.g. the National Currency Council (CMN); Diniz (1989, 113).

12 See, for example, the current articles in the "Forum Nacional."

Part II, Chapter 1

1   This is not the place to go further into the School of Regulation that introduced "Fordism" as a term for the postwar regulatory model based on increases of productivity, the growth in real wages made possible by them, and the welfare-related redistribution mechanisms which, on the whole paved the way to high rates of economic growth; see Lipietz (1987); Hirsch and Roth (1986).

2   Marglin (1990), who argues along Keynesian lines; for the purposes of this study it seems unnecessary to set out the view of Keynesian economists against those of the School of Regulation.

3   Thus the findings of a white book recently published by the British government on the topic of competitiveness; see Financial Times, May 4, 1994, 15, and May 26, 1994, 10.

4   OECD/TEP (1992) provides an excellent survey.

5   Thus Friedman's ironic dictum (1991, 304).

6   This concept should not be confused with the concept of a technological paradigm introduced by Dosi (1982), see below, 1.1.5. For him a technological paradigm is a specific, established view of and approach to a given technical problem: "We shall define a 'technological paradigm' broadly in accordance with the epistemological definition as an 'outlook', a set of procedures, a definition of the 'relevant' problems and of the specific knowledge related to their solution." (Ibid., 148)

7   Brödner (1985, 12) points to the ideological content of this concept: "The at first triumphantly announced 'unmanned factory' might, in times of persistent unemployment, go too far toward arousing the suspicion and resistance of the labor unions. It is here more amenable to speak of the 'factory of the future': who would be unwilling to place his trust in the future?"

8   See Rehder (1988, 184ff.); and Business Week, June 16, 1986, "Detroit Stumbles on its Way to the Future."

9   Though historically oriented industrial sociology is at odds as to whether they even did; Pries (1988) and Freyberg (1989), at least, doubt that Taylorism ever gained a foothold as the dominant model in Germany.

10 See Baethge and Overbeck (1986); Kaplinsky (1985) uses a similar term ("systemofacture").

11   Thus the provocative title of the no less pioneering than controversial study by Kern and Schumann (1984).

12   E.g. Cusumano (1988, 31f.), who points in particular to the narrowness of domestic markets and the sharp competition in them. This is, in the author's opinion, the reason why mass production was not an alternative to flexible manufacturing.

13   *"The actual model from which the clan concept is derived is, however, the Japanese firm with its family-like structuring not only of the internal relations between regular employees and management but also of external transactions with suppliers, customers, and suppliers of capital."* (Deutschmann, 1989a, 85f.)

14   The Adler and Cole (1993) study comparing the Uddevalla factory with the NUMMI factory is not very cogent in that it, so to speak, compares an unripe mango with a ripe apple: when the data were collected, the NUMMI factory had been in operation for a number of years, while the Volvo factory had just begun operations and was still far up on the learning curve; to this extent, the better performance indices for the NUMMI factory are not surprising. Berggren (1993) demonstrates that Uddevalla went through a rapid learning process at the end of which it was producing more efficiently than other Volvo factories. He further convincingly argues that the motivation for closing the factory had to do with firm politics and was not a result of insufficient productivity.

15   A US study came to the conclusion that 46 % of development spending goes for products that fail in the marketplace; see Power (1993).

16   Examples from the electronics industry: 90 % of Fuji-Xerox's parts come from suppliers; the figure for NEC and Epson is 70 %; Canon purchases 65 %; see Florida and Kenney (1991, 37).

17   E.g. Henderson (1989) on the development of microchip design facilities in Hong Kong and Singapore and Watanabe (1989) on the development of software development centers in various developing countries.

18   These are firms that are active only in a limited segment of the value-added chain, typically in design and sales, and in the field of production restrict themselves to organizing a broadly structured network of suppliers; see Normann and Ramirez (1993) on IKEA and Clifford (1992) on the US company Nike.

19   Rotering (1993) notes a failure rate of 45 %, Bleeke and Ernst (1991) 50 % for international alliances.

20   This was the case with 75 % of the already terminated alliances covered by Bleeke and Ernst (1991, 133).

Chapter 2

1   See Crow and Bozeman (1991). They identified a total of 1,341 science and technology institutions, 966 of which responded to the questionnaires sent to them.

678 of them were filled out completely enough to permit clear-cut classifications; see ibid. (166 and 168).

2   The American Rank-Xerox corporation has et up a center for spin-off firms; in it firms are given the opportunity to make use of innovations from the corporation's Palo-Alto research center that Rank-Xerox itself is unable to use; see The Economist, July 11, 1993, 64. This does, however, appear to be an isolated case.

3   Schnaars (1989), quoted after "The Folly of Forecasting Exposed," Multinational Business, No. 1, 1989.

4   See Nelson (1992a). Nelson distinguished three groups: large countries with high income (USA, Japan, Germany, France, England, Italy), small countries with high incomes and a marked agricultural or resource base (Canada, Denmark, Sweden, Australia), and developing countries (South Korea, Taiwan, Brazil, Argentina, and Israel) (352).

5   This is the dictum of Dunning and Cantwell (1991, 53-54); they speak of the *"increasingly footloose nature of international production and innovatory activities."*

6   See "Strenge Gesetze und Vorschriften vertreiben keine Unternehmen. Warum das Gentechnikgestetz den Industriestandort Deutschland nicht gefährdet / Aus einer unveröffentlichten Studie," Frankfurter Rundschau, August 25, 1993.

Chapter 3

1   See "O 1° mundo do pacote," Exame, April 4, 1990; and "Uma vassourada nos cartórois," Exame, Sept. 5, 1990.

2   In 1985, 67 % of imports were products with reduced tariff rates or without any tariffs at all; see Frischtak and Atiyas (1990, 16).

3   This was noted in a follow-up on a study published in 1991; see Meyer-Stamer et al. (1991). One of the then most advanced firms had merged with another less advanced firm, a second firm had been taken over by a multinational corporation, and a third firm had shut down the factory investigated in connection with the study.

4   SMD = surface-mounted devices, i.e. electronic components that are bonded to the surface instead of being mounted and then soldered; this improves quality and reduces costs.

5   280 of the 300 largest national private firms are family companies; see "Damas em crise," Veja, May 12, 1993.

6   The following section summarizes the results of the author's field research (Meyer-Stamer et al. 1991), follow-up surveys of firms (May 1993), and the most important relevant publications – Fleury (1988), Posthuma (1992), Alves Filho et al.

(1989), Ferraz et al. (1990), Tauile (1988), Humphrey (1989), Fleury and Humphrey 1989), Ferraz et al. (1992), Ruas (1993).

7   In April 1991 Autolatina had a total of 12 just-in-time projects with suppliers (author's survey of firms, April 1991).

8   See "País tem menor investimento desde 1947," Folha de São Paulo, May 5, 1993.

9   Outcome of conversations held at BNDES, Rio de Janeiro, May 1993 and June 1994, and the Banco Regional de Desenvolvimento do Extremo Sul, Florianópolis, May 1993.

10 See PBQP (1992, 17). Small firms employ up to 99 persons, medium-sized firms up to 499.

11 By 1993 agreements had been reached in four other chambers (toys, cosmetics, informatics, textiles, and clothing). There are, however, no systematic evaluations of the experiences of other chambers.

12 See "Hope from the north-east," The Economist, Dec. 7, 1991; Haddad (1994, 30ff.); and Amorim (1994).

13 See "Um soco na pobreza," Veja, May 5, 1993.

14 Result of interviews in Santa Catarina, May 1993. This finding has nothing whatever to do with the quality of the study in question; it meets the usual qualitative demands and proposes a number of plausible initiatives.

15 IEDI (1990) contains a self-portrait of the firms that make up IEDI.

Bibliography

Acs, Z.J. / D.B. Audretsch: *Innovation and Technological Change: The New Learning*, Wissenschaftszentrum (FS IV 92-5), Berlin1992

Adler, E.: "Ideological 'Guerillas' and the Quest for Technological Autonomy: Brazil's Domestic Computer Industry", in: *International Organization*, Vol. 42, 1986, No. 3

Adler, P.S. / R.E Cole: "Designed for Learning: A Tale of Two Auto Plants", in: *Sloan Management Review*, Vol. 34, 1993, No. 3

Altmann, N. / M. Deiss / V. Döhl / D. Sauer: "Ein 'neuer Rationalisierungstyp' – neue Anforderungen an die Industriesoziologie", in: *Soziale Welt*, Vol. 37, 1986, No. 2

Alves Filho, A.G. / R. Marx / M. Zilbovicius: "Fordism and New Best Practice: Some Issues on the Transition in Brazil", in: *IDS Bulletin*, Vol. 20, 1989, No. 4

Ames, B.: "The Reverse Coattails Effect: Local Party Organization in the 1989 Brazilian Presidential Election", in: *American Political Science Review*, Vol. 88, 1994, No. 1

Amorim, M.A.: "Lessons on Demand", in: *Technology Review*, Jan. 1994

Anand, R.: "Uruguay Round Text in Perspective", in: *Economic and Political Weekly*, 2.5.1992

Annavajhula, J.C.B.: "Japanese Subcontracting Systems", in: *Economic and Political Weekly*, 25.2.1989

Araujo jr., J.T. de / L. Haguenauer / J.B.M. Machado: "Proteção, Competitividade e Desempenho Exportador da Economia Brasileira nos Anos 80", in: *Pensamiento Iberoamericano*, 1990, No. 17

Asheim, B.: *The Role of Industrial Districts in the Application, Adaption and Diffusion of Technology in Developed Countries*, Background Paper for the UNCTAD/GTZ Symposium on the Role of Industrial Districts, Geneva 1992

Baden-Fuller, C. / J.M. Stopford: "Why Global Manufacturing?", in: *Multinational Business*, 1988, No. 1

Baer, W.: *Industrialization and Economic Development in Brazil*, Homewood: Irwin 1965

—: "The Resurgence of Inflation in Brazil, 1974-86", in: *World Development*, Vol. 15, 1987, No. 8

Baer, W / M.A.R. Fonseca / J.J.M. Guilhoto: "Structural Changes in Brazil's Industrial Economy, 1960-80", in: *World Development*, Vol. 15, 1987, No. 2

Baethge, M. / H. Oberbeck: *Die Zukunft der Angestellten. Neue Technologien / berufliche Perspektiven in Büro und Verwaltung*, Frankfurt/M., New York: Campus 1986

Baptista, M / P. Fajnzylber / J.L. Pondé: *Os impactos da nova política industrial nas estratégias competitiveas das empresas líderes da indústria brasileira de informática*, IE/UNICAMP, Campinas 1993

Barnett, A.: *Technology and Development: The Key Issues*, Science Policy Research Unit, University of Sussex 1991 (mimeo)

Bastos, M.I.: "State Policies and Private Interests: The Struggle over Information Technology Policy in Brazil", in: H. Schmitz / J. Cassiolato (eds.), *Hi-Tech for Industrial Development. Lessons from the Brazilian Experience in Electronics and Automation*, London, New York: Routledge 1992a

—: *The Interplay of Domestic and Foreign Policy Constraints on the Informatics Policy of Brazil*, UNU/INTECH, Maastricht 1992b

—: *State Autonomy and Capacity for S&T Policy Design and Implementation in Brazil*, Maastricht 1993 (mimeo)

—: "How International Sanctions Worked: Domestic and Foreign Political Constraints on the Brazilian Informatics Policy", in: *Journal of Development Studies*, Vol. 30, 1994, No. 2

Bastos, R.L.A.: "Evolução da concentração industrial no Brasil – 1949-80", in: *Ensaios FEE*, Vol. 13, 1992, No. 1

Batista, J.C.: *Debt and Adjustment Policies in Brazil*, Boulder etc.: Westview 1992

—: *A Inserção das Exportações Brasileiras no Comércio Internacional de Mercadorias: Uma Análise Setorial*, BNDES, Estudos No. 23, Rio de Janeiro 1993

Batista, J.C. / W. Fritsch: *A Dinâmica Recente das Exportações Brasileiras (1979-1990)*, no place 1993 (mimeo)

Baumann, R. / H.C. Braga: "Export Financing in LDCs: The Role of Subsidies for Export Performance in Brazil", in: *World Development*, Vol. 16, 1988, No. 7

Becattini, G.: "The Marshallian Industrial District as a Socio-Economic Notion", in: F. Pyke / G. Becattini / W. Sengenberger (eds.), *Industrial Districts and Inter-Firm Co-operation in Italy*, International Institute for Labour Studies, Geneva 1990

Berggren, C.: *Volvo Uddevalla – a Dream Plant for Dealers? An Evaluation of the Economic Performance of Volvo's Unique Assembly Plant 1989-1992*, Royal Institute of Technology, Stockholm 1993 (mimeo)

—: "NUMMI vs. Uddevalla", in: *Sloan Management Review*, Vol. 35, 1994, No. 2

Berkemeier, A.: "Brasiliens Autarkiepolitik auf dem Gebiet der Elektronik", in: *Zeitschrift für vergleichende Rechtswissenschaft*, Vol. 84, 1985

Best, M.H.: *The New Competition. Institutions of Industrial Restructuring*, Cambridge: Polity Press 1990

Bielschowsky, R.: "Ideology and Development: Brazil, 1930-1964", in: *CEPAL Review*, No. 45, 1991

Bleeke, J. / D. Ernst: "The Way to Win in Cross-Border Alliances", in: *Harvard Business Review*, Vol. 69, 1991, No. 6

Blum, V.: "Spaten, Traktor, Keyboard. Bauern und Technologie in den Anden", in: *Peripherie*, 1990, No. 38

BNDES 1988: *Strategic Plan 1988/90*, Rio de Janeiro

Bochum, U. / H.R. Meissner,: *Logistik und industrielle Reorganisation. Neue Herausforderungen einer betrieblichen Interessenpolitik*, Sozialverträgliche Technikgestaltung; Werkstattbericht 79, 1990

Botelho, A.J.J.: "Brazil's Independent Computer Strategy", in: *Technology Review*, May/June 1987

—: *The Political Economy of Professionalization: The Birth of the Brazilian Informatics Policy*, 1988 (mimeo)

—: "The Political Economy of Technology Transfer – the Institutional Basis of the Brazilian Informatics Industry", in: D. Vajpeyi / R. Natarajan (eds.), *Technology Transfer and Third World Countries: Some Managerial and Public Policy Issues*, 1989

Branco, L.C.: *Staat, Raum und Macht in Brasilien. Anmerkungen zur Genese und Struktur der brasilianischen Staats- und Großmachtideologie*, Munich: Fink 1983

Brödner, P.: *Fabrik 2000*, Berlin: Edition Sigma 1985

Bullinger, H.J / J. Niemeier / H. Huber: "Abschied von Taylor. Arbeitsteilige Organisation verhindert Integration", in: *Computerwoche Extra/Focus*, No. 5, 15.12.1989

Calcagnotto, C.: "Soziale und wirtschaftliche Entwicklungsperspektiven der 'Neuen Republik' Brasiliens", in: *Nord-Süd aktuell*, Vol. 1, 1987, No. 1

Callon, M / Laredo P. / V. Rabeharisoa: "The Management and Evaluation of Technological Programs and the Dynamics of Techno-Economic Networks: The Case of the AFME", in: *Research Policy*, Vol. 21, 1992

Cardoso, E. / A. Fishlow: "Latin American Economic Development: 1950-1980", in: *Journal of Latin American Studies* (Quincentenary Supplement), Vol. 22, 1992

Cardoso, F.H.: Versão Resumida da Exposição de Motivos N.395, de 7/12/93, do Ministro Fernando Henrique Cardoso ao Presidente Itamar Franco, no place 1993 (mimeo)

Cardozo, A.C.: *The Implementation of Laws and Regulations on Transfer of Technology: The Experience of Brazil*, UNCTAD (ITP/TEC/15), Geneva 1990

Carey, J.: "Why Washington is Anointing Flat Panels", in: *Business Week*, 16.5.1994

Carneiro, J.G.P.: "Requisitos políticos e técnicos da reforma do Estado", in: J.P. dos Reis Velloso (ed.), *Brasil: a superação da crise*, São Paulo: Nobel 1993

Carvalho, R.Q.: "Why the Market Reserve is not Enough: The Diffusion of Industrial Automation Technology in Braz. Process Industries and its Policy Implications", in: H. Schmitz / J. Cassiolato (eds.), *Hi-Tech for Industrial Development. Lessons from the Brazilian Experience in Electronics and Automation*, London, New York: Routledge 1992

—: "Projeto de Primeiro Mundo com conhecimento e trabalho do Terceiro?", in: *Estudos Avançados*, 1993, No. 17

Cassiolato, J / T. Hewitt / H. Schmitz: "Learning in Industry and Government: Achievements, Failures and Lessons", in: H. Schmitz / J. Cassiolato (eds.), *Hi-Tech for Industrial Development. Lessons from the Brazilian Experience in Electronics and Automation*, London, New York: Routledge 1992

Castañeda, J.G.: *Utopia Unarmed. The Latin American Left After the Cold War*, New York: Alfred A. Knopf 1993

Castilhos, C.C.: "O sistema brasileiro de inovação: uma proposta de configuaração", in: *Ensaios FEE*, Vol. 13, 1992, No. 1

Castro, C.M.: "What is Happening in Brazilian Education", in: E.L. Bacha / H.S. Klein (eds.), *Social Change in Brazil, 1945-1985. The Incomplete Transition*, Albuquerque: University of New Mexico Press 1989

Caulliraux, H.M.: *Organisação da Produção na Indústria de Informática Brasileira. A Flexibilidade no Trabalho Direto*, Rio de Janeiro 1989 (mimeo)

Cavarozzi, M.: "Beyond Transitions to Democracy in Latin America", in: *Journal of Latinamerican Studies*, Vol. 24, 1992, No. 3

CBO: *Using R&D Consortia for Commercial Innovation: Sematech, X-Ray Lithography, and High-Resolution Systems*, The Congress of the United States, Congressional Budget Office, Washington 1990

Cimoli, M. / G. Dosi: "Technology and Development: Some Implications of Recent Advances in the Economics of Innovation for the Process of Development", in: A. Wad (ed.), *Science, Technology, and Development*, Boulder/Co.: Westview 1988

Clifford, M.: "Spring in their Step", in: *Far Eastern Economic Review*, 5.11.1992

Cline, W.R.: *Informatics and Development: Trade and Industrial Policy in Argentina, Brazil, and Mexico*, Washington: Economics International, Inc. 1987

CNI: *Abertura comercial e estratégia tecnológica. 3a pesquisa. A visão de líderes industriais brasileiros em 93*, Confederação Nacional da Indústria, Rio de Janeiro 1993a

—: *Estudo da competitividade da indústria brasileira: a visão empresarial*, Confederação Nacional da Indústria, Rio de Janeiro 1993b

Cohen, L.R. / R.G. Noll: *The Technology Pork Barrel*, Washington: Brookings Institution 1991

Colson, F.: "New Perspectives on the Brazilian Computer Industry: 1985 and Beyond", in: *Multinational Business*, 1985, No. 4

Conca, K.: "Technology, the Military, and Democracy in Brazil", in: *Journal of Interamerican Studies and World Affairs*, Vol. 34, 1992, No. 1

Cooke, P.: "Regional Innovation Systems: Competitive Regulation in the New Europe", in: *Geoforum*, Vol. 23, 1992, No. 3

Cooke, P. / K. Morgan: *Industry, Training and Technology Transfer: The Baden-Württemberg System in Perspective*, Cardiff: Regional Industrial Research 1990

Corbo, V. / J. Melo: "Introduction", in: idem (eds.), *Scrambling for Survival. How Firms Adjusted to the Recent Reforms in Argentina, Chile, and Uruguay*, World Bank, Washington 1985

Corsepius, U. / A. Schipke: "Die Computerindustrie in Schwellenländern – der Fall Brasilien", in: *Die Weltwirtschaft*, 1989, No. 1

Coy, W.: *Industrieroboter. Zur Archäologie der zweiten Schöpfung*, Berlin: Rotbuch 1985

Crow, M. / B. Bozeman: "R&D Laboratories in the USA: Structure, Capacity and Context", in: *Science and Public Policy*, Vol. 18, 1991, No. 3

Cumings, B.: "The Origins and Development of the Northeast Asian Political Economy: Sectors, Product Cycles, and Political Consequences", in: *International Organization*, Vol. 38, 1984, No. 1

Cusumano, M.A.: "Manufacturing Innovation: Lessons from the Japanese Auto Industry", in: *Sloan Management Review*, Autumn 1988

Dahlman, C.J.: *Building Technological Capability in Developing Countries and the Role of the World Bank*, Washington 1990 (mimeo)

—: *New Elements of International Competitiveness. Implications for Technology Policy in Developing Economies*, Paper prepared for the Workshop „Integrating Competitiveness, Sustainability, and Social Devevelopment", Paris, 17.-18.6.1993

Dahlman, C.J. / F.V. Fonseca: "From Technological Dependence to Technological Development: the Case of the Usiminas Steelplant in Brazil", in: J.M. Katz (ed.), *Technology Generation in Latin American Manufacturing Industries*, Basingstoke: Macmillan 1987

Dahlman, C.J. / C.R. Frischtak: "National Systems Supporting Technical Advance in Industry: The Brazilian Experience", in: R.R. Nelson (ed.), *National Innovation Systems. A Comparative Analysis*, New York, Oxford: Oxford University Press 1993

Deutschmann, C.: "Der 'Clan' als Unternehmensmodell der Zukunft?", in: *Leviathan*, Vol. 17, 1989a, No. 1

—: "Reflexive Verwissenschaftlichung und kultureller 'Imperialismus' des Managements", in: *Soziale Welt*, Vol. 40, 1989b, No. 3

Dijk, M.P.: *The Interrelations between Industrial Districts and Technological Capabilities*, Background Paper for the UNCTAD/GTZ Symposium on the Role of Industrial Districts, Geneva 1992

Diniz, E.: "The Post-1930 Industrial Elite", in: M.L. Conniff / F.D. McCann (eds.), *Modern Brazil. Elites and Masses in Historical Perspective*, Lincoln, London: University of Nebraska Press 1989

Dohse, K / U. Jürgens / T. Malsch: "Vom 'Fordismus' zum 'Toyotismus'? Die Organisation der industriellen Arbeit in der japanischen Automobilindustrie", in: *Leviathan*, Vol. 12, 1984, No. 4

Dolata, U.: "Stolpersteine auf dem Weg zur automatisierten Fabrik – Stand und Entwicklungstrends industrieller Automatisierung in der Bundesrepublik", in: *WSI-Mitteilungen*, Vol. 41, 1988, No. 11

Doleschal, R.: *Automobilproduktion und Industriearbeiter in Brasilien*, Saarbrücken: Breitenbach 1987

Dore, R.: "Technology in a World of National Frontiers", in: *World Development*, Vol. 17, 1989, No. 11

Doria Porto, J.R.: *Competitividade do Complexo Eletrônico. Estudo da Competitividade da Indústria Brasileira*, Campinas 1993 (mimeo)

Dosi, G.: "Technological Paradigms and Technological Trajectories: A Suggested Interpretation of the Determinants and Directions of Technical Change", in: *Research Policy*, Vol. 11, 1982, No. 3

—: "Sources, Procedures, and Microeconomic Effects of Innovation", in: *Journal of Economic Literature*, Vol. 26, 1988

Dosi, G / K. Pavitt / L. Soete: *The Economics of Technical Change and International Trade*, New York: New York University Press 1990

Drucker, P.F.: "The Coming of the New Organization", in: *Harvard Business Review*, Vol. 66, 1988, No. 2

Dunning, J.H. / J. Cantwell: "MNEs, Technology and Competitiveness of European Industries", in: *Außenwirtschaft*, Vol. 46, 1991, No. 1

Ebel, K.H.: "Manning the Unmanned Factory", in: *International Labour Review*, Vol. 128, 1989, No. 5

—: *Computer-Integrated Manufacturing: The Social Dimension*, International Labour Office, Geneva 1990

ECOSOC: *Report of the Inter-sessional Ad Hoc Open-ended Working Group on Technology Transfer and Cooperation*, E/CN.17/1994/11, 14.4.1994

Enos, J.L.: *The Creation of Technological Capability in Developing Countries*, London, New York: Pinter Publishers 1991

Erber, F.S.: "The Development of the 'Electronics Complex' and Government Policies in Brazil", in: *World Development*, Vol. 13, 1985a, No. 3

—: "Microelectronics Policy in Brazil", in: *ATAS Bulletin*, 1985b, No. 2

—: "Desenvolvimento industrial e tecnológico na década de 90 – uma nova política para um novo padrão de desenvolvimento", in: *Ensaios FEE*, Vol. 13, 1992, No. 1

—: *The Political Economy of Technological Development – The Case of the Brazilian Informatics Policy*, Maastricht 1993 (mimeo)

Ergas, H.: "Does Technology Policy Matter?", in: B.R. Guile / H.Brooks (eds.), *Technology and Global Industry. Companies and Nations in the World conomy*, Washington: National Academy Press 1987

Esser, K.: "Lateinamerika in der Krise. Neostrukturalismus als wirtschaftspolitische Reaktion", in: Vierteljahresberichte, No. 107, 1987a

—: *Europäische Einflüsse in Lateinamerika und Formen der wirtschaftlichen Entwicklung – Zehn Thesen. Wirtschaft, Kultur und Entwicklung*, 8. Tübinger Gespräche zu Entwicklungsfragen, 8. - 9.5, Tübingen: Institut für wissenschaftliche Zusammenarbeit mit Entwicklungsländern, 1987b

—: *Lateinamerika – Industrialisierung ohne Vision. Neue Determinanten internationaler Wettbewerbsfähigkeit – Erfahrungen aus Lateinamerika und Ostasien*, German Development Institute, Berlin 1992

Evans, P.B.: "State, Local and Multinational Capital in Brazil: Prospects for the Stability of the 'Triple Alliance' in the Eighties", in: D. Tussie (ed.), *Latin America in the World Economy*, Aldershot: Gower 1983

—: "State, Capital, and the Transformation of Dependence: The Brazilian Computer Case", in: *World Development*, Vol. 14, 1986, No. 7

—: "Predatory, Developmental, and Other Apparatuses: A Comparative Political Economy Perspective on the Third World State", in: *Sociological Forum*, Vol. 4, 1989a, No. 4

—: "Declining Hegemony and Assertive Industrialization: U.S.-Brazil Conflicts in the Computer Industry", in: *International Organisation*, Vol. 43, 1989b, No. 2

—: "The State as Problem and Solution: Predation, Embedded Autonomy, and Structural Change", in: S. Haggard / R.R. Kaufman (eds.), *The Politics of Economic Adjustment*, Princeton/NJ: Princeton University Press 1992

Evans, P.B. / P.B. Tigre: "Going Beyond Clones in Brazil and Korea: A Comparative Analysis of NIC Strategies in the Computer Industry", in: *World Development*, Vol. 17, 1989, No. 11

Faletto, E.: "Social Images of Technological Change", in: *CEPAL Review*, No. 45, 1991

Ferraz, J.C.: A *heterogeneidade tecnológica da indústria brasileira: perspectivas e implicações para política*, UFRJ, Instituto de Economia Industrial, Rio de Janeiro 1989

Ferraz, J.C / N. Campos / C.E.F. Young: *Tajetórias de crescimento e a modernização da indústria brasileira: Um cenário para a década de 90*, UFRJ, Instituto de Economia Industrial, Rio de Janeiro 1990

Ferraz, J.C., et al.: *Modernização Industrial à Brasileira*, UFRJ, Instituto de Economia Industrial, Rio de Janeiro 1992

Fiori, J.L.: "The Political Economy of the Developmentalist State in Brazil", in: *CEPAL Review*, No. 47, 1992

Fisher, P.A.: "The Interface Between Manufacturing Executives and Wall Street Visitors – Why Security Analysts Ask Some of the Questions that They Do", in: J.A. Heim / W.D. Compton (eds.), *Manufacturing Systems. Foundations of World-Class Practice*, Washington: National Academy Press 1992

Fleury, A.: *An Institutional Analysis of Policy-Making in Brazil: The Case of Microelectronics*, São Paulo 1986 (mimeo)

—: *The Impacts of Microelectronics on Employment and Income in the Brazilian Metal-Engineering Industry (Technology and Employment Programme)*, International Labour Organization, Geneva 1988

—: *Quality and Productivity in the Competitive Strategies of Brazilian Industrial Enterprises*, Paper prepared for Workshop on Intra-firm and Inter-firm Reorganisation in Third World Manufacturing, Institute of Development Studies, Brighton, 14. - 16.4.1993

Fleury, A. / J. Humphrey: *Human Resources and the Diffusion of New Quality Methods in Brazilian Manufacturing*, Institute of Development Studies, Brighton 1993 (Research Report 24)

Fleury, A. / M. Salerno: *Condicionantes e Indutores de Modernização Industrial*, Texto preparado para o seminário internacional "Padrões Tecnolológicos e Processo de Trabalho: Comparações Internacionais", São Paulo 1989 (mimeo)

Fleury, M.T.L.: "The Culture of Quality and the Management of Human Resources", in: *IDS Bulletin*, Vol. 24, 1993, No. 2

Florida, R. / M. Kenney: "Organizational Factors and Technology-Intensive Industry: the US and Japan", in: *New Technology, Work and Employment*, Vol. 6, 1991, No. 1

Fogaca, A. / L.C. Eichenberg: "Educação básica e competitividade", in: J.P. dos Reis Velloso (ed.), *Educação e modernidade*, São Paulo: Livraria Nobel, 1993

Förster, H.U. / A. Syska: "CIM: Schwerpunkte, Trends, Probleme", in: *VDI-Z*, Vol. 127, 1985, No. 17

Franco, G.H.B.: "Brazilian Hyperinflation: The Political Economy of the Fiscal Crises", in: M. D'Alva G. Kinzo (ed.), *Brazil – The Challenges of the 1990s*, London: British Academic Press 1993

Fransman, M.: "Conceptualising Technical Change in the Third World in the 1980s: an Interpretive Survey", in; *Journal of Development Studies*, Vol. 21, 1985, No. 4

Freeman, C.: *The Economics of Industrial Innovation*, London: Pinter 1982

—: *Technology Policy and Economic Performance. Lessons from Japan*, London, New York: Pinter 1987

—: "The Nature of Innovation and the Evolution of the Productive System. Technology and Productivity", in: *The Challenge for Economic Policy*, OECD, Paris, The Technology Economy Programme 1991

—: "Formal Scientific and Technical Institutions in the National System of Innovation", in: B.-A. Lundvall (ed.), *National Systems of Innovation. Towards a Theory of Innovation and Interactive Learning*, London: Pinter Publishers 1992

Freeman, C. / J. Hagedoorn: *Globalization of Technology*, MERIT, Maastricht 1992

Fregni, E., et al.: *Proposta de Plano Diretor ABICOMP 89/90*, no place 1989

French, J.D.: "The Origin of Corporatist State Intervention Brazilian Industrial Relations, 1930-1934: A Critique of the Literature", in: *Luso-Brazilian Review*, Vol. 28, 1991, No. 2

Freyberg, T.: "Flexibilität – Zur Geschichte eines Schlagworts", in: *Prokla*, No. 76, 1989

Frischtak, C.: "Brazil", in: F.W. Rushing / C.G. Brown (eds.), *National Policies for Developing High Technology industries*, Boulder/Co.: Westview 1986

—: *Learning, Technical Progress and Competitiveness in the Commuter Aircraft Industry: An Analysis of Embraer*, World Bank (Industry Series Paper No. 58), Washington 1992

Frischtak, C. / I. Atiyas: *Industrial Regulatory Policy and Investment Incentives in Brazil*, World Bank (Report No. 7843-BR), Washington 1990

Frischtak, C. / E.A. Guimarães: *O Sistema Nacional de Inovação. V Forum Nacional*, São Paulo, 3. - 6.5.1993

Fritsch, W. / G.H.B. Franco: *The Quest for Efficient Industrialisation in a Technologically Dependent Economy: The Current Brazilian Debate,* Paper Presented to the Symposium on Competition and Economic Development, OECD, Paris, 17. - 18.10.1989

Gaio, F.J.: *The Brazilian Computer Software and Services Sector,* OECD, Paris 1989

Gall, N.: "Does Anyone Really Believe in Free Trade?", in: *Forbes,* 15.12.1986

Gamser, M.S. / H. Appleton / N. Carter: *Tinker, Tiller, Technical Change. Technologies from the People,* London: IT Publications 1990

GATT: *World Merchandise Exports, GATT International Trade 90-91,* Geneva 1992

Gelsing, L.: "Innovation and the Development of Industrial Networks", in: B.-A. Lundvall (ed.), *National Systems of Innovation. Towards a Theory of Innovation and Interactive Learning,* London: Pinter Publishers 1992

Gitahy, L. / M. Leite / F. Rabelo: *Relações de Trabalho, Política de Recursos Humanos e Competitividade: Reestruturação Produtiva e a Empresa, Estudo da Competitividade da Indústria Brasileira,* Campinas 1993

Glos, M.: "Do We Need a Strategic Industrial Policy à la MITI?", in: *Intereconomics,* Vol. 27, 1992, No. 3

Gocht, W. / J. Meyer-Stamer: *Stärkung technologischer Kompetenz in Tansania,* German Development Institute, Berlin 1993

Gonçalves, R.: *Small and Medium-Size Transnational Corporations in Brazil,* UFRJ, Instituto de Economia Industrial, Rio de Janeiro 1992

Gottfried, H.: "The Internationalization of Production, Intra-Core Relations and the State: A Case Study of IBM and the British Computer Industry", in: *Political Studies,* Vol. 34, 1986, No. 3

Grabher, G.: "The Weakness of Strong Ties: the Lock-in of Regional Development in the Ruhr Area", in: idem (ed.), *The Embedded Firm. On the Socioeconomics of Industrial Networks,* London, New York: Routledge 1993

Grossman, G.M.: "Promoting New Industrial Activities: A Survey of Recent Arguments and Evidence", in: *OECD Economic Studies,* No. 14, 1990

Gugler, P.: "Building Transnational Alliances to Create Competitive Advantage", in: *Long Range Planning,* Vol. 25, 1992, No. 1

Guimarães, E.A.: *A Experiência Brasileira de Política Científica e Tecnológica e o Novo Padrão de Crescimento Industrial,* UFRJ, Instituto de Economia Industrial, Rio de Janeiro 1993

Hack, L.: *Vor Vollendung der Tatsachen. Die Rolle von Wissenschaft und Technologie in der dritten Phase der Industriellen Revolution,* Frankfurt: Fischer 1988

Haddad, P.R.: *Os novos pólos regionais de desenvolvimento*. VI Fórum Nacional 1994 (mimeo)

Hagedoorn, J. / J. Schakenraad: "Leading Companies and Networks of Strategic Alliances in Information Technologies", in: *Research Policy*, Vol. 21, 1992, No. 2

Halberstam, D.: "Gewerkschafter von Nissans Gnaden", in: *Die Zeit*, 11.3.1988

Hansen N. / B. Higgins / D. Savoie: *Regional Policy in a Changing World*, New York: Plenum Press 1990

Hearing: *Informatics Trade Problems with Brazil. Hearing before the Subcommittee on Commerce, Consumer Protection and Competitiveness of the Committee on Energy and Commerce*, House of Representatives, 15.7.1987, GPO, Washington 1988

Heaton, G.R.: "The Truth About Japan's Cooperative R&D", in: *Issues in Science and Technology*, Vol. 1, Autumn 1988

Helmschrott, H.: *Technologietransfer und industrielle Forschung und Entwicklung in der Dritten Welt unter besonderer Berücksichtigung von Indien und Südkorea*, Munich etc.: Weltforum 1986

Henderson, J.: "Labour and State Policy in the Technological Development of the Hong Kong Electronics Industry" in: *Labour and Society (Special issue on High Tech and Labour in Asia)*, Vol. 14, 1989

Herbert-Copley, B.: "Technical Change in Latin American Manufacturing Firms: Review and Synthesis", in: *World Development*, Vol. 18, 1990, No. 11

Herzog, H.H.: "Fertigungsinseln – bald mehr als nur Pilotfall?", in: *Jahrbuch Arbeit und Technik*, Bonn: J.H.W. Dietz 1990

Hewitt, T.: *Employment and Skills in the Electronics Industry: The Case of Brazil*, Diss. (University of Sussex) 1988

Hillebrand, W.: *Industrielle und technologische Anschlußstrategien in teilindustrialisierten Ländern. Bewertung der allokationstheoretischen Kontroverse und Schlußfolgerungen aus der Fallstudie Republik Korea*, German Development Institute, Berlin 1991

Hilpert, H.G.: "Japanische Industriepolitik – Grundlage, Träger, Mechanismen", in: *Ifo Schnelldienst*, Vol. 46, 1993, No. 17 - 18

Hirsch, J. / R. Roth: *Das neue Gesicht das Kapitalismus. Vom Fordismus zum Post-Fordismus*, Hamburg: VSA 1986

Hobday, M.: *Telecommunications and Information Technology in Latin America: Prospects and Possibilities for Managing the Technology Gap*, UNIDO (ID/WG.440/2), Vienna 1985

Hoerr, J.: "The Payoff from Teamwork", in: *Business Week*, 10.9.1989

Hoffman, K.: *Technological Advance and Organizational Innovation in the Engineering Industry. A New Perspective on the Problems and Possibilities for DCs*, Brighton 1988 (mimeo)

Hoffman, K. / R. Kaplinsky: *Driving Force. The Global Restructuring of Technology, Labour, and Investment in the Automobile and Components Industry*, Boulder: Westview 1988

Hofmann, J.: *Implizite Theorien in der Politik. Interpretationsprobleme regionaler Technologiepolitik*, Opladen: Westdeutscher Verlag 1993

Holanda, N.: "A crise gerencial do Estado brasileiro", in: J.P. dos Reis Velloso (ed.), *Brasil: a superação da crise*, São Paulo: Livraria Nobel 1993

Humphrey, J.: *New Forms of Work Organisation in Industry: Their Implications for Labour Use and Control in Brazil*, Paper presented to the conference on "Padrões Technológicas e Políticas de Gestão", São Paulo, 16. - 17.8.1989

Hurtienne, T.: "Brasilien: peripherer Kapitalismus oder aufsteigende Industrienation? – Zur Entwicklungsgeschichte eines Schwellenlandes", in: *WSI-Mitteilungen*, Vol. 37, 1984, No. 4

IE/UNICAMP et al.: *Estudo da Competitividade da Indústria Brasileira. Roteiro da Síntese final*, Campinas 1993 (mimeo)

IEDI: *Mudar para competir*, São Paulo 1990

Islam, R.: "Transfer, Dissemination and Adoption of Technology for Small and Cottage Industries: An Overview", in: idem (ed.), *Transfer, Adoption and Diffusion of Technology for Small and Cottage Industries*, ILO-ARTEP, Geneva 1992

Jha, S.: "Biotech and Third World", in: *Economic and Political Weekly*, No. 6, 1990

Johnson, R.R.: *Statement of the Deputy Assistant Secretary for Trade and Commercial Affairs, Department of State. Informatics Trade Problems with Brazil. Hearing before the Subcommittee on Commerce, Consumer Protection and Competitiveness of the Committe on Energy and Commerce*, House of Representatives, 15.8.1987, Washington 1988

Jungnickel, R.: "'Global sourcing' ohne Entwicklungsländer? – Der Einfluß neuer Technologien", in: M. Welge (ed.), *Globales Management. Erfolgreiche Strategien für den Weltmarkt*, Stuttgart: Poeschel 1988

Junne, G / J. Komen / F. Tomeï: "Dematerialisation of Production: Impact on Raw Material Exports of Developing Countries", in: *Third World Quarterly*, Vol. 11, 1989, No. 2

Jürgens, U.: *Internationalization Strategies of Japanese and German Automobile Companies*, Paper presented to an International Symposium at Tohoku University 1991

Jürgens, U. / W. Krumbein (eds.): *Industriepolitische Strategien. Bundesländer im Vergleich*, Berlin: Edition Sigma 1991

Justman, M. / M. Teubal: "A Structuralist Perspective on the Role of Technology in Economic Growth and Development", in: *World Development*, Vol. 19, 1991, No. 9

Kane, C. / J. Morisett: *Who Would Vote for Inflation in Brazil? An Integrated Framework Approach to Inflation and Income Distribution*, World Bank, Washington 1993

Kaplinsky, R.: "Electronics-Based Automation Technologies and the Onset of Systemofacture: Implications for Third World Industrialization", in: *World Development*, Vol. 13, 1985, No. 3

—: *Industrial Restructuring in LDCs: the Role of Information Technology.* Paper prepared for the Conference of Technology Policy in the Americas. Americas Program, Stanford University, 1. -3.12.1988

—: "Restructuring the Capitalist Labour Process: Implications for Administrative Reform", in: *IDS-Bulletin*, Vol. 19, 1988, No. 4

—: *From Mass Production to Flexible Specialisation: A Case Study from a Semi-Industrialised Economy*, Institute of Development Studies, Brighton 1991

—: "The Diffusion of Organizational Reform in Developing Countries: A Case Study from India", in: *IDS Bulletin*, Vol. 24, 1993a, No. 2

—: *Implementing JIT in LDCs: From Theory to Practice.* Paper prepared for Workshop on Intra-firm and Inter-firm Reorganisation in Third World Manufacturing, Institute of Development Studies, Brighton, 14. - 16.4.1993b

Katz, J.M.: "Domestic Technology Generation in LDCs: A Review of Research Findings", in: J.M. Katz (ed.), *Technology Generation in Latin American Manufacturing Industries*, Basingstoke, London: Macmillan 1987

Kaufman, R.R.: "How Societies Change Developmental Models or Keep Them: Reflections on the Latin American Experience in the 1930s and the Postwar World", in: G. Gereffi / D.L. Wyman (eds.), *Manufacturing Miracles. Paths of Industrialization in Latin America and East Asia*, Princeton: Princeton University Press 1990

Kemp, R. / L. Soete: "The Greening of Technological Progress. An Evolutionary Perspective", in: *Futures*, Vol. 24, 1992, No. 5

Kern, H.: "Über die Gefahr, das Allgemeine im Besonderen zu sehr zu verallgemeinern. Zum soziologischen Zugang zu Prozessen der Industrialisierung", in: *Soziale Welt*, Vol. 40, 1989, No. 1-2

Kern, H. / M. Schumann: *Das Ende der Arbeitsteilung? Rationalisierung in der industriellen Produktion*, Munich: Beck 1984

Killick, T.: "East Asian Miracles and Development Ideology", in: *Development Policy Review*, Vol. 12, 1994, No. 1

Kim, L.: "The National System of Industrial Innovation: Dynamics of Capability Building in Korea", in: R.R. Nelson (ed.), *National Innovation Systems. A Comparative Analysis*, New York, Oxford: Oxford University Press 1993

Kinzo, M. D'Alva G.: "Consolidation of Democracy: Governability and Political Parties in Brazil", in: idem (eds.), *Brazil -The Challenges of the 1990s*, London: British Academic Press 1993

Klönne, A. / W. Borowczak / H. Voelzkow: *Institutionen regionaler Technikförderung. Eine Analyse in Ostwestfalen-Lippe und im Östlichen Ruhrgebiet*, Opladen: Westdeutscher Verlag 1991

Kochan, A.: "Simultaneous Engineering Puts the Team to Work", in: *Multinational Business*, No. 1, 1991

Kodama, F.: *Analyzing Japanese High Technologies: The Techno-Paradigm Shift*, London, New York: Pinter 1991

Koshiro, K.: "Japan's Industrial Policy for New Technologies", in: *Zeitschrift für die gesamte Staatswissenschaft*, Vol. 142, 1986, No. 1

Kounides, L.: *Industrial Applications of New and Advanced Materials. Implications for Industrial Policy in Developing Countries*, UNIDO, Vienna 1989

Kubicek, H.: "Organisatorische Voraussetzungen des branchenübergreifenden elektronischen Datenaustausches – Neue Aufgaben für die Wirtschaftsverbände?", in: H. Kubicek / P. Seeger (eds.), *Perspektive Techniksteuerung*, Berlin: Edition Sigma 1993

Lamounier, B.: "Unternehmer, Parteien und Demokratisierung in Brasilien 1974-1990", in: *Lateinamerika. Analysen – Daten – Dokumentation*, No. 16, 1991

—: "Institutional Structure and Governability in the 1990s", in: M. D'Alva G. Kinzo (ed.), *Brazil – The Challenges of the 1990s*, London: British Academic Press 1993

Landler, M. / R. Grover: "Media Mania", in: *Business Week*, 12.7.1993

Langenheder, W.: "Konsequenzen aus der folgenlosen Folgenforschung", in: A. Rolf (ed.), *Neue Techniken alternativ*, Hamburg: VSA 1986

Langer, E.D.: "Generations of Scientists and Engineers: Origins of the Computer Industry in Brazil", in: *Latin America Research Review*, Vol. 24, 1989, No. 2

Lasmar, J.O.: *Descentralização da política industrial: o novo papel dos estados e municípios*. Simpósio internacional sobre política industrial, São Paulo, Rio de Janeiro, 7. - 10.6.1994 (mimeo)

Lavinas, L.: *Polos regionais de desenvolvimento: algumas condições para seu sucesso*, VI Fórum Nacional 1994 (mimeo)

Leff, N.H.: "Entrepreneurship and Economic Development: The Problem Revisited", in: *Journal of Economic Literature*, Vol. 17, 1979

Leite, M.: *O trabalhador e a máquina na indústria metal-mecânica*, LABOR Instituto Eder Sader São Paulo 1989

Lima, R.R.: "Implementing the „Just in Time" Production System in the Brazilian Car Component Industry", in: IDS Bulletin, Vol. 20, 1989, No. 4

Lipietz, A.: *Mirages and Miracles. The Crises of Global Fordism*, London: Verso 1987

Longo, C.A.: "The State and the Liberalization of the Brazilian Economy", in: M. D'Alva G. Kinzo (ed.), *Brazil -The Challenges of the 1990s*, London: British Academic Press 1993

Lucena, C.J.P.: *A Tecnologia de Software no Brasil: a Caminho de uma Participação no Mercado Internacional*, Rio de Janeiro no date a (mimeo)

—: *O Software na Política Nacional de Informática*, Rio de Janeiro no date b (mimeo)

Lüdemann, K.: "Mobilfunk – Ein technischer Überblick für Laien", in: *Wechselwirkung*, Vol. 15, 1993, No. 64

Luhmann, N.: *Soziale Systeme. Grundriß einer allgemeinen Theorie*, Frankfurt: Suhrkamp 1984

Lundvall, B.A.: "Innovation as an Interactive Process: From User-Producer Interaction to the National System of Innovation", in: G. Dosi et al. (eds.), *Technical Change and Economic Theory*, London, New York: Pinter 1988

—: "Introduction", in: idem (ed.), *National Systems of Innovation. Towards a Theory of Innovation and Interactive Learning*, London: Pinter Publishers 1992a

—: "User-Producer Relationships, National Systems of Innovation and Internationalisation", in: idem (ed.), *National Systems of Innovation. Towards a Theory of Innovation and Interactive Learning*, London: Pinter Publishers 1992b

Lutz, B.: "Kann man Technik-Folgen abschätzen?", in: *Gewerkschaftliche Monatshefte*, Vol. 37, 1986, No. 9

Machado, J.B.M. / M.C. Carvalho: *A Escalada Tarifária na Reforma Aduaneira*, FUNCEX, Rio de Janeiro 1993

Mackie, J.A.C.: "Overseas Chinese Entrepreneurship", in: *Asian-Pacific Economic Literature*, Vol. 6, 1992, No. 1

Mahnkopf, B.: "Die dezentrale Unternehmensorganisation – (k)ein Terrain für neue 'Produktionsbündnisse'?", in: *Prokla*, No. 76, 1989

Mainwearing, S.: "Brazilian Party Underdevelopment in Comparative Perspective", in: *Political Science Quarterly*, Vol. 107, 1992, No. 4

Maldonado, C. / S.V. Sethuraman: "Technological Adaptations in the Informal Sector: Conclusions and Policy Implications", in: idem (eds.), *Technological Capability in the Informal Sector. Metal Manufacturing in Developing Countries*, International Labour Office, Geneva 1992

Mansfield, E.: "How Rapidly Does New Industrial Technology Leak Out?", in: *Journal of Industrial Economics*, Dec. 1985

Marcovitch, J.: "Política Industrial e Tecnológica no Brasil: Uma Avaliação Preliminar", in: *Pensamiento Iberoamericano*, No. 17, 1990

Marglin, S. A.: "Lessons of the Golden Age: An Overview", in: S.A. Marglin / J.B. Schnor (eds.), *The Golden Age of Capitalism. Reinterpreting the Postwar Experience*, Oxford: Clarendon Press 1990

Martinsen, R.: "Theorien politischer Steuerung – Auf der Suche nach dem Dritten Weg", in: K. Grimmer et al. (eds.), *Politische Techniksteuerung*, Opladen: Leske und Budrich 1992

Mathieu, H.: "Brazil: Latent Economic Strenght and Manifest Political Weakness", in: *Vierteljahresberichte*, No. 120, 1990

—: *Transnational Corporations, the State, and Class Formation in Industrial Policy Development: The Brazilian Automotive, Chemical, and Electronics Industries in Comparative Perspective*, Draft of a Ph.D. Thesis for Submission to the London School of Economics and Political Science 1991a

—: *The Politics and Political Economy of Economic and Industrial Policy: Industrial Structure, Political System, Interest Groups, and Competitive Strategy in Brazil*, Washington 1991b (mimeo)

Mattelart, A.: *Transnationals and the Third World. The Struggle for Culture*, South Hadley/Mass.: Bergin and Garvey 1983

Mayntz, R.: *Modernization and the Logic of Interorganizational Networks*, Max-Planck-Institut für Gesellschaftsforschung, Cologne 1991

—: "Policy-Netzwerke und die Logik von Verhandlungssystemen", in: A. Heritier (ed.), *Politische Vierteljahresschrift, Sonderheft 24, Policy-Analyse. Kritik und Neu- orientierung*, Opladen: Westdeutscher Verlag 1993

Medeiros, J.A.: *As novas tecnologias e a formação do pólos tecnológicos brasileiros*, Instituto de Estudos Avançados, São Paulo 1990

Messner, D.: "Die südkoreanische Erfolgsstory und der Staat: Von der Allmacht des Entwicklungsstaates zur Krise des 'hierarchischen Steuerungsmodells'", in: *Vierteljahresberichte*, No. 130, 1992

—: "Shaping Industrial Competitiveness in Chile. The Case of the Chilean Wood-processing Industry", in: K. Esser et al. (eds.), *International Competitiveness in Latin America and East Asia*, London: Frank Cass 1993a

—: *Stärkung technologischer Kompetenz in Bolivien*, German Development Institute, Berlin 1993b

—: "Die Netzwerkgesellschaft. Wirtschaftliche Entwicklung und internationale Wettbewerbsfähigkeit als Probleme gesellschaftlicher Steuerung", in: *Schriftenreihe des Deutschen Instituts für Entwicklungspolitik*, Vol. 108, Cologne: Weltforumverlag 1995

Messner, D. et al.: *Weltmarktorientierung und Aufbau von Wettbewerbsvorteilen in Chile – Das Beispiel der Holzwirtschaft*, German Development Institute, Berlin 1991

Meyer, A.D.: "Tech Talk: How Managers Are Stimulating Global R&D Communication", in: *Sloan Management Review*, Vol. 32, 1991, No. 3

Meyer-Krahmer, F. / U. Kuntze: "Bestandsaufnahme der Forschungs- und Technologiepolitik", in: K. Grimmer et al. (eds.), *Politische Techniksteuerung*, Opladen: Leske und Budrich 1992

Meyer-Stamer, J.: "Verblaßt der Stern von Rio? Zur Bedeutung Lateinamerikas als Anlageregion für deutsche Multis", in: *Lateinamerika. Analysen und Berichte*, Vol. 11, 1987

—: *Von der Importsubstitution zur Weltmarktfähigkeit. Probleme und Perspektiven der Informatikindustrie in Brasilien*, German Development Institute, Berlin 1990

—: "Kompetenter Staat, wettbewerbsfähige Unternehmen: Die Schaffung dynamischer komparativer Vorteile in der ostasiatischen Elektronikindustrie", in: *Nord-Süd aktuell*, Vol. 5, 1991, No. 4

—: "Staatlich-private Forschungskooperationen in der Elektronik: Erfahrungen und Perspektiven", in: *Vierteljahresberichte*, No. 131, 1993

—: "Steuerungsprobleme von Medien- und Technikentwicklung", in: O. Jarren (ed.), *Medienwandel – Gesellschaftswandel? 10 Jahre dualer Rundfunk in Deutschland. Eine Bilanz*, Berlin: Vistas 1994a

—: *Perspektiven der europäischen Elektronikindustrie*, Friedrich-Ebert-Stiftung, Bonn 1994b

—: "Wer ist hier unterentwickelt? Erfahrungen mit neuen industriellen Organisationskonzepten in fortgeschrittenen Entwicklungsländern", in: *WSI-Mitteilungen*. Vol. 47, 1994c, No. 2

Meyer-Stamer, J. / C. Rauh / H. Riad / S. Schmitt / T. Welte: *Comprehensive Modernization on the Shop Floor: A Case Study on the Brazilian Machinery Industry*, German Development Institute, Berlin 1991

Mody, A.: *Learning Through Alliances*, Washington 1991 (mimeo)

Mody, A / R. Suri / J. Sanders: "Keeping Pace with Change: Organizational and Technological Imperatives", in: *World Development*, Vol. 20, 1992, No. 12

Moisés, J.A.: "Elections, Political Parties and Political Culture in Brazil: Changes and Continuities", in: *Journal of Latin American Studies*, Vol. 25, 1993

Moreira, M.M.: *Industrialisation and Interventions. The Role of Governments in Developing Countries: Brazil*, UFRJ, Instituto de Economia Industrial, Rio de Janeiro 1993

Moura, A.R.: "Stabilization Policy as a Game of Mutual Mistrust: The Brazilian Experience in post-1985", in: M. D'Alva G. Kinzo (ed.), *Brazil – The Challenges of the 1990s*, London: British Academic Press 1993

Mytelka, L.K.: *Transfer and Development of Technology in the Least Developed Countries: An Assessment of Major Policy Issues*, UNCTAD, Geneva 1990

Nadal Egea, A.:" Choice of Technique Revisited: A Critical Review of the Theoretical Underpinnings", in: *World Development*, Vol. 18, 1990, No. 11

—: "National Innovation Systems: A Retrospective on a Study", in: *Industrial and Corporate Change*, Vol. 1, 1992a, No. 2

—: *The Co-Evolution of Technologies and Institutions*, Columbia University 1992b (mimeo)

Nelson, R.R. / G. Wright: "The Rise and Fall of American Technological Leadership: The Postwar Era in Historical Perspective", in: *Journal of Economic Literature*, Vol. 30, 1992, No. 4

Nobrega, M. da: "A estabilização é questão essencialmente política", in: J.P. dos Reis Velloso (ed.), *Brasil: a superação da crise*, São Paulo: Livraria Nobel 1993

Nochteff, H.: *Government Policies for the Data Processing Industries in Argentina, Brazil and Mexico*, UNIDO (ID/WG.440/7), Vienna 1985

Nomura, M.: "Der japanische 'Produktionismus' am Ende? Die Auswirkungen des Handelskonflikts auf die japanische Arbeitsgesellschaft", in: *Prokla*, No. 66, 1987

—: *Japanese Personnel Management Transferred -Transplants of the Electronic Industry in Asia and Europe*, International Symposium on "The Production Strategies and Industrial Relations" Sendai, 14. - 18.10. 1991

Normann, R. / R. Ramirez: "From Value Chain to Value Constellation: Designing Interactive Strategy", in: *Harvard Business Review*, Vol. 71, 1993, No. 4

Nussenzveig, H.M.: "Research Funding in Brazil: A Case History", in: *Technology in Society*, Vol. 14, 1992

O'Donnell, G.: "Challenges to Democratization in Brazil", in: *World Policy Journal*, Vol. 5, 1988, No. 2

—: "On the State, Democratization and Some Conceptual Problems: A Latin American View with Glances at Some Postcommunist Countries", in: *World Development*, Vol. 21, 1993, No. 8

OECD: *Science and Technology Policy Outlook*, Paris 1988

—: *Major R&D Programmes for Information Technology*, Paris 1989

—: *Main Science and Technology Indicators*, Paris 1991

—: *Industrial Policy in OECD Countries. Annual Review 1992*, Paris1992a

—: *Science and Technology Policy. Review and Outlook 1991*, Paris 1992b

—: *Industrial Policy in OECD Countries. Annual Review 1993*, Paris 1993a

—: *Public Management Developments. Survey 1993*, Paris 1993b

—: *Science and Technology Policy Outlook: Part III – Selected Issues*, Paris (DSTI/ STP(93)19/ REV. 1) 1994

OECD/TEP: *Technology in a Changing World*, The Technology/Economy Programme, OECD, Paris 1991

—: *Technology and the Economy. The Key Relationships*, The Technology/Economy Programme, OECD, Paris 1992

Ortmann, G. / A. Windeler (eds.): *Umkämpftes Terrain. Managementperspektiven und Betriebsratspolitik bei der Einführung von Computersystemen*, Opladen: Westdeutscher Verlag 1989

Ouchi, W.G. / M.K. Bolton: "The Logic of Joint Research and Development", in: *California Management Review*, Vol. 30, 1988, No. 3

PAQ (Projektgruppe Automation und Qualifikation): *Widersprüche der Automationsarbeit*, Berlin: Argument 1987

Pavitt, K.: "Sectoral Patterns of Technical Change: Towards a Taxonomy and a Theory", in: *Research Policy*, Vol. 13, 1984

—: "'Chips' and 'Trajectories': How does the Semiconductor influence the Sources and Directions of Technical Change?", in: Roy M. MacLeod (ed.), *Technology and the Human Prospect. Essays in Honour of Christopher Freeman*, London, Wolfeboro/N.H.: Frances Pinter 1986

—: "What Makes Basic Research Economically Useful?", in: *Research Policy*, Vol. 20, 1991

—: "Internationalisation of Technological Innovation", in: *Science and Public Policy*, Vol. 19, 1992, No. 2

Pavitt, K. / Patel, P.: "Technological Strategies of the World's Largest Companies", in: *Science and Public Policy*, Vol. 18, 1991, No. 6

PBQP: *Pesquisa qualidade e produtividade no meio empresarial*, Brasilia 1992

Pearce, R.D.: "The Globalization of R and D by TNCs", in: *CTC Reporter*, No. 31, 1991

Pellegrin, J.P.: "The Hidden Sources of Employment", in: *The OECD Observer*, No. 185, 1994

Peñalver, M. et al.: *Brazil. Industrial Policies and Manufactured Exports*, World Bank, Washington 1983

Perez, C. / L. Soete: "Catching up in Technology: Entry Barriers and Windows of Opportunity", in: G. Dosi et al. (eds.), *Technical Change and Economic Theory*, London, New York: Pinter 1988

Peters, T.: "Das Ende der Hierarchien. Die Mikroelektronik fordert eine neue Unternehmensorganisation", in: *Blick durch die Wirtschaft*, 22.3.1989

Pinheiro, A.C., et al.: "Composição setorial dos *incentivos às exportações brasileiras"*, *in: Revista* Brasileira de Economia, Vol. 47, 1993, No. 4

Piore, M.J. / C.F. Sabel: *The Second Industrial Divide. Possibilities for Prosperity*, New York: Basic Books 1984

Porter, M.E.: "The Competitive Advantage of Nations", in: *Harvard Business Review*, Vol. 68, 1990, No. 2

Posthuma, A.: "Japanese Production Techniques in Brazilian Automobile Components Firms: A Best Practice Model of Basis for Adaptation?", to be published in: T. Elger / C. Smith (eds.), *Global Japanization? Transnational Transformations of the Labour Process*, London: Routledge 1992

Power, C.: "Flops. Too Many New Products Fail. Here's Why – and How to Do Better", in: *Business Week*, 16.8.1993

Power, T.J.: "Politicized Democracy: Competition, Institutions, and 'Civic Fatigue' in Brazil", in: *Journal of Interamerican Studies and World Affairs*, Vol. 33, 1991, No. 3

Prahalad, C.K. / G. Hamel: "Nur Kernkompetenzen sichern das Überleben", in: *Harvard Manager*, Vol. 13, 1991, No. 2

Price, A / K. Morgan / P. Cooke,: *The Welsh Renaissance: Inward Investment and Industrial Innovation*, Cardiff: CASS 1994

Pries, L.: *Taylorismus: Agonie eines Produktionstyps oder Abschied von einer Schimäre?* (Mensch und Technik; Sozialverträgliche Technikgestaltung; Werkstattbericht 53) 1988

Proença, A. / H.M. Caulliraux: *Criação e Evolução de Empresas de Base Tecnológica. Avaliação Setorial – Indústria de Informática*, Rio de Janeiro 1989

Pyke, F.: *Industrial Development Through Small-Firm Cooperation. Theory and Practice*, International Labour Office, Geneva 1992

Quintas, P / D. Wield / D. Massey: "Academic-Industry Links and Innovation: Questioning the Science Park Model", in: *Technovation*, Vol. 12, 1992, No. 3

Radkau, J.: *Technik in Deutschland. Vom 18.Jahrhundert bis zur Gegenwart*, Frankfurt/M.: Suhrkamp 1989

Ramamurti, R.: *State-Owned Enterprises in High Technology Industries*, New York: Praeger 1987

Rammert, W.: "Wer oder was steuert den technischen Fortschritt? Technischer Wandel zwischen Steuerung und Evolution", in: *Soziale Welt*, Vol. 43, 1992, No. 1

Ramos, A.W.: *Reavaliação do sistema nacional e da infra-estrutura pública de normalização técnica, metrologia e qualidade*, Unicamp, Instituto de Economia, Campinas 1990

Rath, A.: "Science, Technology, and Policy in the Periphery: A Perspective from the Centre", in: *World Development*, Vol. 18, 1990, No. 11

Reddy, N.M. / L. Zhao: "International Technology Transfer: A Review", in: *Research Policy*, Vol. 19, 1990, No. 4

Reese, J.: "Wissenschaft, Gesellschaft und die Rolle der Technologiefolgenabschätzung", in: H.-H. Hartwich (ed.), *Politik und die Macht der Technik*, Opladen: Westdeutscher Verlag 1986

Rehder, R.R.: "Japanese Transplants: A New Model for Detroit?", in: *Business Horizons*, No. 1, 1988

Ribeiro, S. C.: "Educação e cidadania", in: J.P. dos Reis Velloso (ed.), *Educação e modernidade*, São Paulo: Livraria Nobel 1993

Rosenberg, N.: *Inside the Black Box: Technology and Economics*, Cambridge etc.: Cambridge University Press 1982

—: "Why do Firms Do Basic research (With Their own Money)?", in: *Research Policy*, Vol. 19, 1990

Rosenblatt, D. / A.D. Novaes: "O poder regional do Congresso – uma atualização", in: *Revista Brasileira de Economia*, Vol. 47, 1993, No. 2

Rossnagel, A.: "Rechtspolitische Anforderungen an die verbandliche Techniksteuerung", in: H. Kubicek / P. Seeger (eds.), *Perspektive Techniksteuerung, Berlin:* Edition Sigma 1993

Rotering, J.: "Wie strategische Allianzen zum Erfolg werden", in: *Blick durch die Wirtschaft*, 5.1.1993

Roth, S. / H. Kohl: *Perspektive: Gruppenarbeit*, Cologne: Bund 1988

Ruas, R.: "Notes on the Implementation of Quality and Productivity Programmes in Sectors of Brazilian Industry", in: *IDS Bulletin*, Vol. 24, 1993, No. 2

Rush, H.J.: *Manufacturing Strategies and Government Policies*, UFRJ, Instituto de Economia Industrial, Rio de Janeiro 1989

Sader, E.: "The Workers' Party in Brazil", in: *New Left Review*, No. 165, 1987

Salgado, L.H.: "Política de Concorrência e Estratégias Empresariais: Um Estudo da Indústria Automobilística", in: *Perspectivas da Economia Brasileira – 1994*, IPEA, Rio de Janeiro 1993

Sangmeister, H.: "Der Plano Cruzado – Eine Zwischenbilanz. Anspruch und Wirklichkeit des brasilianischen Stabilisierungsprogramms", in: *Lateinamerika. Analysen-Daten-Dokumentation*, Vol. 4, 1987, No. 9

Santos, W.G.: *Razões da desordem*, Rio de Janeiro: Rocco 1993

Sauer, D. / V. Wittke: *Vom Wandel der Industriearbeit zum Umbruch industrieller Produktion*. Bericht aus dem Schwerpunkt Arbeit und Technik. Zur Entwicklung und Nutzung von Technik in Arbeit und Alltag, Verbund Sozialwissenschaftlicher Technikforschung (Mitt., No. 12), Cologne 1994

Saxenian, A.: "Regional Networks and the Resurgence of Silicon Valley", in: *California Management Review*, Vol. 33, 1990, No. 1

Scharpf, F.W.: "Die Handlungsfähigkeit des Staates am Ende des zwanzigsten Jahrhunderts", in: *Politische Vierteljahresschrift*, Vol. 32, 1991, No. 4

Scherrer, C. / T. Greven: "Für zu schlank befunden -Gewerkschaftliche Erfahrungen mit japanischen Produktionsmethoden in Nordamerika", in: *WSI-Mitteilungen*, Vol. 46, 1993, No. 2

Scherer, F.M. / D. Ross: *Industrial Market Structure and Economic Performance*, Boston etc.: Houghton Mifflin 1990 (3rd edition)

Schmitz, H.: *Flexible Specialisation – A New Paradigm of Small-Scale Industrialisation*, Institute of Development Studies, Brighton 1989

—: *Small Shoemakers and Fordist Giants: Tale of a Supercluster*, Institute of Development Studies, Brighton 1993

Schmitz, H. / R. Carvalho: "Der Fordismus lebt. Autoproduktion in Brasilien", in: *Entwicklungspolitische Korrespondenz*, No. 3, 1989

Schmitz, H. / B. Musyck: *Industrial Districts in Europe: Policy Lessons for Developing Countries?*, Institute of Development Studies, Brighton 1993

Schmitz, H. / K. Nadvi: *Industrial Clusters in Less Developed Countries: Review of Experiences and Research Agenda*, Institute of Development Studies, Brighton 1994

Schnaars, S.: *Megamistakes: Forecasting and the Myth of Rapid Technological Change*, New York: Free Press 1989

Schneider, R.: *Wege der Integration zwischen den aufgabenspezifischen Software-Lösungen CAD, CAM (CAP), PPS, Online 86*, V. Kongreß, Velbert 1986

Schneider, V. / R. Werle: "Policy Networks in the German Telecommunications Domain", in: B. Marin / R. Mayntz (eds.), *Policy Networks: Empirical Evidence and Theoretical Considerations*, Frankfurt: Campus 1991

Schultze, R.O.: "Förderalismus als Alternative? Überlegungen zur territorialen Reorganisation von Herrschaft", in: *Zeitschrift für Parlamentsfragen*, No. 3, 1990

Schumpeter, J.: *Theorie der wirtschaftlichen Entwicklung. Eine Untersuchung über Unternehmergewinn, Kapital, Kredit, Zins und den Konjunkturzyklus*, Berlin: Duncker und Humblot 1964 (6th edition; 1st edition 1911)

Schwartz, G.: "Stabilization Policies under Political Transition: Reform versus Adjustment in Brazil, 1985-89", in: *The Developing Economies*, Vol. 28, 1990, No. 1

Schwartzman, S.: "High Technology vs. Self Reliance: Brazil enters the Computer Age", in: A. Botelho / P.H. Smith (eds.), *The Computer Question in Brazil: High Technology in a Developing Society*, Center for International Studies, MIT, Cambridge/Mass. 1985

—: "The Power of Technology", in: *Latin American Research Review*, Vol. 24, 1989, No. 1

Schwartzman, S. (coord.): *Ciência e Tecnologia no Brasil: um nova política para um mundo global*, Fundação Getúlio Vargas, São Paulo 1993

Scott-Kemmis, D.: *Learning and the accumulation of technological capacity in Brazilian pulp and paper firms*, International Labour Organization (Technology and employment programme), Geneva 1988

SEI: *Relatório da comissão especial No. 29 – Automação industrial. Proposta de plano setorial de automação industrial*, Secretária Especial de Informática, Brasilia 1988

—: *Panorama do setor de informática*, Secretária Especial de Informática, Brasilia 1989

SENAI: *SENAI. Desafios e oportunidades*, Subsídios para discussão de uma nova política de Formação Profissional para Indústria no Brasil, Rio de Janeiro 1994

Sengenberger, W. / F. Pyke: "Industrial Districts and Local Economic Regeneration: Research and Policy Issues", in: idem (eds.), *Industrial Districts and Local Economic regeneration*, International Institute for Labour Studies, Geneva 1992

Sequeira, J.H.: *World-Class Manufacturing in Brazil. A Study of Competitive Position*, São Paulo: American Chamber of Commerce Publications Division 1990

Sercovitch, F.C.: "Brazil", in: *World Development* (Special Issue on Technology Transfer from Developing Countries), Vol. 12, 1984, No. 5/6

Shah, R.: "Erfahrungen europäischer CIM-Anwender", in: *VDI-Z*, Vol. 131, 1989, No. 8

Shapiro, H.: *Brazil: Managing Structural Change in the '90s*, Harvard Business School Case Study 9-391-206, 1991

Sharif, M.N.: "Basis for techno-economic policy analysis", in: *Science and Public Policy*, Vol. 15, 1988, No. 4

Sherwood, R.M.: "A Microeconomic View of Intellectual Property Protection in Brazilian Development", in: F.W. Rushing / C.G. Brown (eds.), *Intellectual Property Rights in Science, Technology, and Economic Performance. International Comparisons*, Boulder etc.: Westview Press 1990

Singer, P.: "Linksintellektuelle in Brasilien", in: *Prokla*, No. 70, 1988

Skidmore, T.E.: *The Politics of Military Rule in Brazil, 1964-85*, New York, Oxford: Oxford University Press 1988

Smith, K.: "Innovation Policy in an Evolutionary Context", in: P.P. Saviotti / J.S. Metcalfe (eds.), *Evolutionary Theories of Economic and Technological Change*, 1991

Smith, M.B.: "Statement of the Deputy U.S. Trade Representative, Office of the Trade Representative", in: Hearing, *Informatics Trade Problems with Brazil*. Hearing before the Subcommittee on Commerce, Consumer Protection and Competitiveness of the Committee on Energy and Commerce, House of Representatives, 15.7.1987, GPO, Washington 1988

Soifer, R.: *Information Technology: National Policies and Experiences. Economic and Social Progress in Latin America. 1988 Report*, Inter-American Development Bank, Washington 1988

Soskice, D.: "Innovation Strategies of Companies: A Comparative Institutional Approach of Some Cross-Country Differences", in: W. Zapf / M. Dierkes (eds.), *Institutionenvergleich und Institutionendynamik, WZB-Jahrbuch 1994*, Berlin: edition sigma 1994

Soto B.F.: *Da indústria do papel ao complexo florestal no Brasil: o caminho do corporatismo tradicional ao neocorporatismo*, IE/Unicamp, Campinas 1993

Standke, K.H.: "Kein Geld für hohe Ansprüche. Wissenschaft und Technologie im Dienst der Entwicklung", in: *epd-Entwicklungspolitik*, No. 3, 1987

Stewart, F. / G. Ranis: "Macro-Policies for Appropriate Technology: A Synthesis of Findings", in: F. Stewart / H. Thomas / T. de Wilde (eds.), *The Other Policy. The Influence of Policies on Technology Choice and Small Enterprise Development*, London: IT Publications 1990

Storper, M.: *Industrialization, Economic Development and the Regional Question in the Third World – from Import Substitution to Flexible Production*, London: Pion 1991

Suzigan, W.: *Indústria brasileira. Origem e desenvolvimento*, São Paulo: Brasiliense 1986

—: "Estado e industrialisação no Brasil", in: *Revista de Economia Política*, Vol. 8, 1988, No. 4

Sydow, J.: *Strategische Netzwerke*, Wiesbaden: Gabler 1992

Tajima, M.: "Mechatronisierung der Produktion und Arbeitnehmer in der Werkstatt japanischer Unternehmen", in: *Zeitschrift für Betriebswirtschaft*, Vol. 60, 1990, No. 1

Taucher, G.: "Der dornige Weg strategischer Allianzen", in: *Harvard Manager*, No. 3, 1988

Tauile, J.R.: "Notes on Microelectronic Automation in Brazil", in: *CEPAL Review*, No. 36, 1988

Teece, D.J.: "Foreign Investment and Technological Development in Silicon Valley", in: *California Management Review*, Vol. 34, 1992, No. 2

Teitel, S.: "Towards An Understanding of Technical Change in Semi-Industrialized Countries", in: J.M. Katz (ed.), *Technology Generation in Latin American Manufacturing Industries*, Basingstoke, London: Macmillan 1987

Tetzlaff, R.: "Technologietransfer in die Vierte Welt durch transnationale Unternehmen: Verheißung oder Selbstbetrug?", in: B. Kohler-Koch (ed.), *Technik und internationale Politik*, Baden-Baden: Nomos 1986

Teubal, M.: "The Role of Technological Learning in the Exports of Manufactured Goods: the Case of Selected Capital Goods in Brazil", in: *World Development*, Vol. 12, 1984, No. 8

—: "Innovation and Development: A Review of Some Work at the IDB/ECLA/UNDP Programme", in: J.M. Katz (ed.), *Technology Generation in Latin American Manufacturing Industries*, Basingstoke, London: Macmillan 1987

Thomas, V.: "Lessons from Economic Development. What have We Learned about the Path to Successful Development?", in: *Finance und Development*, No. 3, 1991

Thorp, R.: "A Reappraisal of the Origins of Import-Substituting Industrialisation 1930-1950", in: *Journal of Latin American Studies (Quincentenary Supplement)*, Vol. 22, 1992

Tigre, P.B.: "Brazil: A Future in Homemade Hardware", in: *South*, No. 16, 1982

—: *Technology and Competition in the Brazilian Computer Industry*, London: Pinter 1983

—: *Business Strategies in die Brazilian Electronic Industry*, Rio de Janeiro 1988 (mimeo)

Tyler, W.G.: *The Brazilian Industrial Economy*, Lexington, Toronto: Lexington Books 1981

Tyson, L.D. / D.B. Yoffie: "Semiconductors: From Manipulated Trade to Managed Trade", in: D.B. Yoffie (ed.), *Beyond Free Trade: Firms, Governments, and Global Competition*, Boston: Harvard Business School Press 1993

UNCTAD: *Recent Trends in International Technology Flows and their Implications for Development* TD/B/C.6/145, 1988a

—: *Technology-Related Policies and Legislation in a Changing Economic and Technological Environment*. Report by the UNCTAD Secretariat. Geneva 1988b

—: *Further Consultations on a Draft International Code of Conduct on the Transfer of Technology* TD/CODE TT/56, 1990a

—: *Research and Development Institutes in Developing Countries and Their Contribution to Technological Innovation* UNCTAD/ITP/TEC/11, Geneva 1990b

—: *Transfer and Development of Technology in a Changing World Environment: The Challenges of the 1990s*, TD/B/C.6/153, Geneva 1991a

—: *Trade and Development Aspects and Implications of New and Emerging Technologies: The Case of Biotechnology*, 1991b

—: *UNCTAD VIII.* Analytical report by the UNCTAD secretariat to the Conference, New York 1992

—: *World Investment Report 1994 – Transnational Corporations, Employment and the Workplace*, New York, Geneva 1994

UNCTC (United Nations Centre on Transnational Corporations): *Transborder Data Flows and Brazil*, New York 1983

UNIDO: *Industrial Competitiveness in Brazil: Trends and Prospects*, PPD.225, Vienna 1992a

—: *Brazil's Industrial Policy: An Assessment in the Light of the International Experience* PPD.226, Vienna 1992b

—: *Industry and Development. Global Report 1992/199*, Vienna 1992c

Van de Ven, A.H.: "The Emergence of an Industrial Infrastructure for Technological Innovation", in: *Journal of Comparative Economics*, Vol. 17, 1993

Velloso, J.P.R.: "Reforma fiscal, inflação e sociedade", in: J.P. dos Reis Velloso (ed.), *Brasil: a superação da crise*, São Paulo: Livraria Nobel 1993

Velloso, R.W.R.: "Rigidez orçamentária da União", in: J.P. dos Reis Velloso (ed.), *Brasil: a superação da crise*, São Paulo: Livraria Nobel 1993

Vessuri, H.: "O Inventamos O Erramos: The Power of Science in Latin America", in: *World Development*, Vol. 18, 1990, No. 11

Vet, J.M.: "Globalisation and Local und Regional Competitiveness", in: *STI Review*, No. 13, 1993

Vetterlein, U.: "Die Industriepolitik der Europäischen Gemeinschaft – Implikationen der Maastrichter Beschlüsse", in: *List Forum*, Vol. 18, 1992, No. 3

Vickery, G. / D. Campbell: *Managing Manpower for Advanced Manufacturing Technology*, OECD, Paris 1991

Vietor, R.H. / D.B. Yoffie: "Telecommunications: Deregulation and Globalization", in: D.B. Yoffie (ed.), *Beyond Free Trade: Firms, Governments, and Global Competition*, Boston: Harvard Business School Press 1993

Villaschi, A.: "O Brasil e o novo paradigma tecnológico de desenvolvimento econômico mundial", in: *Ensaios FEE*, Vol. 13, 1992, No. 1

Villeda, R.: "Implementing JIT in a Maquiladora", in: American Production and Inventory Control Society, Inc. (ed.), *33rd International Conference Proceedings*, New Orleans, 8. - 12.10.1990

Voelzkow, H.: "Staatliche Regulierung der verbandlichen Selbstregulierung – Schlüssel für eine gesellschaftliche Techniksteuerung?", in: H. Kubicek / P. Seeger (eds.), *Perspektive Techniksteuerung*, Berlin: Edition Sigma 1993

Wad, A.: "Microelectronics: Implications and Strategies for the Third World", in: *Third World Quarterly*, Vol. 4, 1982, No. 4

Wakasugi, R.: "Why are Japanese Firms so Innovative in Engineering Technology?", in: *Research Policy*, Vol. 21, 1992, No. 1

Watanabe, S.: *International Division of Labour in the Software Industry: Employment and Income Potentials for the Third World*, International Labour Office, Geneva 1989

Weir, M.: "Ideas and the Politics of Bounded Innovation", in: S. Steinmo et al. (eds.), *Structuring Politics. Historical Institutionalism in Comparative Analysis*, Cambridge: Cambridge University Press 1992

Welliver, A.D.: "Going to the Gemba", in: J.A. Heim / W.D. Compton (eds.), *Manufacturing Systems. Foundations of World-Class Practice*, Washington: National Academy Press 1992

Wiemann, J.: "Schutz des geistigen Eigentums im GATT: 'Technologischer Neokolonialismus' oder Schlüssel für den Zugang der Entwicklungsländer zum globalen Industrie- und Technologiesystem", in: J. Henke / J. Noth (eds.), *High-Tech-Transfer in die Dritte Welt – Berliner Erfahrungen aus Ost und West*, Society for International Development, Berlin 1992

Willke, H.: "Staatliche Intervention als Kontextsteuerung", in: *Kritische Vierteljahresschrift für Kriminologie und Gesetzgebung*, 1988

Wirtz, R.: "Die Ordnung der Fabrik ist nicht die Fabrikordnung. Bemerkungen zur Erziehung in der Fabrik während der frühen Industrialisierung an südwestdeutschen Beispielen", in: H. Haumann (ed.), *Arbeiteralltag in Stadt und Land: neue Wege der Geschichtsschreibung*, Berlin: Argument (Sonderband 94), 1982

Wolf, K.D.: "Zwangstransfer zum Nulltarif oder Beitrag zur Überwindung von Unterentwicklung? Probleme der Automatisierung des Technologietransfers durch internationale Abkommen", in: B. Kohler-Koch (ed.), *Technik und internationale Politik*, Baden-Baden: Nomos 1986

Womack, J.P. / D.T. Jones / D. Roos: *The Machine that Changed the World*, New York: Rawson 1990

World Bank: *Brazil. Economic Stabilization with Structural Reforms*, Washington (Report No. 8371-BR), 1991

—: *Money, Debt, Inflation and Forward-Looking Markets in Brazil*, Washington (Report No. 10286-BR), 1992

—: *The East Asian Miracle. Economic Growth and Public Policy*, Oxford etc.: Oxford University Press 1993

You, J.I.: *Capital-labor relations in South Korea: Past, Present, and Future*, Harvard University 1990 (mimeo)

Ziegler, B.: "Calling All Channels", in: *Business Week*, 27.9.1993